CHICAGO
Rink Rats

CHICAGO Rink Rats

The Roller Capital in Its Heyday

TOM RUSSO

Foreword by Darius "D-Breez" Stroud

THE History PRESS

Published by The History Press
Charleston, SC
www.historypress.net

First published 2017

Manufactured in the United States

ISBN 9781625859686

Library of Congress Control Number: 2017948487

I was raised by a roller skate family, one that came together during the war years and socialized as one for decades. Those were the skaters of Chicago's West Side whose home rink was Madison Gardens Rink. This is their story, how they endured the years of World War II and preserved the skate social scene for the boys and girls as they returned home.

I also dedicate this to my grandparents, who faithfully responded to my primitive cursive-writing letters, described as illegible but as faithful grandparents, wrote back! Thomas Gutano Russo (paternal) and Theresa Johnson (maternal). Their praise provided the encouragement to write but it was the keyboard that unleashed the potential they inspired.

CONTENTS

Foreword, by Darius "D-Breez" Stroud 9
Preface 11
Acknowledgements 13

PART I. THE GOLDEN AGE OF ROLLER SKATING 17
The First Decade 17
That Which Is Golden May Not Glitter 25
Chicago Roller Capital 31

PART II. RINKS OF THE GOLDEN AGE, 1937–1959 41
Chicago Rinks 46
Flagship Rinks 76

PART III. CHICAGO RINK RATS 93
From Sidewalk to Rink, 1938–1941 95
Skating the War Years, 1941–1945 102
Mobilizing for Competition, 1946–1959 134

PART IV. THEY KEPT THE HOME FIRES BURNING 147
Mobilization 149
Demobilization 162

PART V. THE ORGANIZATIONS OF ROLLER SKATING 169
The Formative Years 170
Merger Overtures 174
Skate So Others Can Walk: A National Project 176

PART VI. HOW IT ENDS 179
Roller Skating and Pop Culture 181
Roller Rhythms 183

Conclusion 189
Appendix A. Map of Chicago Roller Rinks, 1937–1959 193
Appendix B. Chicago Roller Rinks: Skate Floor Dimensions 195
Appendix C. A Roller Rink Poem 197
Notes 199
Selected Bibliography 223
Index 227
About the Author 237

FOREWORD

I grew up on roller skates in the 1970s and continue to roller-skate as an adult, specializing in Chicago-style JB skating. I had heard stories related to roller skating back in the day from my parents but found Russo's *Chicago Rink Rats* filled with facts that brought those stories to life. It was rumored that the Savoy jazz band played at Al Capone's Rainbo Room but also entertained skaters at the Savoy Roller Rink. Well researched, comprehensive and historical, this book delves into topics that not only portray the heritage of the golden age but also connect it to roller skating today.

Roller skating is about the music! As Russo writes, it is the music that creates the nostalgia we relate to skating, whether it was the organ music, the jazz bands of the 1940s or the rhythm-and-blues we skate to today. It was interesting to learn that variations of rhythm skating had their origins as early as World War II in not only Chicago but the city of Motown as well! Detroit hosted the Forest Club in the Paradise Valley, where black and white skaters loved to skate to the jazzy sounds of Motown music. While Detroit skaters were creating their unique skate style, Chicago skaters adapted their style to the funk of James Brown. We talk often about "old-school style," and what we mean is music used today that dates to nearly forty years ago—or, yes, disco era music. The music evolved, and urban centers adapted and created their unique skate styles. In Chicago, we call it "JB skating." That's the way we roll in Chicago.

Today, many urban areas could claim "roller capital," but the Midwest and the East still seem to dominate the roller scene. Cali surged with roller disco in the 1970s and persists with its gangster rap music and many great rinks today throughout that West Coast corridor from L.A. through Seattle and Portland. But while Detroit and New York still vie for the roller capital title, Chicago's distinctive skate style is recognizable and dominates the roller scene around the nation, especially to anyone who recreates and roller skates! Regardless of style, if you seek a historical perspective on the Golden Age of Roller Skating, Russo's *Chicago Rink Rats* offers insights into its rise to prominence, demise, surge and origins that you will not find anywhere else.

DARIUS "D-BREEZ" STROUD,
Chicago JB Elite Skate Team and Chicago's Independence Roll

PREFACE

My mother's teenage grandchildren frequently asked, "What did you do growing up, Grandma?" Now they have children. While not yet old enough to ask those questions, they will ask the same, and her answers will not waver much: "We didn't tweet or text. There were no cars to drive or a cellphone plastered to our ears." She reminded them that she grew up during the war. There was no TV, no Internet and no computer to sit in front of all day. Lights went out at night to conserve energy, and big cities like Chicago had blackouts to avoid being a target for enemy bombs. They would come back with the same question: "So what did you do?" She quickly quipped, "We roller-skated!"

The idea for this book came out of those stories, as well as asking mother what she would want those great-grandchildren to know of their great-grandparents and what it was like growing up during the war years—the kinds of things we wonder about our own grandparents but either did not have the opportunity to ask or did not take the time to ask.

There persists a rite of passage during the teen years to know what it was like for our parents and grandparents, grilling them with questions in the hopes they will slip and reveal some nuggets on either themselves or our parents that we can use as "stamps" in the event we falter and need something to draw on to remind parents of their own failings when they were growing up. My mother over the years would tempt us with a statement that she and the "gang of girls" hung out at the roller rink. I always envisioned her girls growing up as the female gangs in *West Side Story*. Her tales were a tease, but we never got the full story!

My mother's recollections of her gang of girls during their adolescence took place during the years of World War II. As a result, this book is about those recollections of a teenager whose social scene was the roller rinks of Chicago during what is defined as the "Golden Age of Rolling Skating," 1937–59. The gang would visit other rinks around Chicago, taking the Green Hornet streetcar or the buses. They did not know it then, but the 1940s were the heyday of roller skating across the nation. Roller skating emerged in the wake of the war as the top participatory recreational sport adopted by Americans and returning war heroes. Roller skating took hold during those war years, surged and grew tremendously for two decades.

Today, we describe those who engage in compulsive gym workouts as gym rats. Well, for young people during the 1940 war years, they were Chicago's "rink rats." The rink was their social scene where teens connected with the "gang" gathered at the rink three to five times a week. Rink rats spent hours at a time at the rink. They socialized, skated, laughed and talked about boys, especially those headed off for war. Rink rats also planned going-away parties for the boys leaving for the front. But they also looked for bottles to recycle and get enough change for rink admission—then a modest fee of twenty-five cents. Rink rats did not know it then, but they contributed to the Golden Age of Roller Skating when Chicago vied for America's roller capital.

This is the story the girls would share over and over with their grandchildren. They skate-danced, speed-skated and performed skate tricks at rink center. They grew up during the war years when food was rationed, families were issued ration coupons and gasoline for travel was limited, among other sacrifices. But none of that mattered. This is the story of roller skaters across America as they made the Golden Age of Roller Skating a legacy to be told to their great-grandchildren.

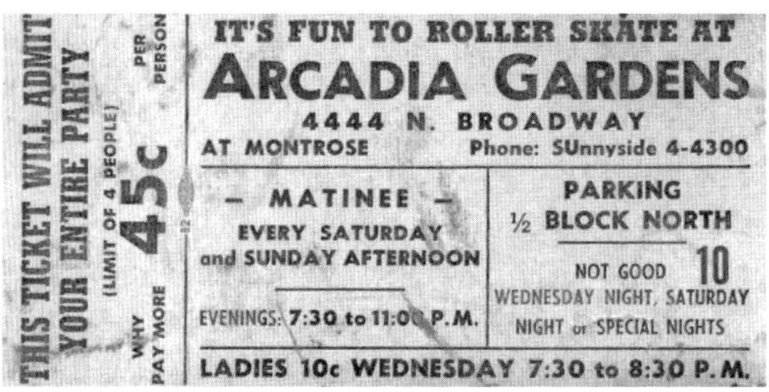

Your $0.45 roller skate admission ticket to Chicago rink rat action. Arcadia Gardens, Chicago, late 1940s. *George "Whitey" Heist.*

ACKNOWLEDGEMENTS

This book project presented many challenges along the way, but the topic deserved patience and the involvement of many contributors whose expertise, knowledge and recollections beyond my capabilities contributed to this story of roller skating's golden age. It also became an emotional journey much more than expected.

A special thanks goes to the many individuals who helped sort images, reviewed and edited images, read drafts, interpreted and extrapolated insurance map schematics and generally provided insight into this unique period in roller skating; Beth Diviacchi for finding the time to read the entire manuscript while three young boys lay wasted after a day of fun with mom; Ryan Harvey, engineer of the City of Myrtle Beach; Doris Knight, originally from Hollywood Rink, who married into the Madison Gardens gang; Deborah Russo for sorting and scanning family photos; William Matteson for his recollections of skating at local rinks during the heyday; and Tom Moro and Katie Geary at Johnny's Icehouse West for photographing the Madison Gardens Rink logo that hangs on the wall in the stadium. A grateful acknowledgement to the entire History Press team that worked diligently to make this a fun project and especially Ryan Finn, senior editor, for the final polish to the manuscript. I'm indebted to Marion Smith Harrison, who teased us over the decades with her stories of the West Side gang of girls and their rink escapades, until one of us asked questions and felt compelled to write the story. To this day, we have yet to hear the details of those antics to truly enrich those rink tales.

Image help came in many forms. The challenge was to ready dated images for publication, especially given the fact that they ranged from fifty-five years old to more than one hundred years old. Technical expertise came in many ways but included Dan Lipps and Tom Brady from Reel Events and photography aficionado Frank Everitt. Ben Gibson, acquisitions editor, provided encouragement as he reviewed early work and provided tools and direction along the way. Frank Perez's knowledge of Manhattan narrowed the search to locate the source of a classic, very early photo of Roller Follies' campaign to Save Gas in 1942.

I call them the cable car guys, but their knowledge and technical expertise provided insights into Chicago's early 1900 public transportation system, as well as helping track down and confirm the origins of Chicago's Madison Gardens Rink—thanks, Roy Benedict, Greg Borzo and William Vandervoort. Greg was particularly encouraging from the very start of the project.

A number of skaters who performed at the national level, past and present, were extremely helpful in sharing their recollections and insights into competitions, whether hosted by ARSA or RSROA. Contributing skaters included Alan Bacon, Jaci Zimmerman Charbonneau, George "Whitey" Heist, James Kohl, Emily MacKay, Ray Quitter and Robert Shaffer. Certainly, D'Breez Stroud would affectionately reference this group as old-school but appreciate their contribution and connection to roller skating today. His insightful foreword connects the heritage of roller skating as a continued recreational sport. And a special thanks goes to Peggy Young at the USA Roller Sports, who carved out the time to locate images from the National Museum of Roller Skating archives. I learned about the use of rosin in speed racing, national dance competitions and the nuance of the ARSA style of competition versus that of RSROA, as well as the challenges owners must confront to remain solvent and keep rink doors open.

Academic papers provided scholarly insight for themes developed throughout this story and put into context the golden age and the times that were so pervasive during the years of World War II. Meghann Mason's master's thesis, "The Impact of World War II on Women's Fashion in the United States and Britain," provided insights and analysis of clothing worn by women in the images included in this work. Carla Intza's master's thesis, "Images of Women on the Home Front," explored the impact of the World War II Office of War Information and its work to incorporate favorable war messages into Hollywood movie scripts and the role propaganda played to influence and change those roles. Romy Poletti's master's thesis, "Residual Culture of Roller Rink: The Media,

Music & Nostalgia of Roller Skating," studied the nostalgia associated with roller skating, the impact of music in that relationship and how these change as the musical tastes of each generation reflect the time. These emerge as major factors in the decline of roller skating's popularity by the end of the 1950s. If Mason's work provided the "what," Intza's work spoke to the "whys." Likewise, Poletti's research gives meaning to the lifecycle of roller skating from the golden age, through the disco roller craze and onward to its experience today.

To conduct the research required to write this historical snapshot would have meant cost-prohibitive travel to the libraries, museums and organizations just a few decades ago. Today's digital collections, whether hosted at the U.S. Library of Congress or a neighborhood library, offer researchers tremendous access to rare images, government documents and academic resources that collectively tell the story of seventy-five years ago. Much appreciation is due to both individuals who support those institutions and those whose passion for the work helps researchers navigate the nation's digital libraries with their unique and historical collections. Those institutions include the Chicago Public Library, Detroit Public Library, Digital Public Library of America, Elmhurst Historical Museum, Lenhardt Library of the Chicago Botanic Garden, Michael Schwartz Library at Cleveland State University, Museum of Flying Collection at the Santa Monica Public Library, Museum of London, National Archives and Records Administration, National Automotive History Collection at the Detroit Public Library, National Museum of American History, National Museum of Roller Skating, National Sports Company, Northwest University Library, 303rd Bomb Group Association, U.S. Amateur Roller Skating Association, U.S. Army Center of Military History, U.S. Library of Congress's Prints and Photographs Division and the World War II Poster Collection at Northwestern University Library.

Perhaps the most surprising find and invaluable resource was Google Books. Through its Internet access, I was able to access archived magazine editions by year and digitized books and locate World War II documents that would have required a visit to a local library decades ago. Today, these are readily available online and at no charge. These become invaluable resources to researchers and are much appreciated.

PART I
THE GOLDEN AGE OF ROLLER SKATING

The First Decade

During the Golden Age of Roller Skating's formative years, there were an estimated four thousand rinks[1] and more than 17 million skaters. The wheels were wooden, roller skating was hep, everyone went to a rink and Chicago was its epicenter.[2] The year was 1943, the world was at war and roller skating promoted itself as a wholesome, social form of recreation[3] that provided relaxation for soldiers, sailors and war workers. It was a time when the boys enlisted, got drafted or worked in the defense industry. The girls' duty was to keep the home fires burning, work and fill the employment gaps, which provided discretionary income used to recreate at roller skating rinks across America. In this same period, roller skating ranked as the second-highest participation sport in the United States, and among West Coast servicemen, roller skating was the favorite sport during leave of duty.[4] By the end of the decade, it had become the top recreational sport in the nation.[5]

The establishment of the Roller Skating Rink Owners Association (RSROA) in 1937 anchored the onset of the Golden Age.[6] Certainly for teen girls during this period, the 1938 roller skate exhibitions of sixteen-year-old Gloria Nordskog, a Chicago girl,[7] inspired a generation to don skates and roll into history. Soon to go professional, Nordskog shortened her name to Nord, and the nation came to know her as Gloria Nord. She won generous plaudits from local roller fans during the September Skating Vanities

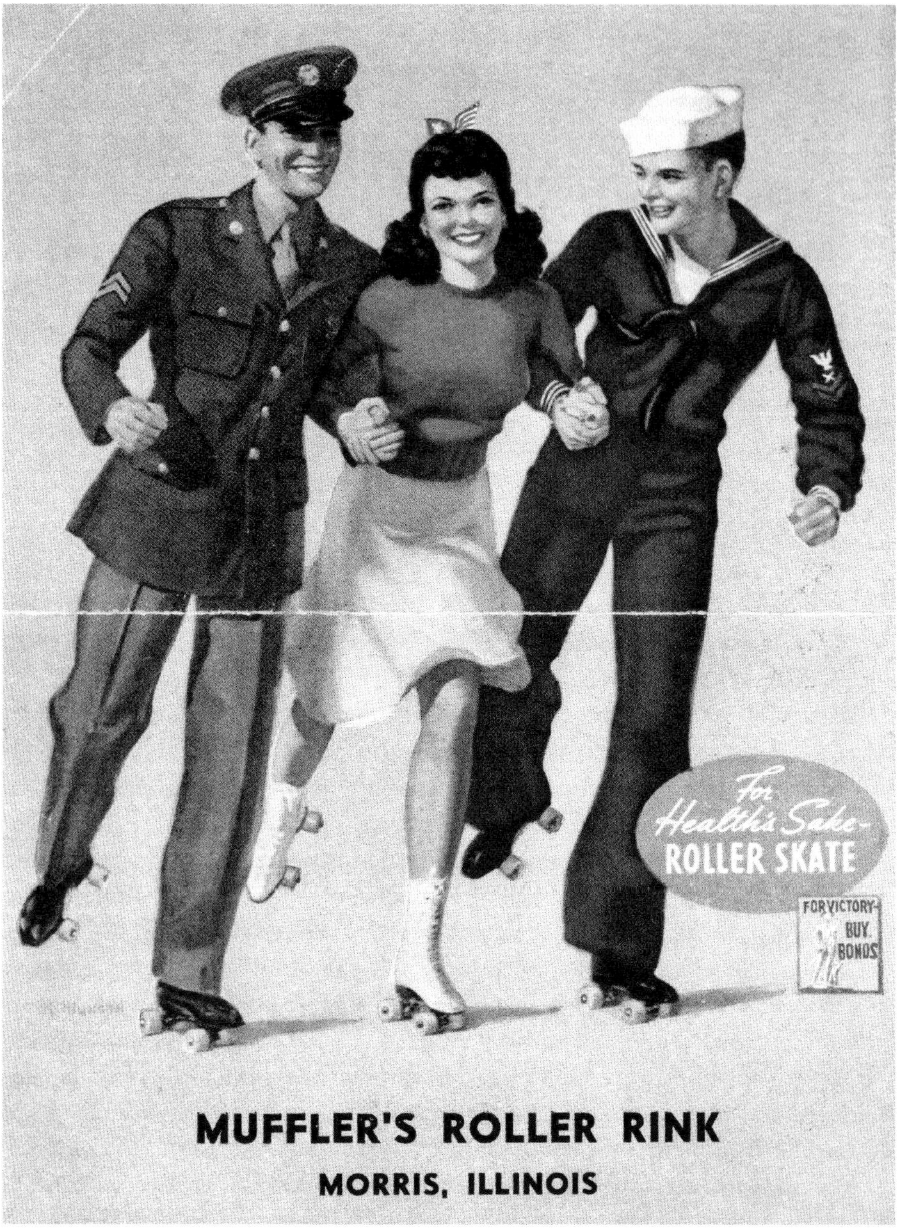

Trio skating was popularized in the early 1940s, along with the rink message "For Health's Sake—Roller Skate!" Muffler's Roller Rink, Morris, Illinois. *Author's collection.*

extravaganza's second season, which opened at the Chicago Coliseum Rink in 1942.[8] As the country distanced itself from the Great Depression of 1929, young people who had stood in rationing lines and watched their parents grow anxious over little work adopted skating rinks as a social outlet and a form of recreation that would define their generation through the war years and into adulthood. Teens experienced the rink as a social scene that was action-oriented, provided a safe venue to socialize with others and defined an age that symbolized their generation. Each generation immerses itself in its popular culture, which draws on their emotional and physical energy and establishes lifetime associations and relationships. We call that nostalgia. In the 1960s, it was the Beatles. In the late 1970s, it was disco. And in the 2000s, there was social media and flash mobs.

If 1937 launched the golden age, then the 1940s were the heyday of skating.[9] Rinks were opening at incredible rates, schools were training professional skate instructors and aspiring entrepreneurs were seeking pro instructors to add to their mix of marketing strategies to attract the best skaters. Rink operators networked and sought to position roller skating as a high-class audience participation sport, creating a niche that distinguished it from ice skating while maximizing public participation for teens and adults.[10] Roller skating went from seventh as a participatory sport in 1937 to second only to bowling a few years later.[11] The war provided tremendous opportunity for roller skating to step up, support the war effort and exploit opportunities at local, state and national levels that would establish a foundation for the growth of the sport in both recreational and competitive modes.

At the center of the frenzy was Skating Vanities, a three-hour production from Harold Steinman, who discovered Gloria Nordskog in California and incorporated her talent into a musical extravaganza on wheels with a cast of eighty-five and a program of twenty-seven numbers. Trained as a ballerina, Nord adopted roller skating and displayed incredible rhythm and grace that the media adored. But the show also pit those roller talents against those of Sonja Henie, the "ballerina on ice skates." Sonja Henie was a Norwegian figure skater, film star and three-time Olympic champion. In an effort to distinguish Skating Vanities, Steinman featured a twenty-two-piece orchestra, a singing master of ceremonies and a roller skating cast as a fun, glamorous and thrilling sport. In addition to skating numbers, the production included stunning costumes, jugglers on wheels, "a chorus of 24 rollerettes and a dozen roller cadets."[12] As Skating Vanities readied for its new season, Nord was profiled in *Newsweek*'s sports column, which described this new roller show as "a rink but no ice" in the August 30, 1943 issue. Its run in Chicago lasted for twelve days.

Gloria took a tumble in the opening performance of the thirteen-night stand of Skating Vanities at the Chicago Arena in September 1943. It was common for skating stars to lose their footing during the opening performance, whether on ice or rink.[13] However, the spill resulted in a disparaging Chicago review that unfavorably compared the roller spectacle to those on ice: "[It] is still a far cry from ice revues playing in similar spots…grace and rhythm are more difficult to achieve on wheels than on blades, this type of show will face an uphill box-office battle. Plenty of talent on tap, though. Standouts are Gloria Nord, blond lively and highly graceful skater, Ann Manion, expert thrill skater, and Lon Hall."[14] The critiques persisted, but the extravaganza with the five-foot-two, 115-pound blonde was effective in shaping a favorable public opinion toward roller skating, a far cry from its roughneck reputation in the 1920s and 1930s.[15] Not only were the "best people of all ages attracted to roller skating," but Steinman had also leveraged a Skating Vanities act from Betty Grable's *Pin Up Girl.* Ms. Nord would become servicemen's favorite new pin-up girl. Roller skating's popularity was without match compared to ice skating—the former with four thousand rinks and 15 million skaters and the latter with two hundred rinks and 1 ice skater to every 20 rollers.

Newspapers and magazines persisted in setting ice skating against roller skating. The January 8, 1944 *Billboard* featured Sonja Henie (the Golden Girl) and the Hollywood Ice Revue in Chicago on January 1, 1944, versus Gloria Nord in Cincinnati with the Skating Vanities on page three. The article noted that Hollywood Ice Revue "has drawn practically capacity business every night and indications are the show will set an all-time record for attendance and receipts."[16] In contrast, the write-up for Skating Vanities read, "Skating Vanities gets Cincy raves: Off slowly but ups."[17] In February 1944, *Billboard* reported that the "Ice Follies" hit a record $400,000 at Boston Garden, while the Skating Vanities grossed $72,955 in ten performances at Olympia.[18]

Billboard drew on this contrast in its January 1944 issue: "She's a screen star dancing with her leading man to a Hollywood background; stops the show in its tracks with a naughty hula; is sweetly decorous as a deb waltzing with her fiancé; clicks with a tango that is a marvel of timing, and winds up with a whirlwind-romp as a Parisian soubrette."[19]

With war underway, the roller skating industry was quick to use its numbers and adopt official civil defense morale and motivation-building campaigns for citizens, war workers and those in military service. The Office of War

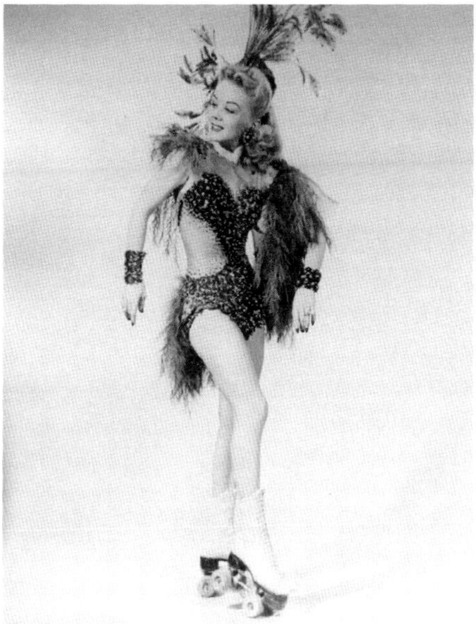

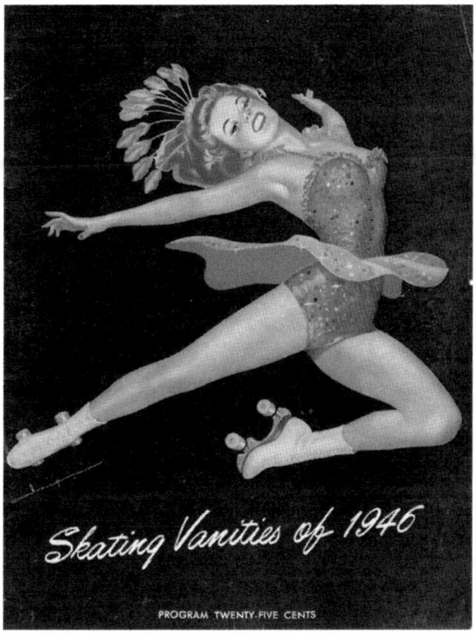

Left: Gloria Nord of the Skating Vanities in costume. *Gloria Nord Collection, donated by Mike Nordskog, great-nephew of Gloria Nord, National Museum of Roller Skating.*

Right: Skating Vanities, 1946 program cover. *Author's collection.*

Information rolled out a propaganda campaign to motivate the civilian force to support the war economy with a "Keep 'em Rolling" campaign. A companion program was a nationwide physical fitness program adopted by the roller industry to rally 12 million roller skaters.[20] While the campaign was created to appeal to those workers who built trucks, tanks, airplanes, ship and artillery, the roller industry was skillful at recruiting industry leaders to incorporate the tagline into their industry-related ads distributed in trade journals, entertainment magazines and neighborhood newspapers.

Rinks and skate manufacturers printed posters, flyers and ads adopting the slogan and printed, published and distributed campaign materials to skate patrons and industry partners. Roller skating was expected to play a major role in the all-sports project division of the Office of Civilian Defense (OCD) to promote better health, higher morale through participation in sports and the motive for mobilization. Skaters in some four thousand rinks were "welded into a 'keep fit' unit," and OCD called for skaters to wear the health shield of the OCD with the pledge to recruit skaters. Skaters who pledged new skate recruits committed to skating with the beginner twice a week for six weeks. They also pledged to skate and instruct the newcomer

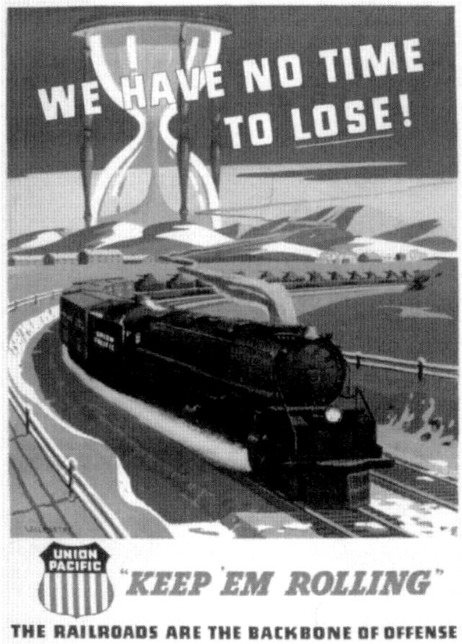

"We have no time to lose!—Keep 'em Rolling!" Productivity campaign propaganda poster from the U.S. Office of War Information, War Production Board. *U.S. National Archives and Records Administration [179-WP-1313].*

in the sport's fundamentals. The newcomer received an identifying button. However, rink operations were heavily hit as the boys left for the front, causing operators to continually recruit and train new skaters for roles in rink management.

The boys overseas were asked often what they would like from home. The top requests were letters along with cigarettes and roller skates. The girls from their home rink kept in touch with the boys, writing millions of letters. It was natural that roller skating was promoted as a wholesome sport, unsurpassed in cleanliness and interest and approved by the physical fitness division of OCD in support of the war effort. Liquor or beer was not sold in rinks (and remains much the same to this day), and those under the influence of intoxicants were promptly ejected. Even school and church groups had regular skating parties at neighborhood rinks.

Ads cited the moral value of roller skating. The Oaks Rink in Portland promoted skating as the best method in the world for helping war workers condition their bodies, toughen muscles, eliminate excess fat, stimulate a zest for work and produce relaxation and sleep. The OCD recommended skating as a sure way to keep trim.[21]

Rolling skating in the early 1940s was not without its troubles. While skating had successfully established itself as an amateur and professional sport, nagging perceptions kept public participation from growing. Skates were described as unwieldy and clumsy and maple wood floors were noisy and dusty, considerations that hampered its development of a favorable public perception.[22] As talk of the war ended, it was believed that skate manufacturers would build better skates with quieter actions, suitable for use by the general public. Optimism was expressed for air-conditioning systems that would vastly improve as materials became available and correct deficiencies in current systems. Hopes were high that A/C systems would improve the sanitation and comfort aspects of roller skate rink environments to operate in the summer, especially in the South! Wish lists also included silent plastic floors, skates that would grip without the need for powdered floors and material that would fill in the cracks and gouges so anticipated with wood floors. Even music could advance with the production of albums that rinks could adopt.

Nonetheless, perception persisted that skating rinks were "pick-up" spots. An anonymous letter to the editor of the *Cleveland Press* charged a Cleveland rink with gross impropriety. Once published, thousands of response letters sent to the editor described the benefits of attending rinks, their practices and how school and church groups regularly held parties at city rinks. Servicemen wrote that rinks offered them a wholesome sport and were among the few places where they could go when off duty.[23] With the likes of the Circle Waltz, the most popular music request, skate dancing had tamed the sport.

Pick-up spot or not, romance flourished at roller rinks, which sometimes became the scene for couples taking vows on rollers. It was called "Roller Romance," complete with ushers on skates and bridal parties rolling down the rink aisle, followed by best men and maids of honor skating down the aisle with a touch of a Wurlitzer organ recital.[24] Only the pastor escaped the requirement of roller skates for all on the rink floor.

Billboard wrote in 1948 that the Roller Skating Institute of America was the best thing that had happened in roller skating since 1942.[25] Its objective was to promote roller skating itself rather than focus on rinks, operators, amateur organization or styles. In 1949, RSROA secretary/treasurer Fred A. Martin reported that roller skating had advanced from a slum sport to become the leading participant sports in 1948–49.[26] By the late 1940s, roller skating had achieved the position of top participant sport in the country[27] and closed out the decade as the top recreation, according to former roller speed-racer Fred Martin.

Questions remain about the basis for the roller industry's claim to be the top recreational sport in America. Competitor numbers steadily increased in state, regional and national competition events. Thirty-five competition classes were defined by rules that involved artistic, dance and speed skating and included pairs and mixed-relay teams. The RSROA reported that in 1949, 12,700 competitors took part in meets across the country. Roller rinks were still being built and numbered five thousand, including outdoor, tents and part-time rinks such as the Chicago Coliseum and Chicago Stadium.

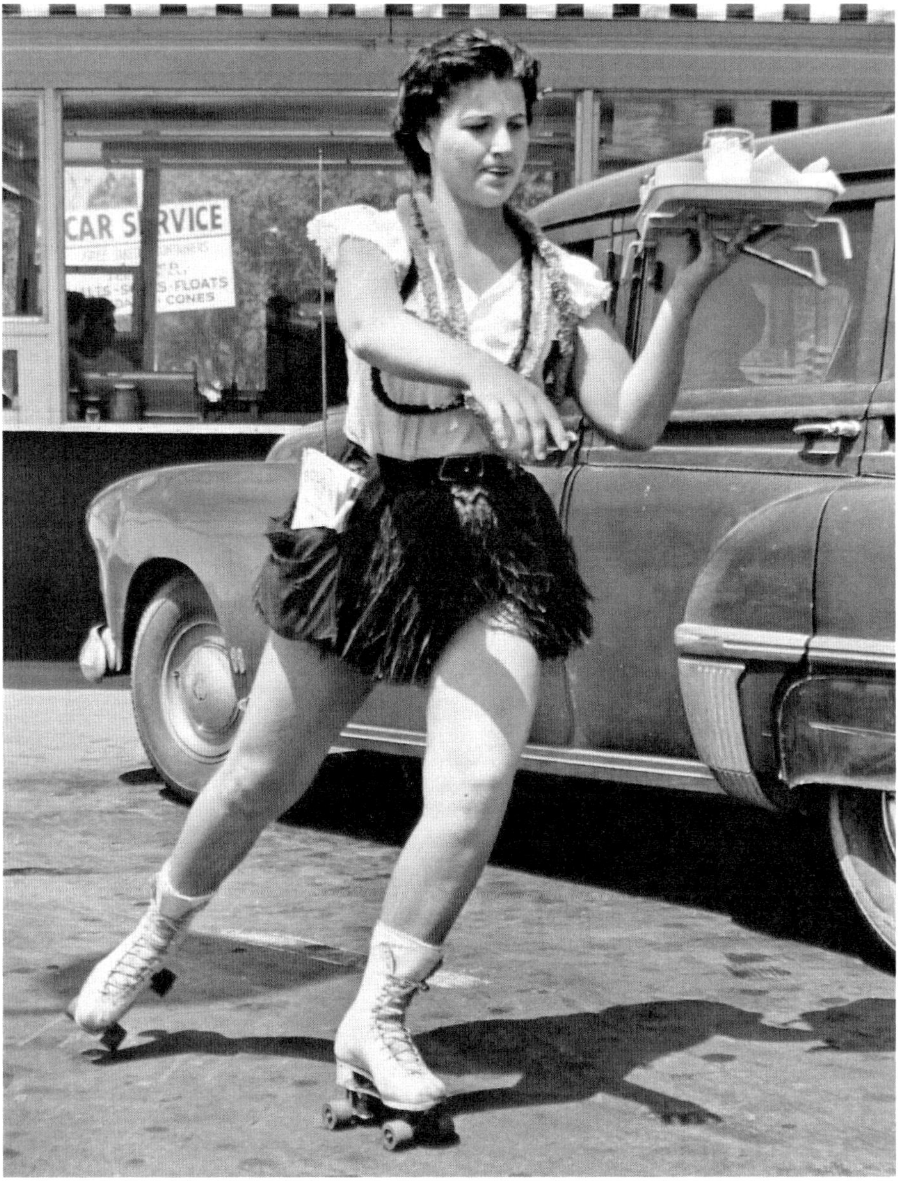

A 1940s drive-in carhop on roller skates skillfully delivers a tray of food to customers, circa 1940s. *From the* New York Daily News.

But there was also a related roller sport that predated the establishment of structured roller sport competition: the Transcontinental Roller Derby, introduced in 1935. Then, in 1948, roller derby merged with television, and suddenly the thrill and danger drew tens of thousands of spectators rink-side, with TV crowds also getting caught up in roller derby fever. By the end of the 1940s, Americans had a choice of watching Skating Vanities live or turning the channel to catch the antics of their favorite derby players. Hardcore fans went to the stadiums with huge rinks to share and take in the feel of roller action, whether it was in the form of organized competitions, the spectacular extravaganzas of Skating Vanities or the action-driven roller derby. This roller action did not escape the attention of publishers. Press reports were frequent, whether it was neighborhood news of rink fundraisers or roller industry news in trade journals. But it was four full pages of roller derby in *Life* magazine—featuring tough-as-nails pretty girls flying around a banked-oval track and, not infrequently, flying over the railings—that caught the nation's attention.[28]

As the Golden Age of Roller Skating entered its second decade, America's favorite recreation became firmly entrenched and expanded into new venues. The 1950s rolled in with drive-in restaurants and waitresses on skates taking orders and delivering product, creating a phenomenon that persists into the twentieth-first century.

THAT WHICH IS GOLDEN MAY NOT GLITTER

Roller skating had numerous public perceptions that it fought to overcome throughout the 1940s to be viewed as clean, healthful and a moral activity for youngsters. While the industry shaped itself for this new image during the early 1940s, the story of the Golden Age of Rolling Skating cannot be told without placing it in the context of World War II and the restrictive conditions of war imposed on the nation's citizenry to fulfill its military material requirements.

When war broke out, the War Production Board (WPB) was mobilized as an emergency war structure to manage the acquisition of war material for the War Department (Army) and the Navy Department. A Department of Defense did not exist to manage procurement for the military branches. As a result, there existed no stockpiles of munitions, ships, planes or tanks. A scramble ensued to identify the status of basic raw materials required to produce equipment to fight a modern war. Volunteers were recruited to lead many of these efforts and were paid one dollar per year (hence were known as dollar-a-year men). For example, studies on the availability of raw materials were requested by Roosevelt to determine their status and what other options the United States ought to pursue. Japan had cut Allies off from rubber tree plantations located in Southeast Asia in 1942. Rubber was one such example of an essential material, used for tires for Jeeps and trucks and even roller skates. Roller skates were actually considered for moving troops around invaded cities without the necessity of gasoline-driven vehicles depicted by cartoonist Bill Mauldin.[29] Stateside, roller skate–related "Save Gas" campaigns sprouted throughout the country as citizen patriots, driven by the recently organized roller skate industry, mobilized to support the war effort.

It would be several years before Congress would pass authorization to create the Department of Defense through the National Security Act of 1947. Studies and proposals had come and gone for decades suggesting unification of the military branches. The nation had yet to learn the lessons of World War I, as well as its emerging role in the world as a superpower, persistently and deliberately posturing itself as an isolationist nation. It would take a second world war and a president under pressure of an emerging cold war with the Soviet Union to push the military branches and Congress for a compromise unification proposal in addition to a National Security Council to address issues of national security. Essentially, the National Security Act of 1947 put the nation on a perpetual war footing by integrating intelligence, military and civilian leadership into an advisory group that reported to the president. But in 1941, prior to December 7, the political will for any sort of war readiness by the public, Congress or a president was absent.

Because the nation was not prepared, a scramble took place for securing raw materials and refitting industry from commercial use to the production of war materials, as well as rationing of all sorts, including metal, leather, food, gasoline, driving for pleasure and even cigarettes. To conserve coal and therefore energy, the government's War Production Board[30] (WPB) issued blackout orders. Big cities like Chicago were hit hard, shutting down recreational and entertainment activities after work hours. At the request of the government, all conventions with fifty or more persons were canceled to ease transportation and housing requirements. For example, the RSROA, in a predictable move, canceled its 1945 amateur championships.[31] These were the shared hardships endured by the nation, and they rippled through leisure, entertainment and recreational industries.

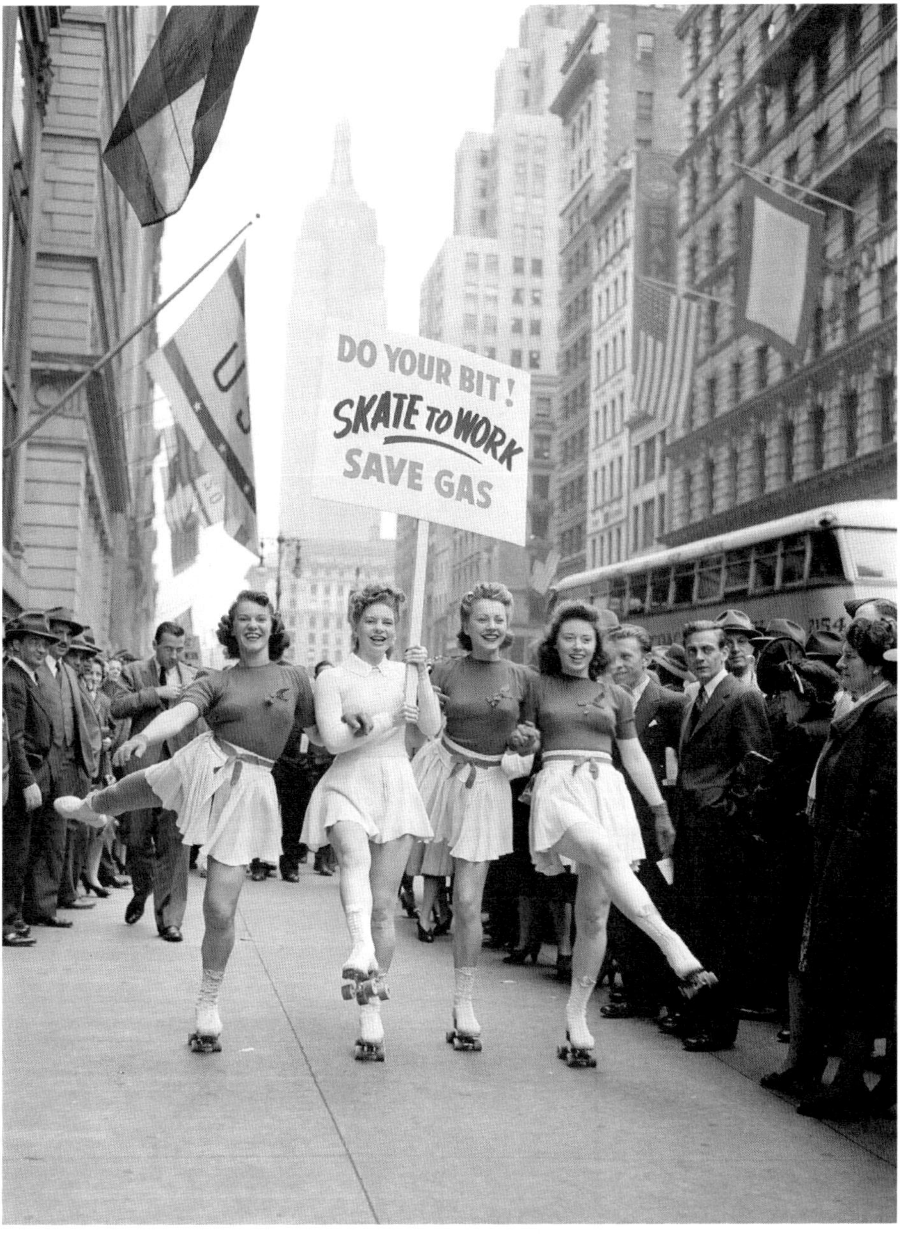

Professional skaters from Broadway's *Roller Follies* skate New York's Fifth Avenue to promote President Roosevelt's "save gas" campaign, June 2, 1942. When Gloria Nord joined the cast, the show was renamed Skating Vanities. *From left to right*: Ronnie Billet, Dolly Durkin, Isabel Newland and Jo Reilly. *Associated Press.*

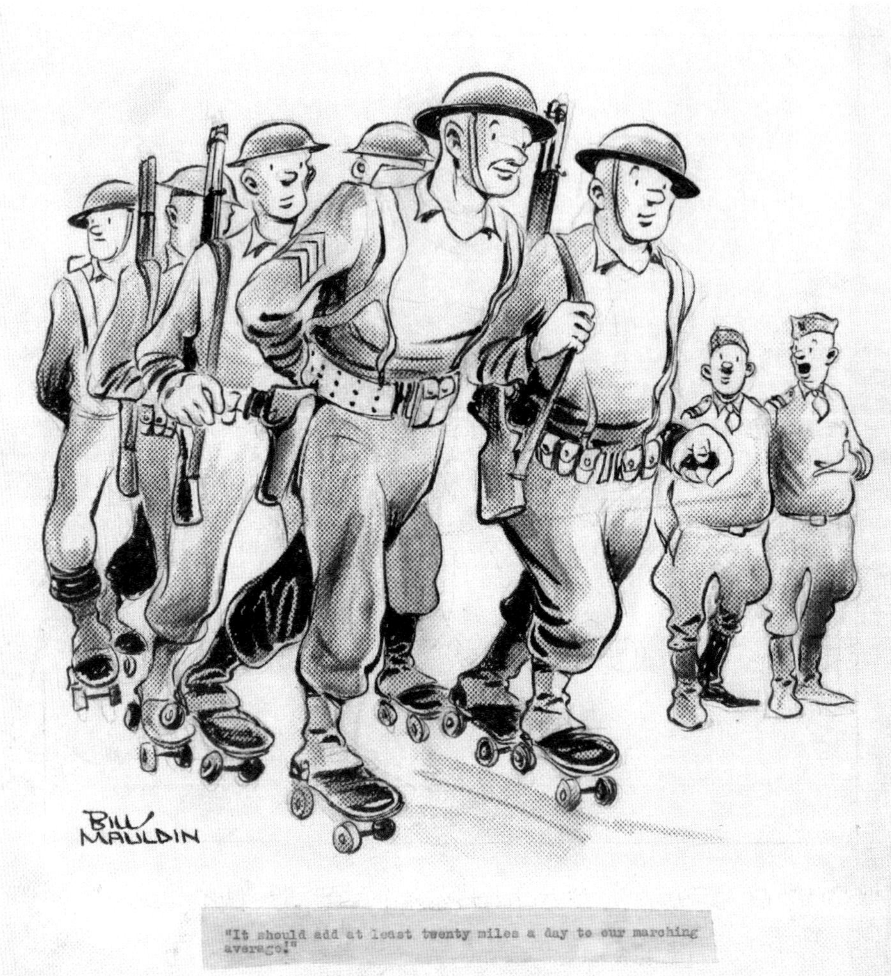

A 1941 Bill Mauldin cartoon from the *Oklahoma City Times'* July 14, 1941 edition depicts military officers and soldiers marching on roller skates. Two officers stand and comment on the benefits of the change in footwear. "It should add at least twenty miles a day to our marching average!" *Library of Congress, Papers of Bill Mauldin, Cartoon Drawings [CD 1—Mauldin, no. 169 (A size)].*

Shoe companies were ordered to make army combat boots instead of roller skate boots, as leather was in limited supply. Scrap metal was conserved and recycled, requiring saving skate parts and rebuilding skates from those parts. Ball bearing manufacturing plants converted and made ball bearings for artillery, tanks and ship cannons. Cotton used to manufacture boot laces was in short supply. Cotton and wool textile mills were ordered to weave service uniforms and make rope cots for ships and used for a number of other military requirements. By 1945, two years had gone by without the manufacture of new skates. Heavy wear on old equipment, both skates and rink materials, forced many rinks to close.[32] By May 1945, Robert Ware Sr. wrote to *Billboard* that Chicago Roller Skate Company had made no roller skate shoes for three years or more since WPB Order M-126 had gone into effect.[33] WPB orders remained in effect until they were withdrawn.

In addition to these restrictions, a "war tax" depicted as an emergency tax or luxury tax was passed on consumption that affected the entertainment industry. These were levied against distilled spirits, nightclubs, theater admissions and coin machines. The entertainment industry anxiously awaited the peacetime dividends and the declaration of a date for the end of emergency taxes, anticipating a return to their low prewar levels.[34] While the war ended on September 2, 1945, it would be July 1946 before the end of emergency was declared. Entertainment insiders recalled that during World War I, a war tax was declared but failed to be repealed once the war concluded.

What was not in short supply were morale-boosting programs or propaganda about how best the roller skate industry, among others, could support that effort, whether it was with the federal Office of Civilian Defense or individual military branches. For example, Rear Admiral D. McLeBreton, commandant of the Fifth Naval District, was the guest of honor at the formal opening of the new Mercury Rink at Norfolk in January 1945. The admiral stated that skating has been a morale builder for the navy during the war.[35] The admiral was accompanied by other dignitaries as well, including the governor of Virginia, mayor of Norfolk and General J. Fulmer Bright.

Other evidence of roller skating's contribution to the war effort is seen through the War Production Board's support of rebuilding the Rollerdrome in Portland, Oregon. A $40,000 project, the rink was expanded from twenty-two thousand square feet to twenty-six thousand square feet "using WPB priorities, reconstruction and enlargement" initiatives, increasing seating capacity from 750 to 1,000.[36] Portland was the site of naval shipbuilding during World War II.

This give and take between the roller industry and war industry persisted from 1941 well into 1946. From war demands to men called to duty in the millions, diversion and rationing of supplies that supported the roller industry, all became constraints the industry worked through and overcame to achieve continued growth by the end of the 1940s. Despite these hurdles, business economics, popular cultural changes and racial undercurrents worked against the industry as it peaked in the mid-1950s.

Former skate enthusiasts have asked, "Why did the Golden Age of Roller Skating end in 1959?" After all, the nation experienced roller disco in the 1970s, roller derby grew in popularity and speed skating expanded its competitive stance with interest…or so it seemed. Was it the snub by the International Olympic Committee to accept roller skating as an Olympian sport?[37] It could have been the death of longtime skate dancer Earl Van Horn, who passed away tragically in 1962. Van Horn claimed the title of his Mineola Roller Rink as the "home of dance skating" and contributed significantly to skate dancing as sport and competition. Author Lou Brooks's *Skate Crazy* concluded that it was the invasion of the Beatles in 1964.

Brooks's thesis is not far off the mark. Romy Poletti studied the relationship between roller skating and music, concluding that this symbiotic relationship contributed to the nostalgia in roller skating by enthusiasts and provided a rationale for the decline of roller skating by the end of the 1950s.[38] A new generation had come of age, and their interest was in rock-and-roll, which differed dramatically from that of their parents and the organ music of the war generation. Rock-and-roll did not offer a rhythm nor a beat that was conducive to roller skating. Rock-and-roll's rebellious nature also rejected the adult world's order and status quo. So, when roller rinks catered to an organ music–oriented audience, rock and rollsters saw that as dated and too adult and found other forms of entertainment.

Organ music was living on borrowed time by the early 1940s. Wurlitzer pipe organs had earned a second life by being repurposed for roller skating rinks across the country. Both pipe organs and organists were first introduced in neighborhood theaters for the silent movie era.[39] The Hammond electric organ was introduced in later years (1940s), but either instrument was a significant investment initially and then to maintain and operate. Large rinks hosted both a Hammond and a Wurlitzer.

However, it would take more than rock-and-roll to end a golden age. It represented but one factor among many that would culminate in the decline of roller skating's heyday. Economic factors included declining gate receipts, increasing liability insurance costs and real estate values that made the return on investment no longer a viable business venture; recreational segregation would persist for decades. This dynamic would eventually erode roller skating's golden age image.

In 1942, interracial groups picketed Chicago's White City Roller Rink, organized by a fledging organization, the Congress of Racial

Equality (CORE). The group sought access but was denied by white operators on the basis of its club membership policy. The "club" method was used to subvert the Illinois civil rights statute, as well as in other states, but CORE demonstrated that white activists gained access while black activists were denied.[40] The incident underscored the widespread desire by African Americans to exercise their civil rights and access public accommodations, including leisure and recreational opportunities afforded to some but denied to others. A nonviolent campaign persisted until a 1946 legal suit by CORE against White City Roller Rink resulted in desegregation of the rink.[41] Subsequently, White City changed its name to Park City Roller Rink.

CORE's disciplined crusade of civil disobedience would serve as a model that would be used in later years for civil rights demonstrations, such as in the 1950s and 1960s in Chicago as well as throughout the nation.[42] This dynamic, the clash of white ownership and its white patron support versus that of black access, with white support, resulted in the movement toward desegregation of public accommodations. Desegregation actions targeted housing, restaurants, amusement, leisure and recreational facilities, rippling through roller rinks for two decades. Its climax was the 1968 Chicago riots along Madison Avenue, which destroyed the oldest, best-known roller rink in their wake. The Golden Age of Roller Skating in Chicago came to an end.

CHICAGO ROLLER CAPITAL

Chicago roller skate enthusiasts had many reasons to advance the claim that Chicago was the roller capital of America during the early years of the golden age.[43] It may well have started with the first silent movie in 1907, *An Awful Skate*, by Chicago's Essanay Film Company. More than likely, that first movie was inspired by the first outdoor public roller skating rink in 1902, which attracted seven thousand skaters. In the initial days of silent moviemaking, Chicago was recognized as the movie capital of the world.[44] Essanay filmed and produced more than two hundred silent movies during that period. While those first movies were silent, Chicago-style roller derby created pandemonium that persists to this day.

On the eve of the roller skating craze as it emerged out of hibernation, Chicago hosted the first "competitive" marathon, the Transcontinental

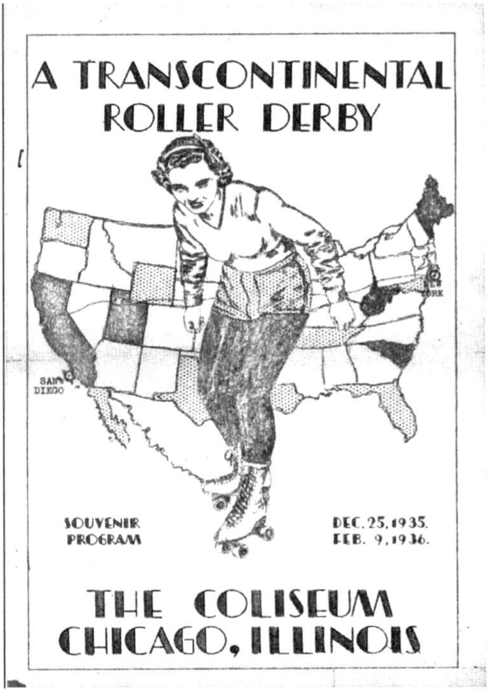

Left: A 1935 souvenir program cover for the Transcontinental Roller Derby. *National Museum of Roller Skating.*

Below: 1950 women's roller derby skaters leap over two who have fallen. *Library of Congress, Prints & Photographs Division [LC-USZ62-133382].*

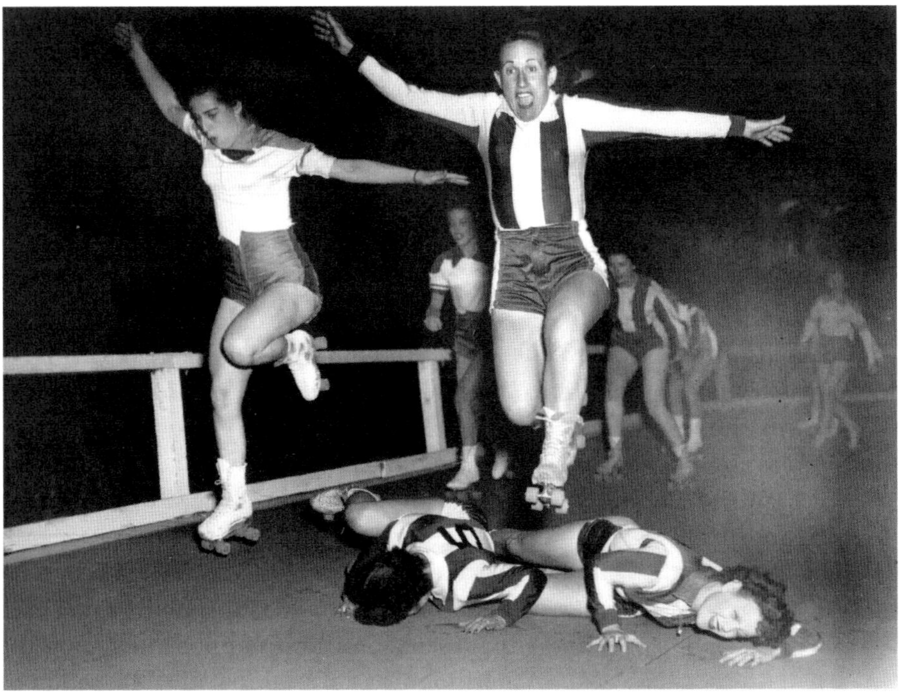

Roller Derby, with a pair of men and a pair of women facing off at the Chicago Coliseum in 1935.[45] As a result the modern version of roller derby was born, and Chicago was its birthplace.[46] The derby was a grueling sixty-four thousand laps, four thousand miles, covering one hundred miles per day over six weeks. Twenty thousand spectators crammed the Coliseum to witness that first event. Initially promoted as a marathon speed event, the roller derby was a test of endurance and stamina.[47] The 1940s team the Chicago Mohicans represented Chicago in those early derby bouts.[48]

Organizer Leo Seltzer discovered that the bank floor, made from white pine, would not hold up to roller derby antics and replaced it with hard maple. A white powder dusted the wooden floor to ensure that wooden wheels would stick to the rink surface, creating clouds of dust—not unlike the smoke that would surround disco skaters decades later. Early contests played with teams of five skaters on each side, with each team consisting of the same number of boys and girls. They raced for fourteen laps on a banked track. The banked track eased the strain of speed, not unlike those tracks featured in roller derby movies. Contestants skated from 1:00 a.m. until 1:00 a.m. the next night. Patrons crammed into the stadium, screaming with excitement for their favorite teams, urging darling players to score and booing bad guys, all of which created thrilling spectator events.

It was 1937 when sportswriter Damon Runyon suggested to Seltzer that more contact be incorporated into the sporting event. Team members scored points and blocking was permitted, but no hands, feet or elbows were allowed; "whipping" was invented to provide instant acceleration for jam skaters. Rules developed further, and roller derby as played today evolved from those early events. The first televised roller derby in 1948 catapulted the sport's popularity, and derby expanded into other cities.

Roller derby evolved from speed skating, whose history dates to the late 1890s and early 1900s. In fact, speed skating on ice was quite popular at the turn of the century (1900) in Humboldt Park, where forty thousand spectators would gather to watch the annual Illinois Championship. Newspapers from the 1900s labeled the contest the world championships. Of course, these speed events required ponds to freeze over sufficiently that skaters would not fall through the ice, which also suggests why rollers became instantly popular, as they could skate at any time of the year.

Whether it was roller derbies, silent movies or the teen blond sensation on rollers Gloria Nord, this attention to roller skating spawned roller fever across Chicago rinks. Initial rehearsals for Roller Follies were held at Arcadia Rink before the show was expanded to become the spectacle

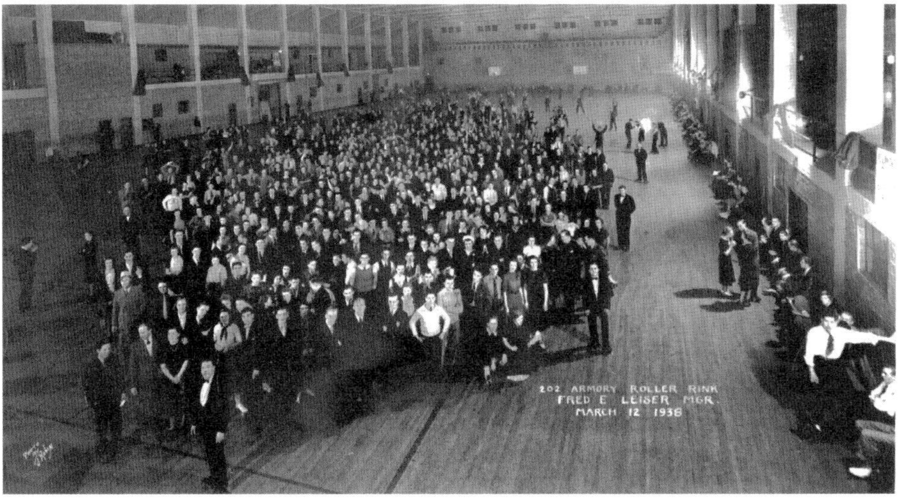

A huge crowd represented by sailors, suits and skirts at the 202nd Armory Roller Rink, the "World's Largest Roller Skating Rink," Chicago, March 12, 1938. *Sandra Levin and Chicago's Orbit Skate Center.*

patrons recalled in later years. The name changed to Skating Vanities with Nord's star recruitment. Nord convinced Steinman that the name Roller Follies would mislead the public into thinking they would be seeing a roller derby.[49] Young people breaking in sidewalk skates were eager to come of roller age at area rinks and see the new stars of roller skating such as Gloria Nord. What they saw and learned was that much more awaited them inside those huge rinks—speed, artistry and the softer, graceful side of skating, dancing on rollers.

Along with the Chicago Coliseum, Riverview Park hosted the early speed skating races at Riverview's huge oval pavilion rink. Other Chicago rinks also formed speed clubs and began to train and develop athletes to compete in speed events, like at Madison Gardens. Inter-rink rivalries emerged and were at the forefront of using their speed clubs to produce competitors for not only local speed events but also those first organized, national competitions formed in the late 1930s and early 1940s. The first of the Armory rinks, the 202nd Armory Rink located at 5917 North Broadway, opened as the "World's Largest Roller Skating Rink" in the late 1930s with a massive 34,500-square-foot rink floor.

Later, Arcadia and Armory formed speed clubs to compete against those of Madison and Riverview. Chicago speed clubs were poised to send a steady stream of seasoned competitors to national competitions hosted

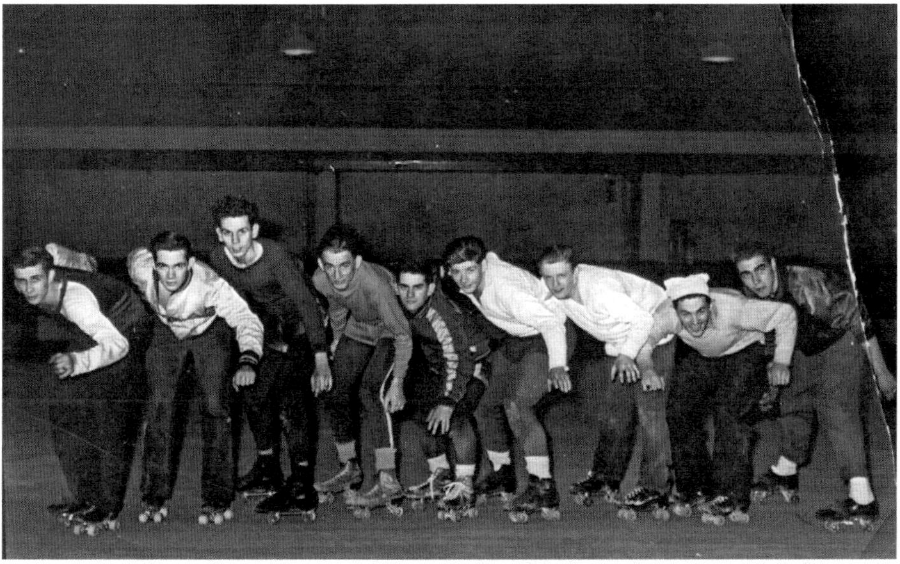

Arcadia speedsters take first at the Illinois meet, Arcadia Speed Club, circa 1946. *Family of Elmer "Bud" Knight.*

by the Roller Skating Rink Owners Association (RSROA), with the first national roller speed skating championship taking place in 1938. It comes as no surprise that Chicago skaters formed the Roller Skating Club of Chicago (RSCC) to develop the next generation of roller speedsters. Chicago roller speedsters found a new niche for their speed skills, dominating state and national speed events for the next decade.

From a spectator's perspective, speed skating was most exciting and often talked about as idle conversation or just jostling at skate events, speed or otherwise.[50] The future of speed skating in a review by C.V. (Cap) Sefferino, who operated the Sefferino Rollerdrome in Cincinnati,[51] referred to Arcadia and Madison Gardens in Chicago as the "hotbeds of amateur speed skating." Sefferino added that less than 5 percent of rinks tolerated speed skating and less than 10 percent of rink operators furnish the talent for competition. Arcadia and Madison Gardens rinks developed competitors but also represented well-managed operations, setting aside set times—essential to support speed skating. The Rollerdrome did likewise and reserved Saturday and Sunday afternoon sessions for speed skating races. Sefferino claimed that the fog (rosin that rises up with speed) goes with competition and ensures the safety of speed skaters; while not great, it is required for competition.

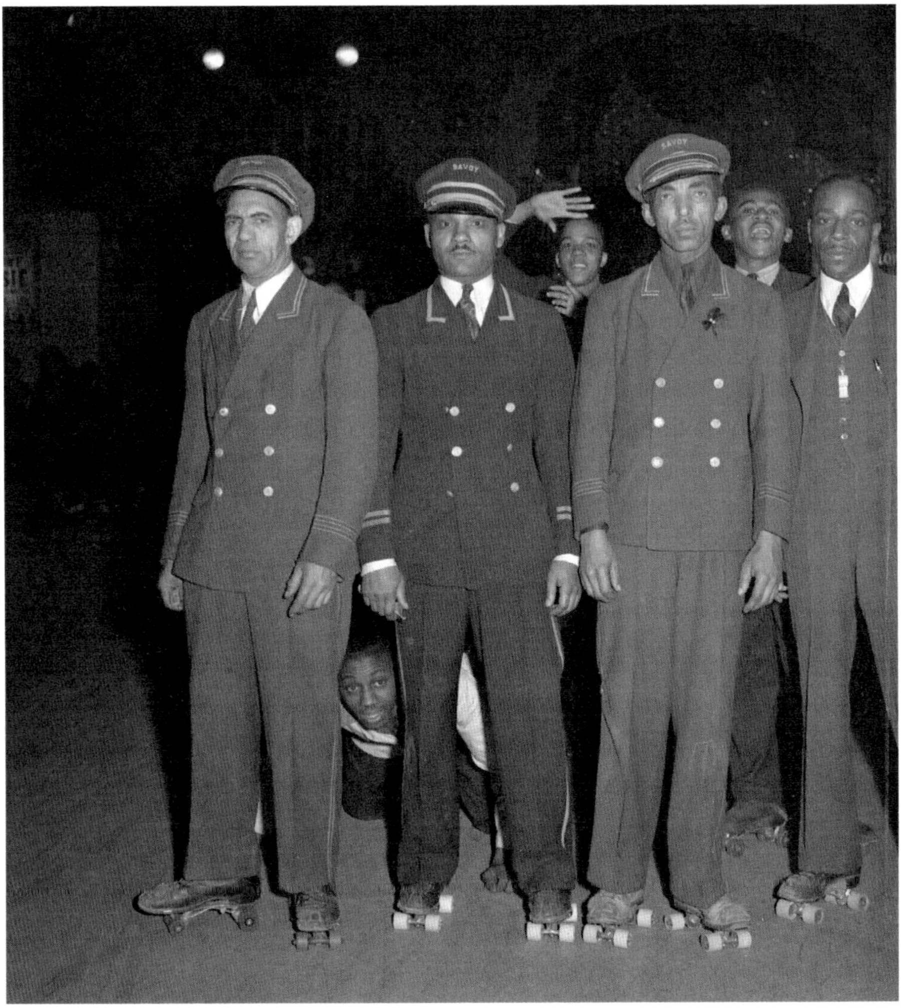

Instructors and floor guards in uniform at the Savoy Roller Rink, 1941. Jimmy Davis was the lead instructor, with the leader suggested by the dark suit in the center. *Library of Congress, Prints & Photographs Division, FSA/OWI Collection [LC-USF34-38551-D].*

Ironically, while white Chicago skaters dominated national competition, unknown Chicago black speed skaters dominated an all-black skater league organized by Savoy's Jimmy Davis in cooperation with Detroit and Cleveland. The league lasted only a few years as Chicago's skaters hauled home the cache of trophies. Black skaters lacked the proficiency to compete with whites due to limited access to rinks, instruction and trainers. Chicago's Savoy Ballroom set aside a night each week for black rollers. By the early 1940s, floor time was devoted to the roller sport, and its popularity among black residents grew throughout the Chicago area and the Midwest.

The rinks of Chicago offered an array of sizes and character, new and old, each hosting a style of skating with great skaters to carve out a unique niche among Chicago's roller rinks. The longtime and best-known Madison Gardens anchored the West Side and was among the few rinks that survived Prohibition, the Depression and a honky-tonk reputation, but Madison Gardens emerged to produce the next crop of speed skaters. The Armory rinks and Arcadia cornered the north side of the city. Each hosted numerous competitive events, while Arcadia attracted performers and professionals like Gloria Nord,[52] who used the rink to work out new routines.[53] Ms. Nord practiced new routines at the Arcadia Rink during the off season and became a regular celebrity for Chicago North Side rollers. Organist Berry described Nord's ability to interpret the music as exceptional and very much like those in ballet. The far South Side had the Swank Rink and White City, while the near West Side featured the newest rink, the Roller Bowl. The giant Hub Rink secured the northwest outpost.

During those early years, when the roller skating industry established national championships, it was Arcadia, Madison Gardens and the Armory that produced competitors who would dominate championships, in not only speed but figure and skate dancing as well, throughout the decade of the 1940s. Skaters with speed, skill and motivation traveled to the North Side for training and competition. For example, Russell Brown, from Madison Gardens Speed Club, set records in 1941 at the Cleveland Rollercade that remain unbroken to this day, while Maxine Rosser, also of Chicago, set speed records for the junior ladies.[54] Ted Rosdahl, who won as a junior in 1944, returned in 1952 as a senior to win national figure championship in freestyle. That same year, he and Betty Rosdahl won senior dance at the Great Lakes Regional championships.

A century ago, there were numerous roller rinks in Chicago. Most are forgotten, but a few survived, establishing rivalries that energized Chicago's place in the Golden Age of Roller Skating. The Chicago Coliseum was at the center of many spectator roller events where speed records were made and broken. In 1904, Coliseum operators gave thought to a national speed roller circuit, claiming that "the fastest men on roller skates has been developed there, have been incentive for making roller skating popular."[55] It was the birth site of the legendary roller derby,[56] a sport that continues to awe crowds a century later. But it was Harley

Davidson who dueled with speed skater contemporaries such as Fred A. Martin, Art Eglington and Roland Cioni, of Chicago, setting records at the Riverview Rink in 1907. These early speed events instigated roller speed skating, and despite the Great War and the Depression, skaters found solace in speed skating that endured until its time would rise once again.

As interest grew in other forms of roller skating, instigated by the silent movies, roller derbies and professionals like Gloria Nord,[57] the demand for quality skate equipment increased. While the nation's attention was riveted to skate events, the inventor of the modern roller skate and the major manufacturers of roller skates based out of Chicago produced skate equipment, advertising and promotional literature that positioned Chicago for a new era in an industry that rolled from coast to coast. Their continued innovation brought roller skates to the masses, whether it was ball bearings, sidewalk skates or boot skates designed for a new generation of roller skate rinks. Headquartered in Chicago, Chicago Roller Skate Company[58] and the Richardson Ballbearing Skate Company were the major skate manufacturers in the world.

In 1957, Chicago Roller Skate Company[59] celebrated its fifty-year anniversary and was credited for building a roller skate suitable for those maple rink floors as the Golden Age began its boom in the 1940s.[60] This was before the existence and use of plastic coatings such as polyurethane, used on maple wood floors to avoid the use of rosin to provide the "stick" skaters needed to keep wheels on the rink floor.

But a challenge to the company's owners, the Ware brothers, came early from Paddy Harmon, famous sports promoter and builder of the Chicago Stadium. He became interested in bringing roller skating to the stadium. The Ware brothers were building three-wheel skates, and Harmon challenged them to build a better skate by throwing the three-wheeler at them. Wheels were made with steel, vulcanized fiber, aluminum or boxwood. The boxwood was Turkish and came over to the States on ships used as ballast. It was wet, sawed by hand and punched out with a punch press. According to Harmon, the three-wheeled skate and boxwood were tired concepts, inferior and could not hold up to the new demands of an emerging new industry. This challenge brought about the improved quad skate as we know it today. When Harmon saw the new four-wheel skate, he was elated. Soon maple wood wheels were adopted by major rinks across the country.

Paddy Harmon is credited with reviving the sport of roller skating in 1904 and earned the title of "father of roller skating" at the turn of the twentieth century.[61] It was Harmon who opened the Riverview Park Roller Rink, at that time promoted as the world's largest rink, and started the first world's championship race. Once Harmon built the Chicago Stadium, he whetted the sports appetite of citizens by attracting a range of events from boxing to hockey, basketball and roller skating. For example, in 1929, world championship roller races were brought to the Chicago Stadium, where its seventeen-thousand three-tier seating capacity could be filled. An eighteen-foot track with eight laps to the mile was built for the races with no banking. Later, the stadium would host Skating Vanities.

Claims can be made by Chicagoans to grab the moniker of "roller capital" during the Golden Age of Roller Skating, but if the preceding were not sufficient for Chicago's claim to the title, then surely Chubby completes the case. Chubby was outfitted with two pair of Chicago roller skates by Robert Ware Jr. of Chicago Roller Skate Company.[62] While Ware Jr. fitted the skates, he was wise enough to bring onboard Freeman Clark, animal trainer from Wichita, Kansas, to train Chubby to skate.[63] You see, Chubby was no ordinary skater but a roller-skating horse trained to skate and perform tricks. His start: Chicago!

PART II

RINKS OF THE GOLDEN AGE, 1937–1959

Roller skate rinks during the Golden Age competed for the best skaters and largest skate clubs, hosted competition-driven meets and recruited the best organists to keep skaters on the floor. Chicago-area rinks were no different, as rink operators vied to become Chicago's flagship roller rink. Madison Gardens Rink on the West Side used the tagline "Oldest and Best Known." Somewhat out of the mainstream of Chicago rinks but well established was the South Side White City Roller Rink. The 202nd Armory bragged with the "World's Largest" (34,500 square feet), but Gloria Nord returned to Arcadia Gardens Rink to work out the mechanics of new routines. The Riverview Rink carved out its niche as "Chicago's courteous rink." The Roller Bowl remained the newest skate rink in the 1940s, opening in 1942 with a 24,000-square-foot floor, the largest rink in Chicago, to be rivaled by the Hub, which opened in 1950. The Swank Rink represented the far South Side with the only knee-action skate floor in the country.

Rink owners established dress codes in the late 1930s to upgrade rink perception while distancing the view that they were gang-centered facilities. But dress codes were not adopted by all clubs. The Mineola rink in Long Island, New York, called for men to wear jackets or sweaters while skating. Sweaters had to have sleeves and collars, and ties had to be worn unless the skater were wearing a neat sport shirt, subject to the approval of management. So-called polo shirts were not to be confused with sport shirts and were not permitted. Women's skating dresses had to be no shorter than two inches above the knees. Under no circumstances were

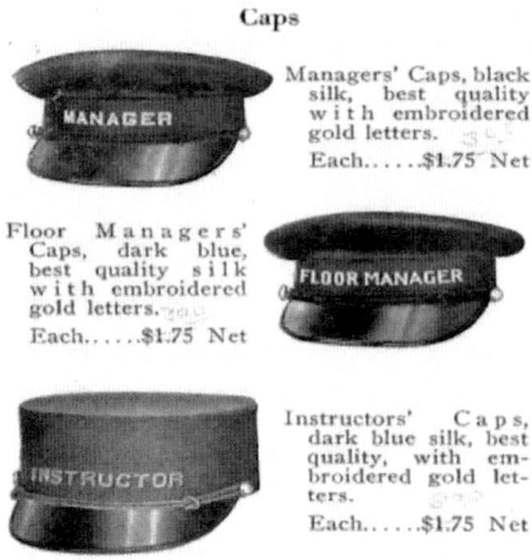

Roller skate rink uniform caps. Most rinks required staff to wear uniforms, accompanied by dress codes for patrons. *National Museum of Roller Skating.*

women permitted to skate in slacks, pajamas or trousers of any kind. And alcohol was banned!

New services were established to accommodate the new look of roller skating. Most rinks offered "learn to skate" classes that ranged from basic steps to the advanced maneuvers and even skate dancing by music type. The latest equipment included quality maple wood floors, skate rentals and attendants to help fit those skates. Rink "floor guards" assisted by keeping decorum and halted action to minimize floor pileups. Special events were held and advertised to attract skaters from other clubs in the hopes that the host rink could lure them to adopt their rink as home rink. Skate programs were set and published, providing a certain level of rink decorum that separated the new style of rolling skating from the old perceptions. The weekly skate program would detail the evening's events and include an all-skate, skate dancing, couples only and even the newest fad, trio skates! The organist served as not only musician but also emcee, but the best had the ability to write organ music that catered to the steps of skaters.

Rink amenities grew during the 1940s as owners expanded the skate floor, upgraded facilities and outfitted with new equipment to compete against other neighborhood rinks while also hoping to host state and national competitions. In addition to the main rink floor, basic features included a beginners' rink, a skate dancing rink, spectator stands, a lounge, equipment rooms that served as check-in for shoe skates, a clubhouse and adequate restroom facilities. As rinks grew in size, owners incorporated additional features, such as at the Rollarena in Detroit. It included space for skate-boys along an outer wall so that they would not interfere with traffic. The Rollarena even included a penthouse at one end to provide living quarters for the owner family that was equipped with special privacy glass, allowing visibility from the penthouse into the rink but not the reverse.[64]

The names of roller rinks during the golden age say as much about the popularity and spectacle of roller skating as about the size and magnificence of 1940s-style roller rinks: Rollercade, Rollerdrome, Rollarena, Rolladium, Skatorium and more. As the popularity of roller skating increased, coupled with crowd size, operators were encouraged to expand.

For example, Pontiac, Michigan's original rink was a converted dance hall, with a small rink floor size of 72 by 72 feet (5,184 square feet) and eight posts around the edge. When the Pontiac Rolladium was rebuilt, the rink floor size was expanded to 90 by 190 feet with no posts on the floor. The Rolladium opened in Pontiac, Michigan, in January 1950[65] with its 17,100-square-foot floor size, considered huge in comparison to the original rink. In later years, national roller skate organizations grouped rinks by skating surface size in classifications of small (floor size under 7,000 square feet), medium (7,000 to 10,000 square feet) and large (10,000+ square feet).[66]

However, floor noise remained a distraction. Typical rink floors consisted of a wood base, with maple boards as the primary rink floor cover. However, this allowed air cells between both the wood layers and between boards that contributed to excessive floor noise. For the USARSA National Championships in 1946 at the Norwood Rink, the floor was designed by a construction engineer to minimize noise and was deemed successful. To accomplish this, the floor was constructed with twelve inches of cinders over which a concrete floor was poured. On top of the concrete, a composition of aspheldium mastic[67] was poured, with the boards imbedded in this mastic on their sides similar to the construction of a bowling alley floor. Nails were then driven into each board from the side as laid down, resulting in a solid floor. The end result was a nearly echo-proof floor.[68] When Chicago's Roller Bowl opened in 1942, it featured its soundproof maple wood floor.

Once the war ended, rinks began to experiment with plastic floors. This did not eliminate the use of wood, and maple wood in particular was spared. Six coats of plastic were placed over the wood. The end result produced a non-skid floor that did away with the need for rosin powder.[69] Most rinks were constructed with a suspension hanger, post-free maple floor, gables and poles. The preferred wood for rink floors was white northern maple in 50- by 120-foot planks.

By 1947, competitions had grown tremendously in terms of both spectators and contestants. It was not unusual to have one thousand spectators, while contestant entries had expanded to include all parts of a state and its rinks. The competition season began with state meets in April or May, and then first-, second- and third-place winners moved on to nationals. As the sport grew in later years and the number of competitors increased, regional meets were held to ensure attracting flagship sites with sufficient support amenities. Regional were hosted by both the RSROA and the U.S. Federation of Amateur Roller Skaters by the late 1940s.[70]

Rink owners also had challenges to expand their clientele and track the turnover of new customers. Owners estimated that the turnover rate ranged from 80 to 95 percent among adults who tried roller skating but became disappointed in their progress and dropped the sport. This meant that tremendous effort had to be expended to not only increase participation but also provide services and amenities that would retain skaters.

The perception by many adults who tried and quit was that the sport was dangerous. That was not the case for young people. The chairman of the RSROA Dance Committee wrote that situations of this nature could be overcome by teachers who taught skating versus scooting and could be averted by avoiding "scooter" skates.[71] Scooter skates were designed for straight lines versus roller skates, which were intended for curved lines and the oval nature of a roller rink. The committee writer argued that to ensure the safety, happiness and enthusiastic participation of adults, skaters and rinks should stick with roller skates and avoid scooter skates.

Clamp-on skates (scooter skates) with alloy wheels were popular in the 1940s, the intent being to serve as a "sidewalk" skate versus a rink skate. The argument against the scooter skates was that when the quad skate was invented by James L. Plimpton in 1863, it was designed to be flexible and allow a skater's body weight to make curves when pressure was applied to the skate edge. The skater used their body to lean and direct the skate to one side or the other. As a result, the skater maximizes the joy, thrill and safety when the skater controls the direction of their activity. Sidewalk skates were low-cost street skates designed as an economic alternative to the flexible skate but resulted in a stiff skate.

National conventions, in addition to individual and couples competitions, offered instructor training techniques in rink management and association management duties. Meetings addressed issues such as those described earlier, whether they were image policies (dress code), quality of skate equipment, new materials and maintenance for rink floors—services and amenities that would retain the client base. In all, rink associations supported rink operators with a full range of strategies to build their rink roller skate business, led by successful old-timer rink-operators such as C.V. (Cap) Sefferino[72] of the Sefferino Rollerdrome (1937–56) in Cincinnati.

Often, young, accomplished amateurs who competed, exceled and earned accolades (i.e., a national championship) for skate athletic ability would be confronted with a choice between taking their championship credentials and transitioning to a professional career or leaving the sport and pursuing a college degree. Being a professional, or going pro, meant that the young star was making a career decision to serve as a pro at a rink, provide instruction, teach classes, coach and manage rink operations. Going pro also meant skating in shows, such as the likes of Gloria Nord or those who became the stars of Skating Vanities or other specialized skate performances. Flagship rink operators, whether in Chicago or elsewhere, sought the best, most accomplished skaters to run the rink's competition development program, which attracted the best young skaters to their rink. Those young people who achieved the highest levels, still in their youth, were making lifelong career decisions. For many men, this also meant leaving the sport and joining the military.

By 1950, mechanized rink music, or recorded music, was being introduced that would replace the organist. To keep work, old-timer organists prompted newcomers to develop their own style rather than get too dependent on the redundant "um-pa-pa, um-pa-pa" that drove skaters nuts and became boring. It was the organist's creative style that kept patrons coming back and onto the skate floor. He, or she, was a key figure and not only played the instrument but also maintained a skate tempo, the skate playlist and skate program.[73] In most rinks, the number was announced by the organist followed by a two-bar opening by a "terribly heavy down beat" that many loved and others found annoying. Rinks had their own unique sound and feel, given the style, experience and preferences of the organist, including rink theme music and a music number that would serve as a cue for patrons that a new skate number was about to start.[74] But the trend among most rinks was a rhythmic background followed by rink theme music, whether it was a waltz, jitterbug style or tango barn dance. All of this tied back to the rink's tagline. In 1942, the most requested ballad of skaters, popularized by organists, was the "Sleepy Lagoon,"[75] a Harry James waltz trumpet instrumental that became a favorite of U.S. servicemen.

The inaugural Skating Vanities hit Madison Square Garden in 1942 but scored only modest success according to Elliot Colfer, a writer for

Billboard.[76] Plans were to expand the show, make it bigger and better as it headed to Chicago Arena for its September 9–20, 1942 series. It included a tour that would take the Skating Vanities throughout the Midwest until it headed west.[77] Skating Vanities was back at the Garden in June 1944 and better than ever, with servicemen's favorite pin-up girl, Gloria Nord, starring in two numbers. The spectacle was described as a symphony of color and springtime, highlighted by an elaborate first act finale. Russian dances wrapped up the event.[78] Additional performances included a tapping routine on skates, tricks, a tango, comedy, a unicycle act, clowns, juggling, a badminton exhibition and a vaudeville-style act. Audiences loved it!

CHICAGO RINKS

Most Chicago roller rinks were constructed for purposes other than roller skating, including as dance ballrooms, National Guard armories and even a cable car powerhouse. As facilities fulfilled their original intent and purpose, buildings were retrofitted for other purposes. With roller skating's popularity expanding and the dance craze waning, ballrooms became ideal structures for the conversion to roller rinks. Their size and column-free floor space made them relatively straightforward for entrepreneurs.

Floor size was a feature that set the feel of a rink, its following and the purpose that drew skaters to the rink. Competitive skaters were drawn to the larger rinks with clubs that supported training and coaching for competition. Most recreational skaters sought a local neighborhood rink that provided an intimate mood without the cavernous feel of huge rinks. It was not unusual for competitive skaters to hold dual club memberships. However, rink rats visited them all and were quick to size up rinks based on feel, music and the social scene.

Charles Sengstock in *That Toddlin' Town* compared floor sizes of dance ballrooms that operated in the early decades of the twentieth century and incidentally grouped dance floors based on size.[79] This informal comparison, when applied to roller rinks, offers insights into rink floor sizes and may explain why patrons preferred some over others. Consider Arcadia, constructed as a dance ballroom but ending its lifecycle as a roller rink with an estimated 15,300 square feet of rink floor. It hosted a number of regional roller competitions. By ballroom dance floor standards, it

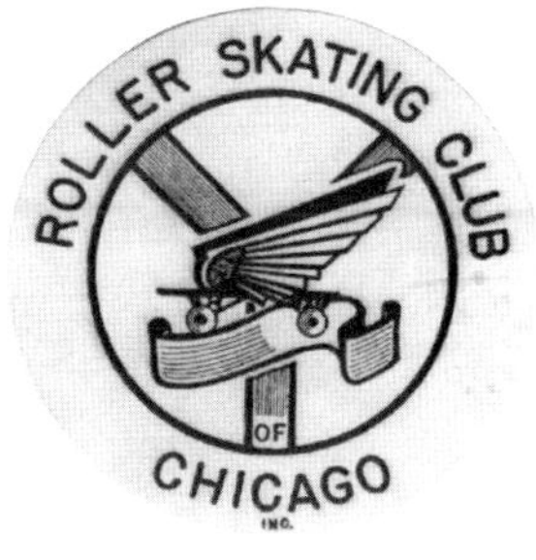

Roller Skating Club of Chicago. *Author's collection.*

was considered a midsized floor but was large compared to contemporaries of the day.[80] The Princess Ballroom was an upstairs dance floor at 1519 West Madison and a medium-sized ballroom with an 8,500-square-foot dance floor. Farther west on Madison, there was the Danceland Ballroom at 3825 West Madison Street with a fairly large dance floor of 13,500 square feet.

In contrast, the Trianon[81] dance ballroom (1922–58) was mammoth with its 29,580 square feet of floor space that could draw 3,000 dancers or 1,500 couples. Described as a reproduction of the palace of Versailles built by Louis XVI for his queen, Marie Antoinette,[82] the Trianon was extravagant, luxurious and sufficiently elegant that it was labeled "the world's most beautiful ballroom."[83] The Trianon also upheld a moral dance policy that prohibited couples from dancing any closer than ten inches, a dance policy common for upscale ballrooms in the 1920s.[84] White City Ballroom (South Side) hosted the largest dance floor in the city at 33,800 square feet, constructed in 1904.[85] After a fire in 1927 destroyed the park, tower and Ferris wheel, only the ballroom and roller rink remained. In contrast, the Willowbrook Ballroom, with its small-sized 5,000-square-foot dance floor, was successfully promoted as the "ballroom with the country club atmosphere" and offered what many considered exceptional intimacy.[86]

Most Chicago roller rinks operated with rink floors in excess of 20,000 square feet (see Appendix B). The armories were the most extreme at 34,500, but most rinks were built or renovated with 20,000- to 24,000-square-foot floors. Madison Gardens Rink was a midsized rink at 11,400 square feet, but it was smaller than Arcadia's 15,300-square-foot floor yet still deemed a medium-sized rink.[87] Madison Gardens used the tagline "Best Known and Most Favorite" roller rink. Why? Skaters, not unlike dancers of the period, were impressed by floor size and sought the intimacy that only a smaller rink could provide. Skaters liked rinks that were large enough to accommodate an all-skate using perimeter space while offering sufficient center rink space for exhibitionists who enjoyed tricks and couples who practiced dance technique. Large rinks could accommodate both a center rink of perhaps 12,000 square feet and a perimeter space that was used by singles, free-skaters and speedsters. The Swank Rink on the far South

Side, while offering the intimacy sought from a neighborhood rink, was described as even smaller than Madison Gardens. Both rinks had a loyal following that persisted for decades due to the intimacy of rink size and the emotional connection with skaters.

When *Skating News* was asked in 1949, "What is a 'Small rink'?" its response was, "One in which it would be impossible or nearly to skate a dance on its regular pattern or in any manner which 'would preserve the symmetry of the dance.'"[88]

Rinks came and went, but at any one time during the golden age, twelve to eighteen rinks were in operation, if not more. Some made it because the sites were the neighborhood rink and offered intimacy sought by regulars. But the larger rinks offered the venue for competitive events accompanied by the thrill of competition. The roller rinks of Chicago during the 1940s formed a unique and cooperative but competitive network that worked to benefit skaters and the Greater Chicago Area best seen by the triumvirate that persisted of Arcadia, Madison Gardens and the Roller Bowl. In later years, other area rinks worked to secure and host state, regional and national competitions, such as Elm and the North Avenue Rollerway in the western suburbs. It had become ingrained among Chicagoland roller rinks that a great city hosted great sport events, and since roller skating was the nation's top recreational sport, it was no different. New rinks understood this role as they watched older rinks succumb to decline, fire and the ravages of time.

By the 1970s and 1980s, most of Chicago's golden age rinks had disappeared from the Yellow Pages and *Chicago Tribune* articles,[89] yet activities at Aurora, the Elm, Fleetwood, Hub, Playdium and Orbit still occurred. No longer was there mention of the old-timer rinks whose heydays were back in the golden age.[90] James Dvorak with Chicago's United States of America rink on the North Side, one of twenty-nine operated in the 1980s by the group across the nation, stated that the nation experienced a roller skating craze in 1979–80. That craze was short-lived, and by 1981, roller skating interest had declined.

Championship events—whether state, regional or national—were bid for, but the cooperative nature among rink operators was such that those bids rotated among the various rinks so all would benefit from the influx of skaters, promotional benefits and the pre-events that were held to ready competitors for the events of national significance. But each rink also planned events that would bring media attention to its particular venue. Operators were master planners of special events and used roller skating as the vehicle to achieve success. A look back today at this collaborative effort reveals a paper trail of evidence (perhaps a digital trail by twenty-first-century standards) by the number of competitive skaters produced by Chicago rinks who won state and national titles. Similar stories among flagship rinks in other competitive metro areas demonstrate an equally collaborative frenzy among rink competitors.

Roller skate stickers started as a promotional method in the 1940s but soon became a rink souvenir item that gained great popularity by the 1950s. Rink operators saw barren metal skate cases, recognized the free advertising opportunity and gave rink stickers away, encouraging skaters to plaster their cases with them. Stickers were only one type of promotional item. Others included window cards, matchbooks and mailing lists along with club membership benefits. Many roller rinks adopted as a logo the winged sandal and foot of Mercury/Hermes, the fleet-footed messenger of the gods, to symbolize skate speed. The son of Zeus and Maia (daughter of Atlas), Mercury was graceful and swift. He wore winged sandals and a low-crowned winged hat, and he carried a magic staff called the "Caduceus."

Whatever the design, the stickers symbolized a proud roller skater who wore them as a badge of pride. Skaters plastered their skate cases with stickers of those rinks they visited, whether locally or nationally. Stickers were often traded, and the exchange often became a primitive form of social networking, as skaters would visit other rinks and proudly state, "I skated there!" International rink stickers were rare and the most sought-after by skaters. It was quite fashionable, especially for those who traveled and participated in competitions. By 1948, sticker collectors had organized the Universal Roller Skating Sticker Exchange (URSSE) and held annual conventions. At the conventions, stickers were traded, and attendees would talk skate stickers. The last meeting of URSSE was held in 1989, and the organization's membership included four thousand collectors.

Roller skate stickers capture the character, the mood and the feel of a rink and remain quite collectible to this day. Often the only thing that remains of those roller rinks is the rink's sticker and the recollections of those who collected and plastered them onto their roller skate cases during the Golden Age of Roller Skating. Perhaps inside that case is an old worn-out pair of Chicago skates with maple wood wheels.

Arcadia Gardens Rink (1936–59)

4444 North Broadway at Montrose
Tagline: "Home of Roller Dancing"
Nicky McMichael, Pro (December 1942)
Phil Hayes, Owner and Operator

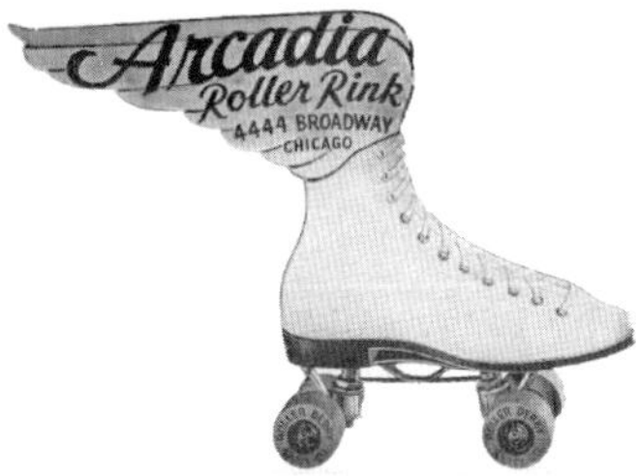

Arcadia Gardens Roller Rink, "Home of Roller Dancing," at 4444 North Broadway. *Author's collection.*

Built as a dance hall in 1906, Arcadia Gardens, formerly the Arcadia Ballroom, was among the first dance halls in Chicago and one of the few North Side places that would book African American jazz bands in the 1920s and 1930s.[91] In the 1930s, Arcadia hosted other sport events, such as boxing matches. The Aragon became the major draw for band performances when it opened in 1926, resulting in the decline of Arcadia's popularity as a dance venue. Arcadia opened in 1936 as a roller rink and continued operation through the next two decades. Leon Berry as the Gardens' "ace" organist—with his ability to write, adapt and play popular tunes to roller skating—underscored the tagline "Home of Roller Dancing." Arcadia ads would tout that skaters "learn to dance skate on roller skates to the swinging rhythm at Chicago's best organist."[92] Berry gained a reputation as the dean of roller rink rock and is credited with introducing classical music to roller skating rinks. In addition to Arcadia, he played the Hub in Norridge and Orbit in Palatine.[93]

A 1946 fire from an electric motor caused an estimated $100,000 damage.[94] Leo A. Seltzer and Fred A. Morelli purchased the rink in November 1946 for $53,000.[95] Arcadia reopened to a record crowd on January 4, 1947, with renovations. A new floor included Chicago's only plastic floor; at the Hammond organ was Ted Day, and the pro was Fred Wickman.[96] Wickman replaced Nicky McMichael (1942) as pro in the early 1940s. To celebrate the opening, Arcadia hosted USO night on Thursday, January 13, with all proceeds going to the service organization. Jackie Nelson defended her Chicago speed title; Gloria Nord, the professional of Skating Vanities, was present and performed for the capacity crowd. Ms. Nord was a regular at Arcadia, where she practiced new routines for the show.

Over the years, Arcadia hosted a number of state and regional competitions, including the 1946 and 1947 Illinois state championships.[97] The 1947 meet was the most successful Illinois event staged by a sponsor up to that time.[98] Due to its high profile, Arcadia attracted competent staffing, including LaVerne Beutlich, 1942 runner-up in state ladies' figure skating contest, and Fred Wickman, pro in charge of club's special sessions, doubling as instructor. In the late 1950s, the Chicago Westerners of the women's professional roller derby league played home matches at Arcadia Gardens.[99] Arcadia burned down on January 4, 1959,[100] and was demolished afterward.

202nd Armory Rink (circa 1937–42)

5917 North Broadway, Chicago
Tagline: "World's Largest Rink"

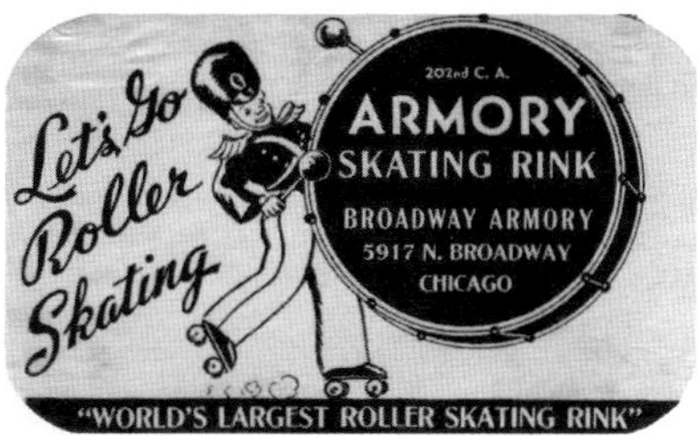

202nd Armory Rink, at 5917 North Broadway, circa late 1930s. *Author's collection.*

The North Side 202nd Armory Rink used the tagline "World's Largest Rink," but it closed in 1942 in support of World War II when it was reclaimed by the Illinois National Guard. It was followed by the Armory Roller Skating Rink at 1566 South Michigan by the same operators.

It was originally built in 1916 as the Winter Garden Ice Skating Rink with the purpose of offering the growing North Side community indoor recreational amenities that featured an enormous ice skating rink. The building included a 55-foot ceiling and a rink floor that was 115 by 300 feet (a huge 34,500 square feet). The Winter Garden Ice Skating Rink opened on March 1, 1917, with five thousand attending an evening opening event.[101] But the facility's tenure as a rink was brief. In the 1920s, it hosted boxing matches and saw its first usage by the National Guard. By 1928, the Illinois National Guard converted the building to its headquarters for the 202nd Coast Artillery, using it for drills and training. It became known as the Broadway Armory.

During the interim period (from World War I to World War II), the facility continued to be leased for sporting events, including ice skating, rolling skating, tennis and boxing, among others. For example, in 1926, the *Chicago Tribune*

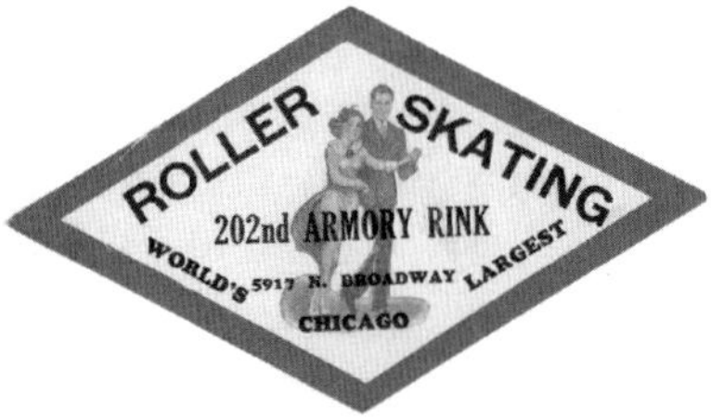

202nd Armory Rink, circa 1940s. *Author's collection.*

reported that Captain Peshmalyan of the 202nd Coast Artillery Broadway Armory had been granted a permit by the Illinois Athletic Commission for the armory to host an all-star middleweight bout in January.[102] It comes as no surprise that business entrepreneurs sought a lease for the dormant facility and opened it as the "World's Largest Rink" to coincide with roller skating's rise in popularity in the late 1930s. In April 1937, Chicago's Armory Rink sent three male speed skaters to the first U.S. Amateur Speed Roller Skating Championship Races in Detroit's Arena Gardens. While the Gardens' floor size was 22,000 square feet, race laps were set at one lap equaling 440 feet, while a mile was a twelve-lap track.[103]

Today, the 202nd Armory is owned and operated by the Chicago Park District. In 1978, the district took out a twenty-five-year lease with the State of Illinois, investing $2 million and opening the site in 1985 as a multipurpose recreational facility.[104] After considerable upgrades and investment, the park district purchased the facility from the state in 1998. The state had concluded that the facility would no longer be required for military purposes.

Armory Roller Skating Rink (1943–65)

1566 South Michigan Avenue (16th Street and Michigan Avenue)
Tagline: "Chicago's Largest Rink"
Phil J. Hayes and Lois Reynolds, Owners and Managers

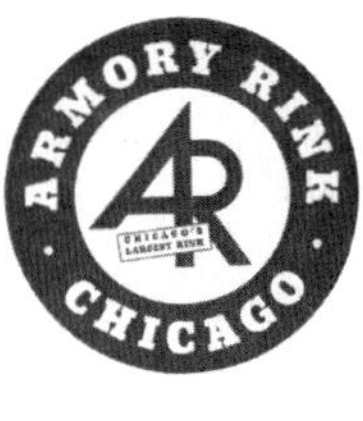

Armory Roller Skating Rink, "Chicago's Largest Rink," at 1566 South Michigan. *Author's collection.*

A new Armory rink opened on June 19, 1943, in the 16th Street Armory with the largest floor space of any in Chicago since the 202nd Armory had been commandeered to support guard readiness. The 202nd Armory Rink had carried the title of "World's Largest Rink," but the new Armory rink sported 34,500 square feet and became "Chicago's Largest Rink." Phil Hayes served as manager and also managed Arcadia Gardens. Norvel Hall was organist.[105]

The Armory operated out of the building built in 1890 for the 1st Regiment of the Illinois National Guard. When first constructed, the Armory included plans for clubrooms, a two-story banquet hall, a library and a gymnasium.[106] The castle-style Romanesque architecture, with its forty-foot entranceway, dominated South Michigan Avenue for decades.

Not unlike its predecessor, the 202nd Armory, the Armory at 16th Street hosted all sorts of events, including boxing, military reunions and even roller derby, before opening as a roller rink in 1943. The *Chicago Tribune* reported in 1942 that the fifteenth roller derby, which opened on October 21, "embraced features of football as well as skating, sending two teams of men and girls against each other."[107] The color commentator reporter wrote, "Roller derby, a quaint mélange of several sports including football, hockey, bike racing, and such minor pastimes as hair pulling and sticking-out-of-the tongue." Of course, this was an early rendition of roller derby that included the new contact rules.

The Armory hosted the Roller Skating Club of Chicago (RSCC). RSCC was truly a dedicated community service organization and conducted all sorts of events to promote roller skating and improve community relations. Members traveled throughout the Chicago area and visited neighborhood rinks, supported competitions and raised funds for all sorts of community needs. For example, the organization planned an event for February 29, 1948, at Madison Gardens Rink, a leap year party. RSCC also planned a party at Armory and an afternoon bus trip to Ing Rink in Rockford. There was also an Armory speed club.

Most impressive of its sponsorships was RSCC's hosting of the Blink Bats, a group of Chicago Braille Center skaters. The team wore blue-and-gold sweaters with the Braille emblem on the chest and a bat on the back, symbolic of the club name.[108]

Chicago Coliseum Roller Skating Rink (1900–1982)

1513 South Wabash Avenue, Chicago

The *Chicago Daily Tribune* reported on December 29, 1902, the grand opening of the Coliseum Roller Skating Rink, which would feature Richardson Skates along with De Baugh's Military Band and fancy skating.[109] The Coliseum's ties to roller skating continued in 1935, when it hosted the Transcontinental Roller Derby, starting a derby craze that continued into the twenty-first century.

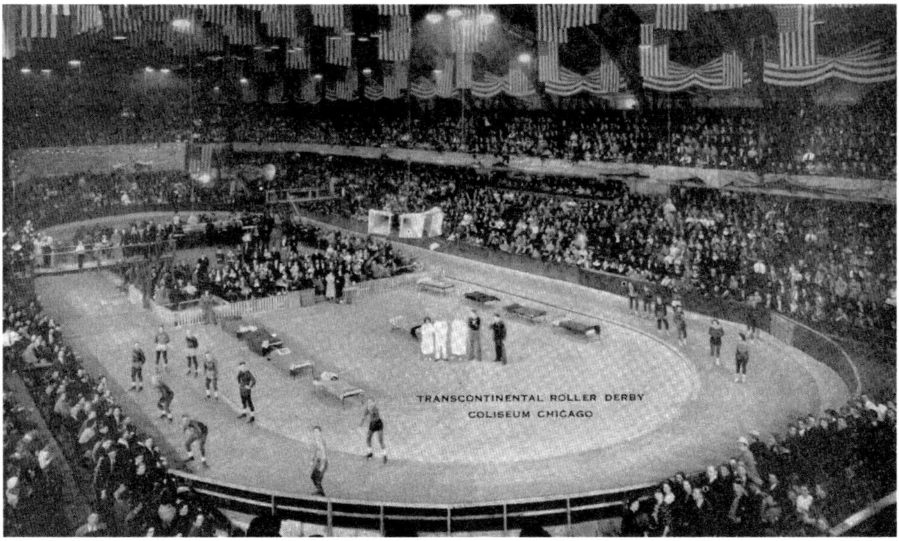

Coliseum Roller Skating Rink, Chicago Coliseum, at 1513 South Wabash, site of the 1935 Transcontinental Roller Derby. *National Sports Company.*

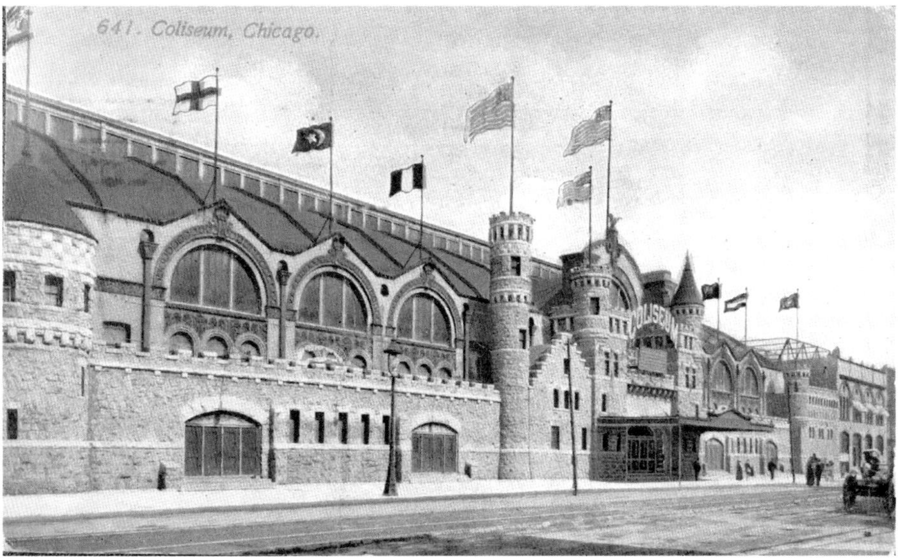

Chicago Coliseum, 1912. The exterior medieval wall housed a Civil War museum for the Confederate Libby Prison. Builder Charles Gunther purchased and shipped Libby Prison by rail from Richmond, Virginia, to Chicago and reconstructed it brick by brick at 1513 South Wabash. *Rare Book Collection, Lenhardt Library, the Chicago Botanic Garden.*

Commonly referred to as the Chicago Coliseum, in January 1944 the Coliseum made a comeback resulting from a deal whereby politician Fred Morelli and roller derby promoter Leo Seltzer acquired the facility. The building was rehabilitated for sports events, conventions and shows.[110] Prior to that, the Coliseum was used by the Army Air Corps from 1942 to 1943.

Pipe organs of the period were huge instruments that were described as equivalent to a giant orchestra, with the capability of producing the sounds of brass instruments, xylophones, marimbas, glockenspiel bells, tambourines, cymbals, string instruments and roll, bass and kettle drums. Dance ballrooms used pipe organs, and later the Hammond electrical organ, to save costs and replace the personnel required for a full orchestra.

Despite the significant amenities that the Coliseum offered to skaters—such as huge pipe organs, spectator stands, banked rink floors (speed skaters loved it) and transportation accessibility—neither the Coliseum nor the Chicago Stadium were able to establish themselves as a neighborhood rink with the character and intimacy that other Chicago rinks achieved, though that was not its purpose.

Chicago Stadium (1929–95)

1800 West Madison Street, Chicago
Tagline: "Madhouse on Madison"
Paddy Harmon, Owner

The profiles of Chicago rinks reveal few built for the sole purpose of a roller skate rink. Harmon's Chicago Stadium, the largest sports arena in the world, was built as a multipurpose sports center rather than a roller rink, with a capacity of twenty-five thousand. Paddy Harmon wasted no time filling it with roller events. The first event invited the best roller racers from around the world for the 1929 world speed championship. Later, the stadium was used for roller derby and Skating Vanities, all of which offered qualifications to be included among those Chicago rinks that contributed to the title of Chicago roller capital. Harmon also built the Arcadia Ballroom on Broadway and the Dreamland Ballroom. The Arcadia Ballroom would later become the Arcadia Gardens Rink.

Of notable interest to Chicagoans is the stadium's location on Madison Street, down the street from the older Madison Gardens Rink. Today, across the street is the United Center, home of the Chicago Blackhawks, while

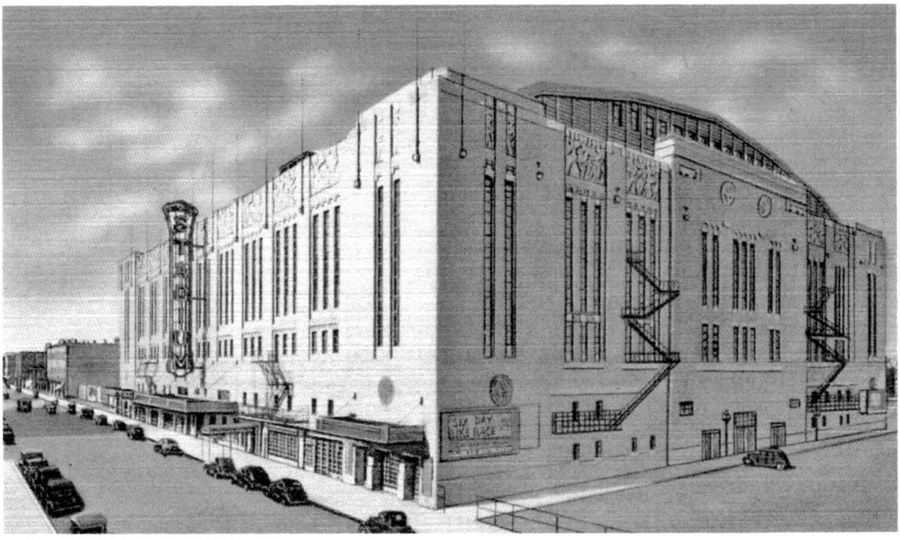

Chicago Stadium, 1800 West Madison Street, site of the 1929 world speed championship and, in the 1940s, host for roller derby and Skating Vanities. *Author's collection.*

down the street is the primary training center for the Blackhawks, Johnny's Icehouse (former location of Madison Gardens Rink, an ironic twist to a century of hotbed roller racing).

The character associated with the Chicago Stadium was delivered by the massive theater organ that was built into the building by the Barton Organ Company of Oshkosh, Wisconsin, in 1929. The Barton pipe organ was one of a kind, designed to fill the huge stadium and its expected capacity of twenty-five thousand. Ralph Waldo Emerson opened the Chicago Stadium, introducing the gigantic organ to Chicagoans.[111] But it was Al Melgard, the "nine-fingered" staff organist for four decades, who brought fame to the pipe organ. The Barton organ reportedly could equal the volume of twenty-five brass bands.[112]

Only once did Melgard pull out all the stops. A riot had broken out after a boxing match decision, and Melgard, deciding to quell the outbreak, played a memorable but rousing rendition of the national anthem that broke windows, shattered light bulbs and sent the crowd fleeing for the exits. Melgard was rewarded with a lifetime position.

Elm Skating Rink (1956–89)[113]

357 West Roosevelt Road
Elmhurst, Illinois
Bill and Lynn Fuchs, Owners and Operators
Elm Dance & Figure Skating Club

The trademark feature of the Elm Skating Rink was a pair of green doors, but the huge, distinctive sign caught the attention of both visitors and regulars. The Elm hosted a twenty-thousand-square-foot hard-maple floor surface, but its construction was the envy of Chicago rinks. Underneath the maple wood lay yellow pine in two subfloors followed by a vapor barrier, a Homasote insulating layer, a coat of tar, a slab of concrete and several inches of sand.[114] The result was a surface built for speed but also one that absorbed the sound that ensued from the roll of wood wheels on its surface.

If the Elm's trademark were those green doors, its loudspeaker was the Geneva Cannock Chase organ with its four-manual console and one thousand pipes. Tony Tahlman brought fame to the Elm for more than twenty years where he served as first chairman of the console.[115] Over his reign, he built the massive organ by investing in pipe organ performance parts, not unlike what racecar teams do when building a high-performance car. It was described as the equivalent to a two-car garage in size, and its parts came from the Rockne Theatre in Chicago; the pipework came from

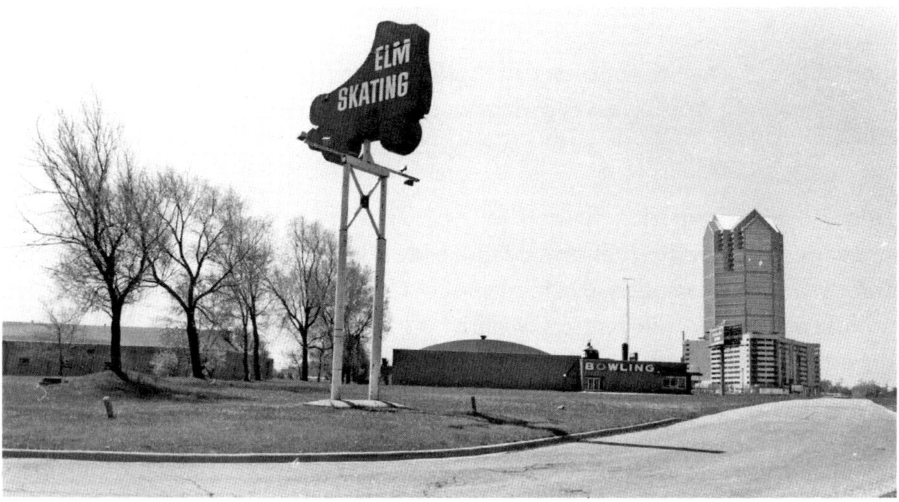

Elm Skating Rink, 357 West Roosevelt Road. *Elmhurst History Museum.*

the Milwaukee Riverview Rink. During its tenure, Elm flaunted the largest rink and best organist in the Chicagoland area.

In the late 1950s and early 1960s, the Elm was a top Chicagoland roller rink and producer of competitive skaters. The Elm skating club was hosted by the Elm, and the rink continued to lead the RSROA rinks in its division (large rinks) for six years with most RSROA-registered amateur skaters from the later 1950s to the early 1960s.[116] During this period, the Elm skate club hosted several of the Great Lakes Regionals for RSROA. In 1965, the Elm rink set the pace in the large rink division for the most amateur registrations for seven consecutive years.[117] The Elm rink had joined RSROA in July 1956, the year it opened its green doors for business.

The Elm nearly closed in 1985, when owner Bill Fuchs learned that his liability insurance was to be canceled. Roller skate rinks, bowling alleys, amusement parks and go-kart tracks had become victims of the inability to buy insurance. Insurance companies jettisoned riskier industries in favor of "safe" customers, according to a *Chicago Tribune* article in November 1985.[118] In 1989, when the Elm closed, the owners gave the organ to a part-time organist. The organist and friends took five weeks to dismantle and move the pieces, some of which weighed five hundred pounds. The organist's plans were to restore the organ. Today, the site is occupied by Lexington Square of Elmhurst.[119]

Hollywood Roller Rink (1941–?)

4825 North Kedzie Avenue
Tagline: "Friendliest Crowd on Wheels"
F.A. Scheive, Manager

The Hollywood Roller Rink was located in Albany Park, just north of Lawrence on Kedzie, in a once predominantly Jewish neighborhood[120] and operated as early as 1941. Hollywood Rink hosted a farewell party for Fred Wickman on June 1, 1941, while Wickman was the pro at Hollywood. By 1943, Wickman was representing Arcadia Gardens in Chicago as its professional. Hollywood Rink—along with Madison Gardens, White City, Armory and Riverview Rinks—all reported excellent business in September 1943.[121] This business report showed that despite the early war years, business flourished among rinks with great access, located in urban areas at the nexus of public transportation (bus and train) despite gas rationing.

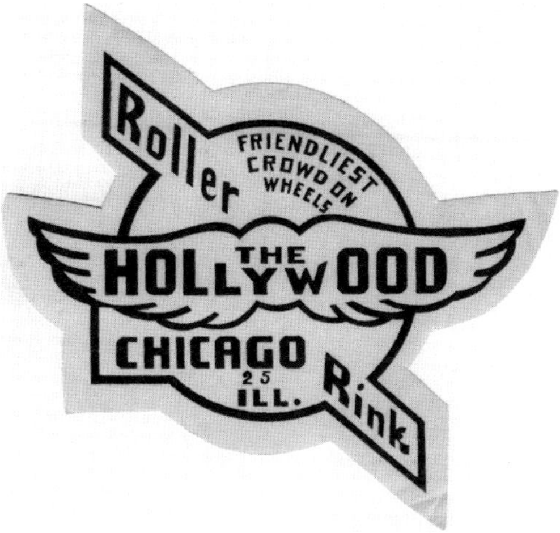

Left: The Hollywood Roller Rink, "Friendliest Crowd on Wheels," at 4825 North Kedzie Avenue. *Author's collection.*

Below: The Four Hollywood Blonds, a farewell party for Fred Wickman at the Hollywood Roller Rink. *Author's collection.*

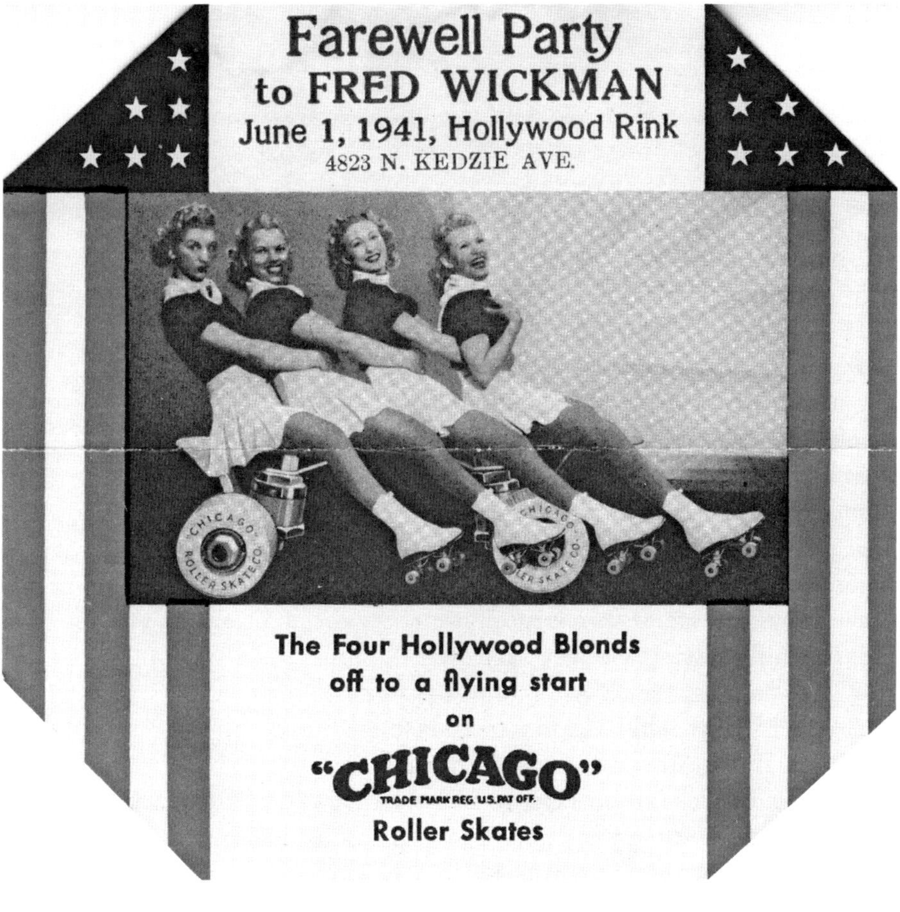

A skate label was produced for the farewell party and featured the "Four Hollywood Blonds off to a flying start on Chicago Roller Skates!"[122] The label illustrated the clever approach to marketing by the Chicago Roller Skate Company. Four of Hollywood's blondes sported identical, trendy skate outfits with roller skates and sat on a large model Chicago Roller Skate. This particular sticker was adopted by numerous rinks around the country that had "Hollywood" in their name. Those rinks used the template label and printed their rink name, tagline or message for souvenir-collecting skaters.

The Hub Roller Rink (1950–74)

4510 North Harlem, Harlem and Montrose
Tagline: "Newest and Largest"

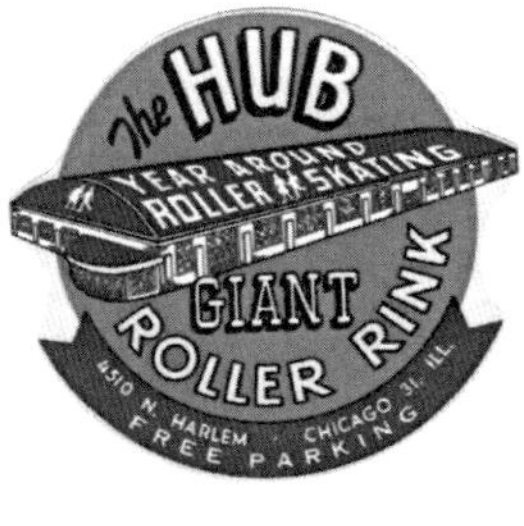

The Hub Roller Rink, "Newest and Largest," at 4510 North Harlem. *Author's collection.*

The Hub, a popular giant in its day with a 26,125-square-foot skating surface, opened on October 27, 1950, was renamed the Axle in 1974 and closed on October 31, 1985. The Hub was built exclusively for roller skating on the far northwest side by William A. Benson and Charles A. Bendler. A grand opening celebration was held on February 13, 1951.

While rink size attracted many, it was the small dance floor and jukebox that appealed to the Hub's shyest skaters. It was built with all the expected amenities, such as a Wurlitzer pipe organ, a snack bar, restrooms, a beginner rink and a mirrored ball that hung above the huge skate floor. A large lighted sign displayed "styles of skating" as the organ changed tempos. While "All-Skate" occupied the majority of the sign, other skate styles signaled to skaters that it was time for "Couples Only," "Waltz," "Fox Trot," "Collegiate" and the "14-Step." A skate style extension of the "Couples Only" skate was the "Trio" and the "Romp"—"Trio" was three skaters in tandem, while the "Romp" featured groups of skaters that ranged from four or more skating in tandem, though the end person would get whipped around the turns.[123] Too much speed and the whole group caused a floor pileup. Today, a very similar skate style is called a train. Skater's arms are intertwined with numbers that range from three to up to a dozen. Trains snake around the floor, whipping each end to the front. Of course, trains require tremendous amounts of real estate, and pileups still happen.

In 1974, the Hub became the Axle Roller Rink and was among those rinks that began operations on the eve of roller disco. By 1978, *Saturday Night Fever* had created a disco frenzy, and large rinks, like Axle with its huge skate floor, became epicenters. George Pickard with the Roller Skating Rink Owners Association reported that 70 percent of RSROA members dropped organ music in favor of disco music during this period.[124] But the Axle stayed true to old-school rollers and its Wurlitzer pipe organ music.

It was promoted as the "Newest and Largest" with year-round skating from 7:30 p.m. to 11:00 p.m. to music of the "mighty Wurlitzer Pipe Organ" played by Leon Berry. The rink remained 275 by 95 feet (26,125 square feet).[125] At some point, floor size was reduced to 265 by 96 feet (25,440 square feet).[126] Rink operators were constantly renovating facilities, adding amenities and increasing a service area. At times, the floor surface was sacrificed to benefit other needed amenities. With its closing in 1985, the Axle left only memories. The property was redeveloped for other commercial purposes.

Madison Gardens Rink (1906–circa 1968)

2560 West Madison Street
Madison Gardens Roller Skating Rink (prior to the 1940s)
Tagline: "Chicago's Favorite Rink!"
J. Charles McCormack and Virginia McCormack, Owners

In 1941, Madison Gardens Rink was Chicago's oldest roller skating rink, located at the intersection of Madison and Rockwell Street. Established by Harry McCormack,[127] Madison Gardens gained a national reputation for operating on a high moral plan and being clean and well managed. J. Charles McCormack, Harry's son, took over operations when his father passed away in 1919. The rink's reputation was built around the loyalty of employees associated with the rink for more than twenty years and the large Wurlitzer organ with "Happy" Johnson at the console. In the late 1940s, Billy Phillips took over organ duties.[128] Skaters reported that the music was best at Madison.[129] It hosted the Madison Gardens Speed Club for many years.

The Madison Gardens history began in 1906, when the two indoor roller rinks in the city fought for flagship status. Each anchored roller action, with Riverview Rink on the North Side and White City on the

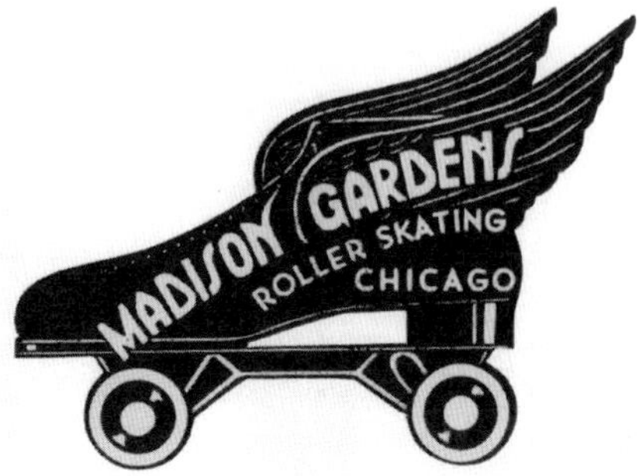

Madison Gardens Roller Rink, "Chicago's Favorite Rink," at 2560 West Madison Street. *Author's collection.*

South Side. Madison Gardens was mid-city, where Madison Street is Chicago's dividing line between north and south. Harlem was the east–west dividing line, placing Madison Gardens at the epicenter of roller activity in the Windy City. It was this early history that let Madison Gardens establish itself as a speed skate rink, competing with the huge rinks on the North and South Side. Carl Carlson won the first Chicago speed skate marathon in 1909, beating the second-place contestant by ten seconds. A number of early prominent speed skaters called Madison Gardens their home rink. In 1915, the rink hosted a professional three-mile roller skate race.[130]

Madison Gardens opened as a rolling skating rink in 1906; survived World War I, Prohibition, the Depression and the decline of roller skating during the 1920s and 1930s; and emerged in the 1940s as the oldest and best-known rink in Chicago. Its origins are unique in that the building, the Rockwell powerhouse, was first rented from the West Chicago Street Railroad Company (WCSR).[131] The building began operation in 1890 as a cable car barn and powerhouse for the Madison street line. The west side of the building was the car barn, while the east side was reserved for the two 1,200-horsepower engines that pulled the underground cable for cable cars. Backup cable cars and those requiring repair were kept in the car barn. By 1906, the line had been replaced with electric trolley cars.

The WCSR operated three powerhouses along the Madison street line.[132] The principal powerhouse was located at Madison and Rockwell (2560 West Madison Street) and was 210 by 225 feet (47,250 square feet). The Rockwell powerhouse operated the Madison street line cable cars from 1890 to 1906. The building was sold before 1922.[133]

At the turn of the century (1900), Chicago had the largest cable car network in the country, but as electric-powered streetcars were introduced, cable systems lost favor.[134] By 1906, in Chicago, the conversion was completed, and the powerhouse facility was adapted to other purposes.[135] The Rockwell cable car powerhouse at 2560 West Madison Street was no longer needed.

Initially rented as a roller skating rink, by 1922 the barn had been purchased. George Harry McCormack was listed as the manager in 1917, when the rink operated as the Madison Gardens Roller Rink. The barn was configured for a 60- by 190-foot rink floor, a balcony on the east side that sat over the ladies' room, an office and a skate rental booth.[136] A musicians' platform anchored the north end of the rink, while a snack bar and two smaller beginner rinks secured the back end toward Warren Avenue. The building was 90 by 270 feet. The 11,400-square-foot rink floor was set against the west wall, toward the front of the building, and was considered a medium-size rink by standards of the day.

Many old-school rollers have asked, "What happened to Madison Gardens Rink?" Madison Gardens' sixty-year run as Chicago's oldest rink ended with the West Side riots in the aftermath of Martin Luther King Jr.'s assassination on April 4, 1968. A two-mile stretch of Madison Avenue from 2200 to 3300 on Pulaski was scorched by rioters over three days on the weekend that followed King's murder.[137] A fire started Friday, April 6, in a furniture store at 2235 West Madison Avenue and continued westward up Madison toward Pulaski.[138] Spectators noted that trucks loaded with gas cans traveled westward up Madison, with young men igniting fires along the way. The first targets were white merchants. In the end, more than 260 stores and businesses were destroyed, with 116 located along the twenty blocks of Madison Street from Damen Avenue to Pulaski.[139]

Johnny's Icehouse West is located at 2550 West Madison Street today and is a popular rink for ice hockey school and training center. It serves as the official practice facility for the Chicago Blackhawks. The Madison Gardens Rink logo is on display in the Stanley Club—a fitting tribute to an early venue (once Chicago's oldest) that prospered for more than a half century, through two world wars and a depression, and watched three generations of West Side rink rats skate dance.

New Planet Roller Rink (1941–circa 1958)

7534 South Racine Avenue
Taglines: "Learn to Dance on Skates at Chicago's Friendliest Rink"; "Skating Promotes Pep and Personality"
Fred E. Leiser and Frank Moser, Owners and Operators

The New Planet Roller Rink opened in 1941 on the South Side as the roller skating craze began its ascent. New rinks were opening at incredible rates, all of which happened on the eve of the nation's entry into World

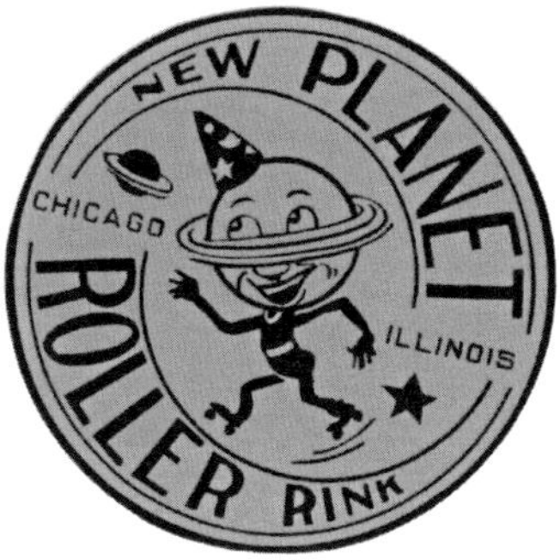

New Planet Roller Rink, "Chicago's Friendliest Rink," at 7534 South Racine Avenue. *Author's collection.*

War II. The rink floor measured 80 by 220 feet (17,600 square feet). Steve Barron banged out tunes on the "Golden Voice Hammond Electric Organ" and would get the crowd involved in an early version of karaoke by holding a contest on "your favorite song—and why?"[140] In December 1949, a new floor was installed. Music was played on a Hammond organ, with Joe Kopiz at the console, while Gene Alders orchestrated the pipe organ.

The Planet's rink size made it popular for skate dancing, with the tagline, "Learn to Dance on Skates at Chicago's Friendliest Rink." Trio skating with two boys and one girl dancing in rhythm was a skate style that showed up regularly on the sign board.[141]

The Planet Rink was an example of how small rinks competed successfully over many years by hosting parties of all sorts. Not only did the Planet Rink host Girl Scout Troops, Camp Fire Girls, church groups and school groups, but it also recruited business association meetings. For example, in April 1955, the Southtown Economist's first Industry and Food Exhibition was in town. The event was held at the twenty-one-thousand-square-foot Planet rink, and its purpose was to showcase the tremendous development of industry in the South Side area for the past fifty years (1905–55), to coincide with the fifty-year anniversary of the Southtown Economist. One of the exciting new devices to be introduced by the Illinois Bell Telephone Company among the four hundred types of phone equipment and services was a telephone that permitted customers to talk or listen without picking up the receiver. Telephones also took on colors to match the décor of any room in a house. The show opened Thursday and closed Sunday.[142]

The Southtown Economist trade show was hosted at the Planet rink for four years, with the last mention in 1958, but the show continued to grow. News accounts in the *Suburbanite Economist* report that as the trade show grew, parking was available in the parking lot of its neighbor, the Continental Can Company. Once the Planet closed in 1962, reports in the early 1970s indicate that the trade show was in its seventeenth year at Continental, former site of the Planet Roller Rink.[143]

News reports next mention the Planet in 1962, when it was announced that a "skaters reunion for those who skated at White City or Planet Roller

Rinks was hosted at the Oak Lawn Roller Rink." After this, few formal mentions of the Planet can be found, except for the anecdotal nostalgic recollections of skate forum posts.[144]

North Avenue Rollerway Skating Rink (1940–98)

8490 West North Avenue, Melrose Park
Steve Seipp and Verlin Seipp, Owners and Operators
North Avenue and River Road, Melrose Park
Tom Seipp and Carol Seipp, Owners and Operators

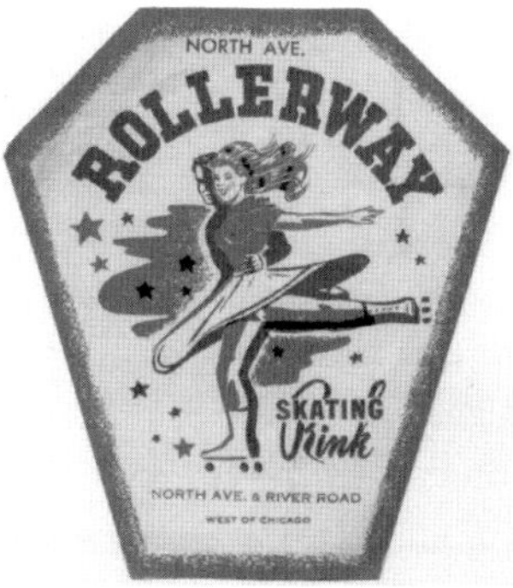

North Avenue Rollerway Skating Rink, at 8490 West North Avenue. *Author's collection.*

Known locally as North Avenue, the Rollerway opened in 1940 and operated continuously as an artistic skate center, with music from an old-time pipe organ, and remained exclusively an all-quad skate rink—no rollerblades! The Rollerway's legacy includes sending a steady stream of successful dance competitors to the ARSA nationals over its decades of operations. Tom and Carol Seipp were ARSA national intermediate dance champs in 1953. Later, in the 1960s, Robert Shaffer and Jacqueline Zimmerman, representing Rollerway at the 1962 ARSA National Championships, were among the many dance champions who represented North Avenue. Interestingly enough, the 1962 ARSA nationals were held at Art's Rolle-Aire Rink in Harvey, Illinois. That same year, Shaffer and Zimmerman would take bronze in dance at the world championships.

In October 1948, North Avenue was destroyed by fire. The renovations resulted in expanded floor size from the original 190 by 100 feet to a huge 240 by 100 feet (24,000 square feet).[145] Rollerway joined United Rink Operators (URO) in 1951 and remained over the decades a home for skate dancing with the North Avenue Dance and Figure Skating Club. Rollerway hosted the 1964 Illinois State Amateur Roller Skating Association state championship[146] and also hosted the USARSA 1956 and 1964 nationals. The July 1964 national championship included artistic, dance and speed events.

In the early 1950s, North Avenue was among a number of rinks that shifted in favor of ARSA status. ARSA reported membership growth in both North Avenue Figure & Dance Club and Swank Dance & Figure Club among the eleven skate clubs and state associations that joined ARSA in 1952. ARSA ranks had swelled to 186 during the early 1950s.[147]

During the 1978–81 roller skate boom, when rinks opened in the wake of roller disco, celebs donned skates and rock videos ruled, but Rollerway remained vigilant to those old-time skaters and their love for pipe organ music.[148] When the high-tech roller disco craze moved on and rinks closed, Rollerway organists were still pumping out rhythms to which skaters could shuffle, fox trot or waltz. When it closed in 1998, North Avenue was among the last of its kind in the nation that played full pipe organ music, described as "that throaty, joyous symphony of sound" that had persisted since the North Avenue opened in 1940.[149]

The last organist to reside over the seventy-year-old pipe organ and its throne-like organ console was Paul Grosnick, who played and maintained the pipe organ for the last decade. Grosnick, not unlike other rink organists, had his back to skaters, with a mirror above his head to watch the floor action while surrounded by rows and rows of buttons and keys of the massive pipe organ. But it was Fred Arnish who rescued and played the organ early on, saving it from its 1920s origins in Chicago dance halls and theaters. Between Arnish and Gornick was Joe Skubish, who ruled over the console for nearly twenty-five years.[150]

When North Avenue closed in 1998, it was the last large roller rink (twenty-four thousand feet) with a pipe organ in the Chicago area whose emphasis was a teaching institute for elegant, aesthetic and artistic roller skating. The Seipps contrasted the rink style of North Avenue with that of social skate rinks, where skating was a free-for-all for the "round and rounders."

The North Avenue Rollerway's demise came about from a decision made by Carol Seipp, daughter of Steve Seipp. She had operated the rink with her brother, Tom, who battled Alzheimer's disease. Carol wanted the rink to operate as it had for nearly six decades and was unwilling to compromise with its traditional roller rink legacy established over that period. As tributes and tears flowed at the Rollerway's last skate in March 1998, one old-time roller stated, "It's easy to see how the grace of old-time roller skating and the magic of the pipe organ create an experience that's somehow grander and more enjoyable than zipping around on blades [rollerblades]."

Riverview Roller Rink (1904–71)

Belmont and Western Avenue, Chicago
Tagline: "Chicago's Courtesy Rink"
Paddy Harmon, Owner
Bill Henning, Skateroom and Repair Department

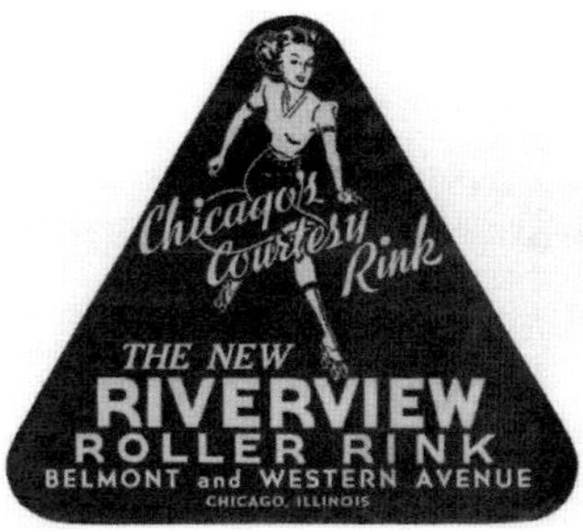

Riverview Roller Rink, "Chicago's Courtesy Rink," Riverview Amusement Park at Belmont and Western. *Author's collection.*

The "father of roller skating," Paddy Harmon, opened the Riverview Roller Rink in 1904 on the North Side with the largest roller rink floor in the world.[151] Harmon called attention to this enormous rink by hosting a world roller skate championship. Harmon would call on this marketing scheme once again when he opened the Chicago Stadium in 1929, with world championship roller skate races on an eighteen-foot track built with eight laps to a mile. It attracted one hundred of the fastest skaters from not only the United States but Canada as well. Prize money was set at $3,000.

When the floor was constructed, it was the only one of its kind in the country.[152] It was in the shape of an ellipse and used ribbon maple wood strips. Once completed, it could accommodate 3,500 skaters. Exact specifications of the rink floor are not known, but given that its South Side rival, White City Roller Rink, boasted the largest rink with its 33,500 square feet when built in 1905, Riverview Rink safely approached 30,000 square feet.

Riverview Rink led a life overshadowed by Riverview Amusement Park and the tremendous promotional campaigns for it. For example, the amusement park hosted an annual, nearly month-long Mardi Gras series of themed events, ending on Labor Day. Special events such as the Tournament of Music were intended to draw patrons and participants from surrounding states. About one hundred youth bands were invited to play, with two competing each night. By the end of the month, the field would be narrowed to a few that would compete for tournament honors.

Riverview Speed Club, in the Harmon style, hosted numerous speed skating events in the early decades, capitalizing on the skating craze early in the century. For example, in 1922, Riverview Roller Rink hosted the Illinois Amateur Rolling Skating Championship. What makes this interesting is that the championship was about speed skating and included three events: the half-mile, the two-mile and the one-mile sprint. Thus, roller skating competitions in the first few decades of the twentieth century were limited to speed skating. Artistic, dance and figure styles on rollers had yet to appear. Riverview Rink returned to a state of prominence during the roller skate craze of the late 1940s, according to the *Chicago Tribune*, becoming "Chicago's Courtesy Rink."[153]

Riverview Rink was active in hosting numerous community events to raise funds for special events, as well hosting church and community groups. Once World War II broke out, Riverview was at the forefront of support for the war effort. It set evenings aside for fundraisers, with management contributing its usual rink rent to match employee contributions along with patrons' entry fees. October 12 was Chicago Service Men's Center night in the Riverview Roller Rink. Proceeds were donated to the Service Men's Center and went toward cigarettes and refreshments for servicemen visiting Chicago.[154] Tickets were fifty cents. Riverview Roller Rink was destroyed by a fire in 1971.

Roller Bowl (1942–circa 1958)

1058 West Washington Street, Chicago
Tagline: "The Most Modern Skating Rink in Chicago"
Samuel Schaffer, Owner
Edward Hershenson, Operator

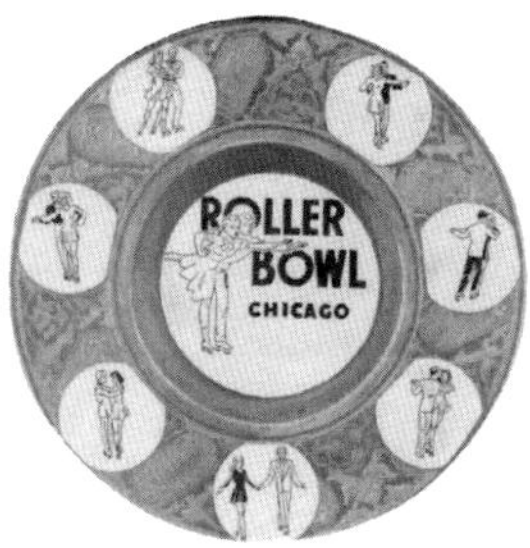

Roller Bowl, "The Most Modern Skating Rink in Chicago," at 1058 West Washington Street. *Author's collection.*

Each Chicago roller rink is a story unto itself, and the Roller Bowl is no exception, in both its origins and its passing. While few of the original buildings that hosted roller rinks stand today, only one remains standing—though it's rumored to be haunted by a "Gray Lady." Those who have sighted the lady reported that she wore an ornate hat and a long dark-gray dress, walked the halls and disappeared into the walls. It is recounted that the Gray Lady was the spirit of a mourner looking for her family but left behind a bit of herself.[155] Samuel Schaffer may not have been acquainted with the hauntings in 1942 when he set up a roller rink on West Washington, a former armory, but employees of Harpo Studios described numerous sightings, sounds and the clinking of glasses.

The Roller Bowl opened on the West Side in what was a cold storage warehouse[156] and, previously, a temporary morgue after the 1915 *Eastland* steamer disaster.[157] The building hosted the 2nd Regiment of the Illinois National Guard from the late 1800s until Schaffer began rink operations in 1942.[158] It opened on July 3, 1942, after a delay in acquiring materials,[159] with Novachord[160] tunes furnished by Al Beckwith and William Backman.

Located east of Madison Gardens Rink, the Roller Bowl became one of the largest and finest in Chicago, with a skating surface of 107 by 220 feet (23,540 square feet) and modern equipment and furnishings.[161] The maple floor was installed in a system that soundproofed the rink floor, and there was also air conditioning, spacious and comfortable rest rooms, a well-furnished lounge room and walls of knotty pine. Soft drinks were served in the lounge. A special 40- by 90-foot rink for figure skaters and beginners was provided. The Hammond organ provided skate music. A 7-foot mirrored globe hung with 2,500 individual mirrors above the center of the rink, and Chicago Roller Skates equipped the rink.[162] With 88,000 square feet to work with, Schaffer added a game room in 1943. Admission price when the Roller Bowl opened was set at fifty-five cents. That same year, on October 31, Schaffer announced that Roller Bowl had become a center for figure skating enthusiasts and, in its short history, had built up a sizable skate club, the Roller Bowl Figure and Dance Club.[163] As a result, Bob Ryan, 1941 men's senior figure skating champion, and then on staff at the Roller Bowl, conducted thirteen-week courses in roller dancing.[164]

In October 1943, Roller Bowl was drawing large crowds nightly. Madison Gardens, White City, the Armory, Riverview and Hollywood all reported excellent business on September 25, 1943.[165] Despite the war and gas rationing, their central location and proximity to streetcar and bus stations ensured that public transportation was useful and served a loyal skate population that sought relief from talk of war and the weekly reports of boys headed to the front.

While this skate frenzy is difficult to convey today, rinks in cooperation with RSROA encouraged all kinds of community service events. For example, later in the 1950s, the Roller Skating Club of Chicago (RSCC) conducted classes to teach skate dancing to Chicago Braille Center members. Both the Roller Bowl and Arcadia rinks hosted class time and set aside special nights for blind skaters.[166]

The Roller Bowl hosted the May 1944 National Amateur Roller Skating Association (ARSA) Championships.[167] Sentiment was strong for holding future championships at rinks built for the purpose of roller skating, with floors adapted for skating and public appeal established at a location.[168] The ARSA national attracted thirty entrants over five days and was particularly significant, attracting the active support of the Amateur Skating Union, Amateur Skating Association and the Middle Atlantic Skating Association.[169] Roller Bowl's management was applauded for handling the large number of contestants with adequate dressing rooms, practice rinks and so on.

In the 1950s, Fred A. Niles Studios used the building for commercial film production. The 100,000-square-foot wooden floor with tall ceilings was ideal for a studio. In 1988, a group of investors acquired the property, and *The Oprah Winfrey Show* began its twenty-five-year run, during which time the building was named Harpo Studios. Winfrey later moved what remained of Harpo Studio's operations to Los Angeles. In 2016, the complex was demolished, as McDonald's planned to build and move its corporate headquarters from Oak Brook to the near West Side. Whether or not the Gray Lady found peace with the unearthing of those lost souls from 1915 is not yet known.

Roller Dome Rink (circa 1943–75)

5955 South Halsted, Chicago
Roller Dome Club of Chicago
Tagline: "Make a Date to Roller Skate!"

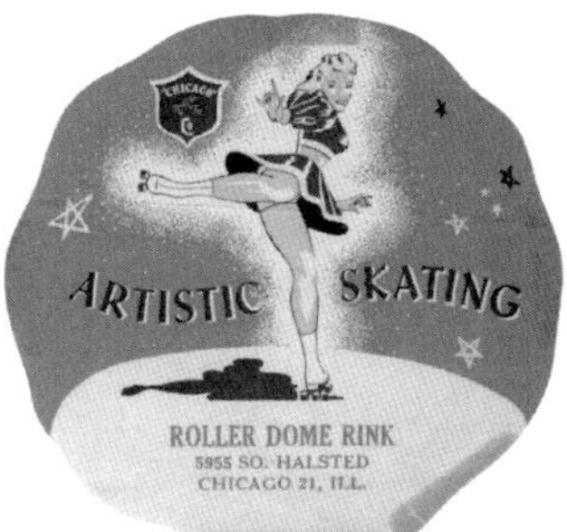

Roller Dome Rink, at 5955 South Halsted. *Author's collection.*

Opened as Skate-Land,[170] Southtown's newest roller rink in 1943 used the tagline "Make a Date to Roller Skate!" Taken over by Joseph Wolak, Skate-Land was renamed in 1947 and principally became known as Roller Dome Rink.[171] Wolak, co-owner and manager, closed Roller Dome on May 5, 1951. It later reopened under new management.

The Roller Dome's 80- by 125-foot plastic floor, laid in 1949, was the first in the city to use the Rink Cote plastic surface. Organist Eddie Hollenbeck, one of the country's finest organists, was credited with the large crowd draws in Roller Dome's early years as Skate-Land. Hollenbeck was able to deliver roller rhythm music to popular tunes that "adds wings to your skates."[172] This made Skate-Land popular, as it built a reputation for the new roller craze skate dancing. It emphasized instruction by Tony Miller with the new international dance styles.

Known for its bebop rhythm style of skate music,[173] the Roller Dome operated well into the 1970s, hosting parties for school groups, churches and clubs of all sorts. Its club, the Roller Dome Club of Chicago, was very active and traveled to many area rinks, including the Palladium Roller Rink in Michigan City, Indiana, and to the grand opening of the Lansing Roller Rink in Illinois to try out its 85- by 185-foot maple wood floor and fluorescent lighting. The Roller Dome played host to a club with one of the more clever names, the Rolling Squirrels Club.

Roseland Roller Rink (1939–1940s)

23 East 115th Street, Chicago

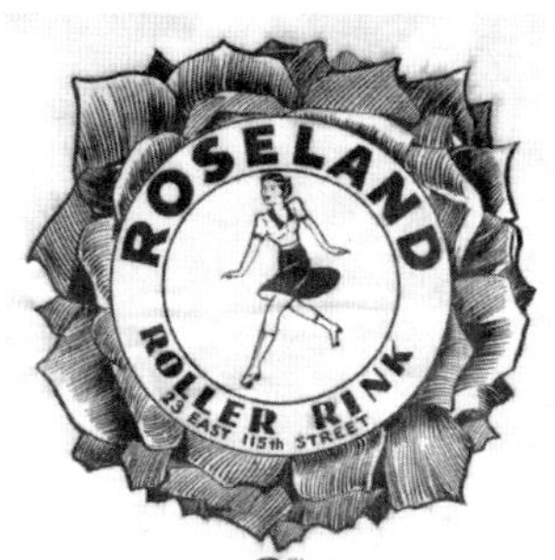

Roseland Roller Rink, at 12 East 115th Street. *Author's collection.*

Roseland Roller Rink is symbolic of communities across the country whose golden age civic pride inspired entrepreneurs to establish a neighborhood rink. Roseland was located within a few miles of the Swank Roller Rink. Both coexisted within a similar timeframe, so there must have persisted a cross-town rivalry. Roseland's tenure was brief given the larger dynamics of change that eventually brought about not only its demise but also those of other neighborhood rinks.[174]

The village of Roseland was the jewel of the South Side, with Michigan Avenue running through the heart of the town. Roseland Rink was accepted by its community, but its short-lived lifespan left a limited paper trail to document its neighborhood contributions and intimate home rink feel. Located on the far South Side, Roseland Roller Rink was rebuilt from a former Roseland post office with a five-year lease in 1939.[175] A new maple floor, ventilation system, special lighting and sound system were installed to ready the building for roller action.

Savoy Roller Rink (Ballroom) (1938–48)

4733 South Parkway

Not to be confused with Harlem's Savoy in New York, Chicago's Savoy also featured African American jazz bands and became a favorite of whites who sought the latest dance crazes.[176] Its location was the hub of Chicago's African American community. Built as a ballroom in 1927, by 1938 the Savoy had become the rink of choice for African American skaters who had few rink options.[177] It became the first African American roller rink during the golden age and was named the Savoy Roller Rink by skating enthusiasts.[178]

The Savoy rivaled the elegance of Harlem's Savoy with the feel for luxury and comfort that included lounges for men and women, a hat and coat check room and an estimated 12,500-square-foot dance floor.[179] It attracted top jazz bands. Later, to help generate revenue, the Savoy hosted sporting events, community meetings and eventually roller skating parties. Louis Armstrong and Duke Ellington were regular and familiar faces at the Savoy.[180]

In 1938, Jimmy Davis lobbied white owners for the Savoy to dedicate one evening a week for roller skating. In keeping with the distinction set for ballroom dancing, the rink operations maintained a dress code for patrons, while floor guards and instructors wore uniforms. Davis, an assistant manager and black roller enthusiast, also worked with rink owners in Detroit and Cleveland and formed an all-black league for competition. Chicago's African American skaters dominated, but eventually the league disbanded, as skaters representing non-Chicago rinks became discouraged and quit.[181] He would later open his own rink, also called the Savoy, in a former Masonic temple at 61st and Cottage Grove. A new version of the Savoy opened in 1963 at 78th and Cottage Grove.

The Savoy Roller Rink differed from other Chicago rinks rather significantly and culturally in terms of music and skate dance style. Both ballroom and rink patrons were entertained by jazz bands. Rink crowds skated to the rhythm-and-blues of a jazz band versus the organ music characteristic of Chicago's predominantly white roller rinks. The Savoy was "jamming" to R&B, a musical genre that would persist underground among the mainstream white roller rinks.[182] Later, jam skating would characterize the roller disco era.[183] Jamming is also a mainstay of roller derby.

The Savoy was demolished in the early 1970s after remaining vacant for more than two decades. A new project, Lou Rawls Theater & Cultural Center, was beset with "years of infighting, politicking and frustration"

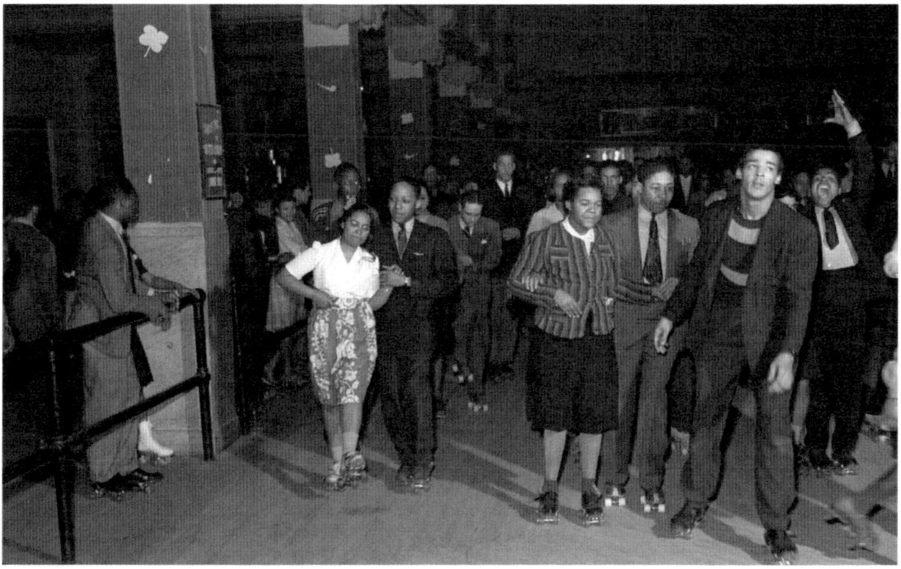

Skaters at Savoy Roller Rink in appropriate dress code, 1941. *Library of Congress, Prints & Photographs Division, FSA/OWI Collection [LC-USF34-38545-D].*

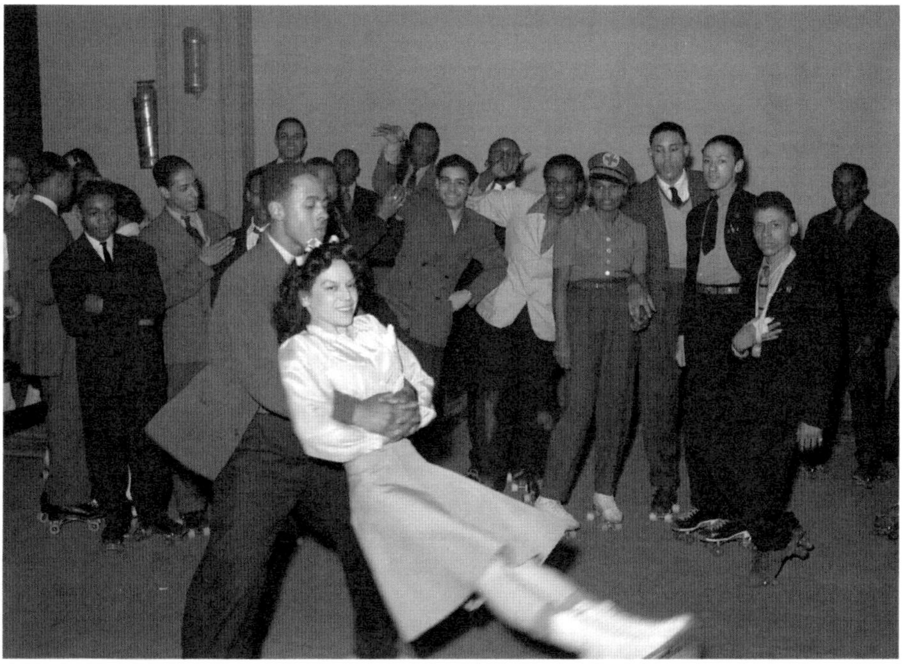

Skater swings partner at Savoy Roller Rink, 1941. *Library of Congress, Prints & Photographs Division, FSA/OWI Collection [LC-USF34-38538-D].*

before a groundbreaking ceremony in May 1998.[184] Promoted as a public/private partnership by Mayor Richard Daley, the project raised only $23,000 in private donations prior to its 1998 groundbreaking.[185] The theater was conceived as a site for a musical resurgence for the South Side to rival that of the 1930s. In 2010, the City of Chicago took control of the center, exercising its lien against outstanding debt.

Today, the Savoy Roller Rink is the site of the Harold Washington Cultural Center. Gone is the brick-and-mortar Savoy, yet its version of a rhythm-and-blues roller dance style that emerged during the 1940s, unique to African American roller skating, kept skating alive for the next generation. Not only would it find life during the roller disco era, but it would also remain a dominant roller dance style among urban rinks throughout the nation in the twenty-first century.

Swank Roller Rink (1940–circa 1965)

2345 West 111th Street/Western Avenue at 111th Street
Taglines: "The Only Knee Action Skating Floor in the Country"; "Where Skating Is a Pleasure"
Elmer Byrnes, Rink Manager

The Swank's tagline, "The Only Knee Action Skating Floor in the Country," was an obvious reference to the new style of rink surface that had become the high-tech floor of the late 1940s. This tagline came much later, when the Swank installed a new floor, at which time the Swank promoted itself as "Chicago's Only Plastic Floor—Free from Dust—Where Skating Is a Pleasure." The rink floor was considered small by rink standards in those days, with an estimated 60- by 135-foot surface (8,100 square feet). But not unlike other rinks, it was probably the small dance floor and jukebox in the back that kept the crowds coming back. Managed by Elmer Byrnes, the Swank enjoyed sizable crowds in spite of its South Side location.

John Powers, a South Sider, described his personal experience of skating at the Swank dating to the mid- to late 1950s.[186] His depiction of skaters who fell and rose out of a cloud of dust illustrated that during this period, the Swank still used rosin to offer skaters the needed stick for the maple wood floor. As they rose up from the floor, the white powder engulfed their every roll. But Powers's description of the ninety-proof air typified most rinks of that era. He wrote, "A mixture of Vitalis, Hair Arranger, Brylcreem and

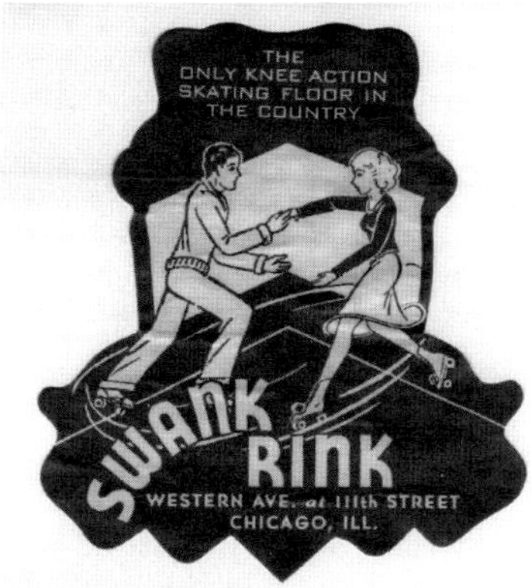

The Swank Roller Rink, "The Only Knee Action Skating Floor in the Country," at 2345 West 111th Street. *Author's collection.*

Vaseline Hair Tonic for Men plus a healthy dose of that gas exclusively produced by forest-preserve outhouses" produced an air quality "that no one ever inhaled twice."

The Swank Skating Club held all sorts of activities, such as teaching blind students to roller skate, and conducted an annual Illiana (multi-state) invitational roller meet.[187] Of particular interest is that even though the Swank was a smaller size, it was successful in hosting the 1956 ARSA Illinois state artistic skating and speed events.[188] Robert Shaffer recalled that skaters had to watch those posts at rink center during competitions to ensure that their pileup was not with the unforgiving posts. The Swank held a "Reunion on Wheels" in November 1960, inviting rollers back to 1940.

As often was the situation with roller rinks of the past, it is easy to find reports of activities. The challenge is to find reports that confirm the end of operations; this often depends on anecdotal reports. For example, ARSA national speed champion, Jack Countryman (1965–70), reported that his first roller experience was at the Swank in 1964,[189] which shows that Swank operated well into the mid-1960s. Neighborhood newspapers[190] reported the Swank hosting skate parties, church groups, Girl Scouts, Brownies and athletic groups well into the mid-1960s, at which point reports about Swank Rink activities go silent. In 1966, a legal notice alerted the Swank Roller Rink Inc. that it must report to the secretary of state. By the 1970s, what remained were the memories of young people gathering at the Swank. *Billboard* magazine reported that Sam Schaffer simultaneously operated the Swank rink, Roller Bowl and White City.

White City Roller Rink (1905–49)

63rd Street and South Parkway (now Martin L. King Jr. Drive)
H.W. "Buck" Plain, Manager

White City was a South Side amusement park with electric lights so intense it could be seen fifteen miles away. The park was described as

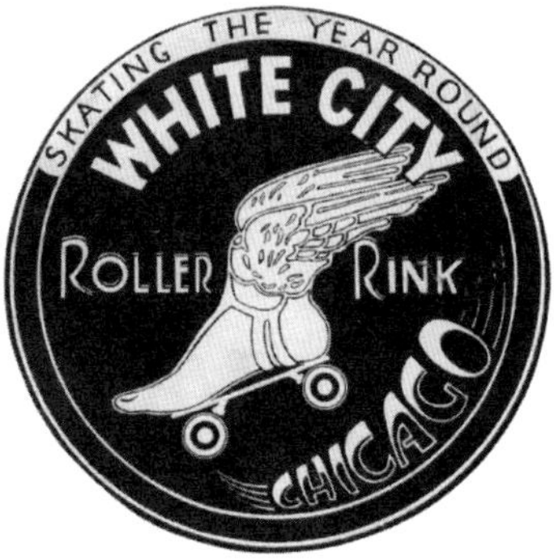

White City Roller Rink, White City Amusement Park, at 63rd Street and South Parkway. *Author's collection.*

"sentimental, gaudy spectacular and seamy where romances were born on its boardwalks and tunnel of love."[191] The park was patterned after the midway of the 1893 World's Columbian Exposition, also known as the World's Fair, and contributed to Chicago's reputation as a mecca for amusement parks in the early 1900s. Among the many amusement rides and Ferris wheels was a tower, a dance ballroom, a sports arena and, of course, a roller skating rink. The rink boasted one of the largest rink floors in the city at 33,500 square feet.

As a result of fire and the Depression, the White City Amusement Park closed in 1933, leaving the White City Roller Rink as the remaining vestige of the park. The roller rink was one source of entertainment among others, including a penny arcade, a ballroom, a beer garden and a boardwalk. In the 1920s, the roller rink was quite popular, with music provided by a brass band.

In 1942, demonstrations against the White City Roller Rink by racially diverse crowds were held by the fledging organization the Congress of Racial Equality (CORE). These protests became a model that would be used in future demonstrations of not only white owned and operated roller rinks but also other amusement venues where African Americans were prohibited from attending.[192] In 1946, CORE brought a lawsuit against White City for its discrimination against black patrons. The name was later changed in 1947 to Park City due to its racial connotations. Park City closed in 1949.

The 694-unit Parkway Gardens housing project was built on the site in the 1950s.[193] A November 1959 fire destroyed the last standing vestige of White City/Park City, seemingly a fitting ending to the South Side amusement center.[194]

FLAGSHIP RINKS

Chicago rinks and their seasoned veterans competed against the foremost rinks of America's big cities during the 1940s and well into the 1950s. Within urban centers, rinks competed for a city's "flagship" title—with rink

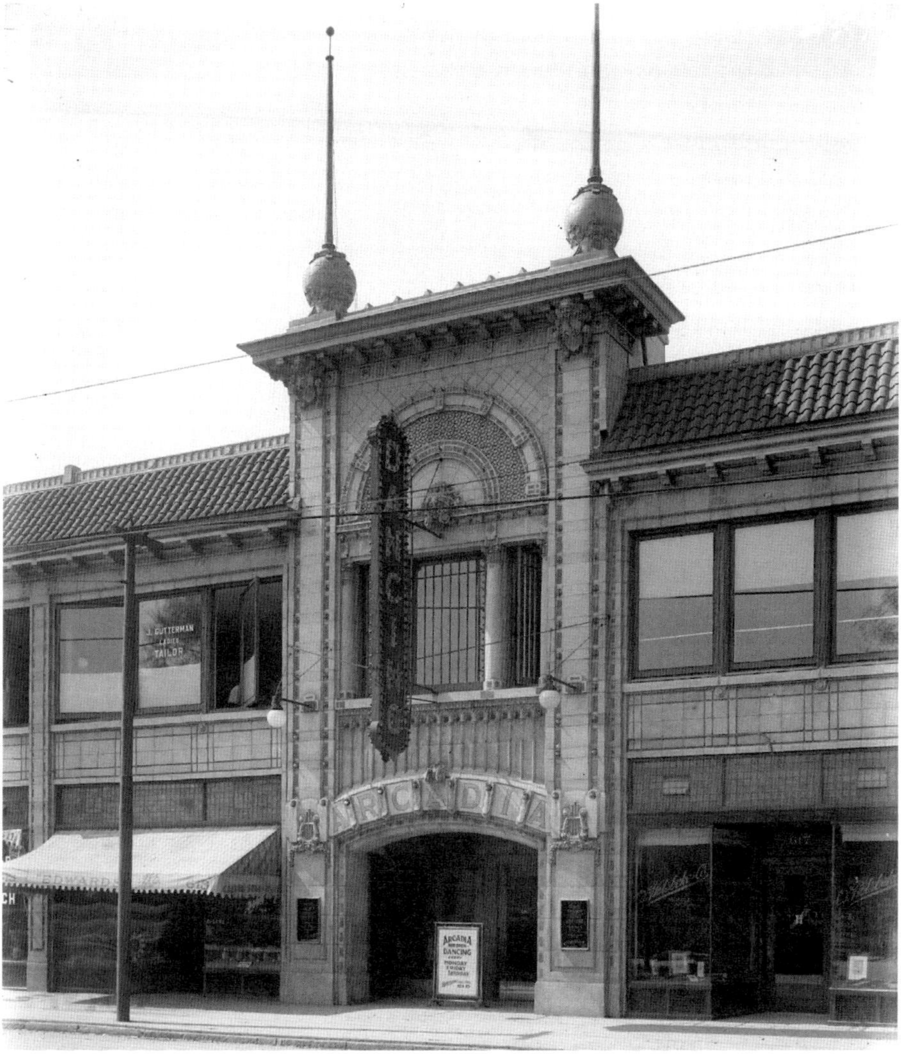

The Arcadia Ballroom's ornate front entrance. Ballrooms were ideal structures to repurpose for roller skating given floor sizes and unobstructed views. Opened in 1912 as one of the largest ballrooms in the country, in 1941 it was converted to the Arcadia Roller Rink. *National Automotive History Collection, Detroit Public Library.*

size, spectator capacity and expected crowd amenities as the barometers—to attract national competitions. Flagship rinks were those where the disciplines of roller skating were incubated, nurtured and became national competitive events such as speed skating, artistic skating and skate dancing. Much of this former glamour is captured in a rink's tagline.

American cities hosted impressive facilities dominated by not only floor size but also personalities that loved roller action with a passion and made it a lifelong ambition. The Midwest was led by Detroit, Cincinnati and Cleveland, as well as Chicago. To the west were Denver and Portland. In the Northeast, New York dominated with several rinks, including the Empire, which would become the birthplace of roller disco decades later. Strong personalities distinguished flagship rinks from others as they carved out a niche to work the national stage and maintain a spirited but cooperative edge over local competitors. Regardless of size or location, rinks succeeded when they catered to the local crowd, kept an evolving entertainment program and created that feel where skate dancing and romance were one at the neighborhood roller rink.

The competitive nature of flagship rinks in America's great cities made roller skating rinks arenas of excitement, romance and spectacle. During the war years, this was particularly true, given the spirit of patriotic cooperation to support the boys overseas. It is in this context that we look at select rinks around the nation that strove to excel, carving out a unique niche as a neighborhood, family-oriented recreational venue. This collective effort across the nation pushed roller skating to become the nation's top participatory sport by the end of the 1940s.[195] By the 1950s, the number of roller rinks across America totaled nearly five thousand.

Arcadia Roller Rink (1941–62)

3527 Woodward Avenue
Detroit, Michigan
Tagline: "The Ultimate in Roller Skating"
Bill Holleman, Owner (also a Wurlitzer organist)
Orville W. Godfrey, Operator

The Arcadia Roller Rink was described as Detroit's most luxurious skating rink at its October 15, 1941 grand opening party. Following in the tradition of large dance ballrooms converted to roller skating rinks, the "Arc," as it was known, opened in 1912 and by 1915 had been converted to a concert hall and theater. It reverted to a ballroom after it was discovered that its acoustics were inadequate to host Detroit orchestra symphony bands. In 1941, it became a roller rink for the next two decades.[196]

In 1947, the Detroit School for Roller Skating Teachers, the first of its kind, sought accreditation through RSROA. The school had been awarded accreditation through the Michigan State Board of Education as a trade school where aspiring roller pros were taught all phases of roller skate competition.[197] Arcadia hosted the school and established its rink as a teaching institution.

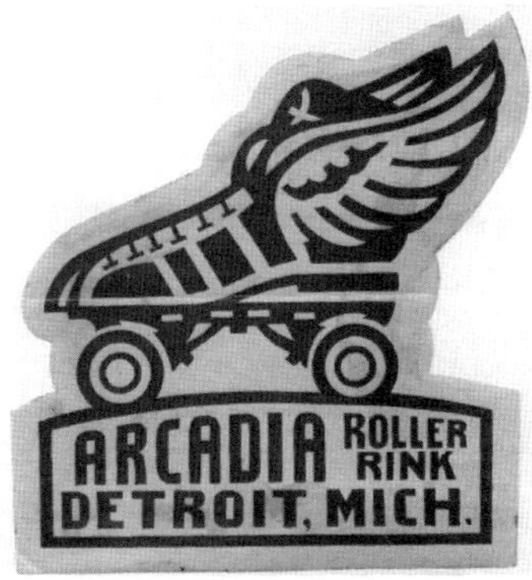

Arcadia Roller Rink, "The Ultimate in Roller Skating," at Woodward Avenue and Myrtle Street, Detroit. *Author's collection.*

Arcadia was the home rink to George Pickard, one of the greats of roller skating, who served in a variety of roller skate association roles, including executive director of RSROA (1972–88).[198] He was among the first recreational skaters at Arcadia when it opened in 1941. In 1972, the Arcadia Roller Rink was demolished and replaced with a 246-unit high-rise apartment building.

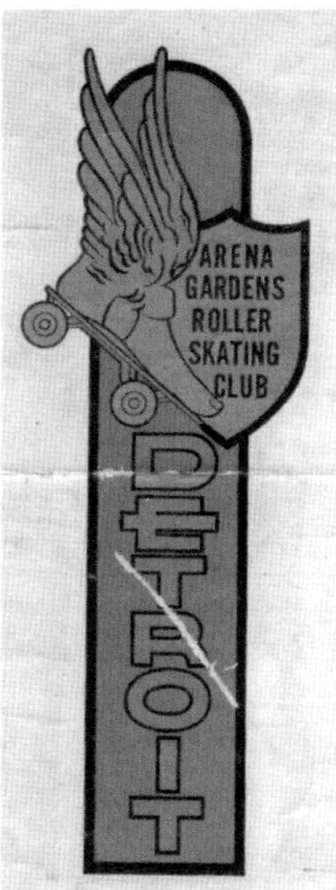

Arena Gardens Roller Skate Club, "Michigan's Largest and Finest Rink: Where Roller Skating Is a Pleasure," Detroit. *Author's collection.*

Arena Gardens Roller Rink (1935–53)

Woodward and I-94
Detroit, Michigan
Tagline: "Michigan's Largest and Finest Rink: Where Roller Skating Is a Pleasure"
Fred A. Martin, Partner and Manager, RSROA President

The Arena Gardens Roller Rink, once the home of "Detroit's Premier Sports Palace," was a former boxing venue in the 1930s and site for dance marathons, as portrayed in the movie *They Shoot Horses, Don't They?* The Arena opened as a roller skating rink in 1935 as the epitome of roller skating in America. Management wore tuxedos, and floor attendants donned custom, tailored, red fitted uniforms. Patrons adhered to a strict conduct and dress code. Its roller skating club, the Arena Gardens Roller Skating Club, was one of the largest in the country. The Arena Gardens hosted the first speed skating national championship in 1938.[199]

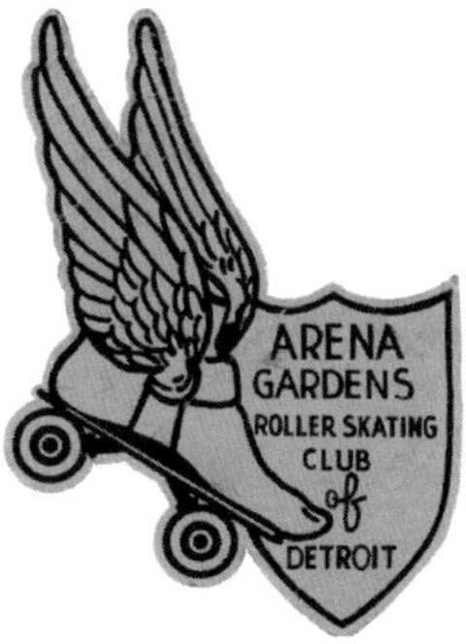

Arena Gardens Roller Skate Club, Detroit. *Author's collection.*

The first official U.S. Amateur Speed Skating Championship, hosted by RSROA, led the way to artistic and dance championships. The Arena's Wurlitzer organ drew huge crowds to events. The site was the first rink in Detroit to equip its sound system with a Wurlitzer.

Its last day of operation was May 3, 1953, closing its doors to make way for the Edsel Ford Superhighway. The Arena had served as point organization and headquarters for the Roller Skating Rink Owners Association (RSROA). A number of U.S. championships were held at the Arena.[200] Fred A. Martin was a founding member of RSROA and served as an officer in several capacities, including as president. Prior to rink management and RSROA duties, Mr. Martin was among those old-time speed skaters from the early 1900s.

Cleveland Rollercade Skating Rink (1941–68)

6800 Denison Avenue, Cleveland
Tagline: "World's Largest and Finest"
Jack Dalton and Clarence and D.J. Reynolds, Owners/Operators

Cleveland's Rollercade, built in 1929 by the Cleveland Union Stockyards Company, was used for livestock shows, polo matches and riding contests and known as the Equestrium.[201] It was repurposed and became the Rollercade in 1940, with a rink floor that measured 120 by 260 feet (31,200 square feet). By contrast, a football field is 48,000 square feet. The floor was featured and promoted as the world's largest and finest, featuring a triple-cushion, floating, soundproof floor. Initially, an electric organ supplied music; seating could accommodate three thousand. The Rollercade acquired a Wurlitzer from the Cleveland Palace Theatre in the mid-1960s.[202] It was removed in 1968. Renovations followed Rollercade's opening, adding a separate 2,550-square-foot figure skating practice rink (30x85 feet). Parking space accommodated five thousand vehicles.

After renovations, Rollercade continued to be promoted as the largest and finest rink in the world. At 23,400 square feet, the Rollercade hosted the 1948 RSROA National Championship in July 12–17, with 9,000 spectators

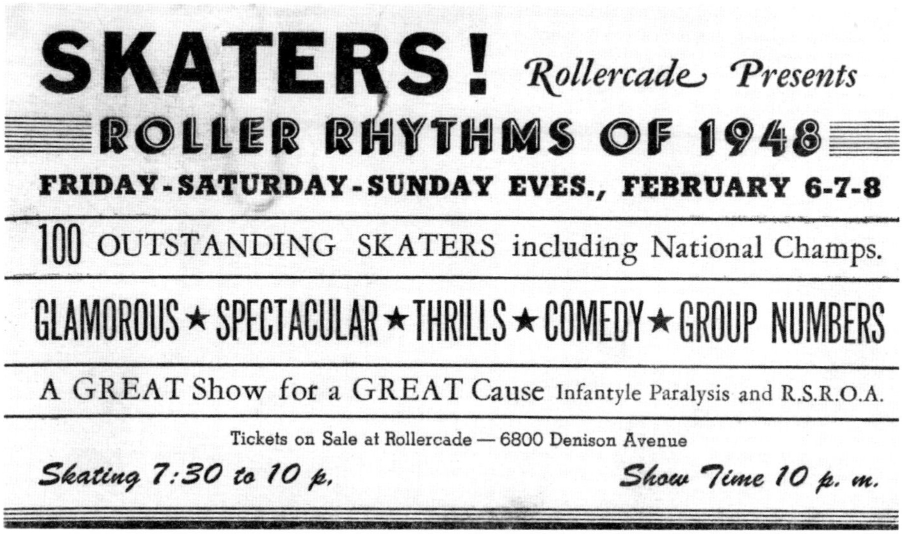

Rollercade ticket. Roller Rhythms of 1948 at the Cleveland Rollercade Skating Rink. *Author's collection.*

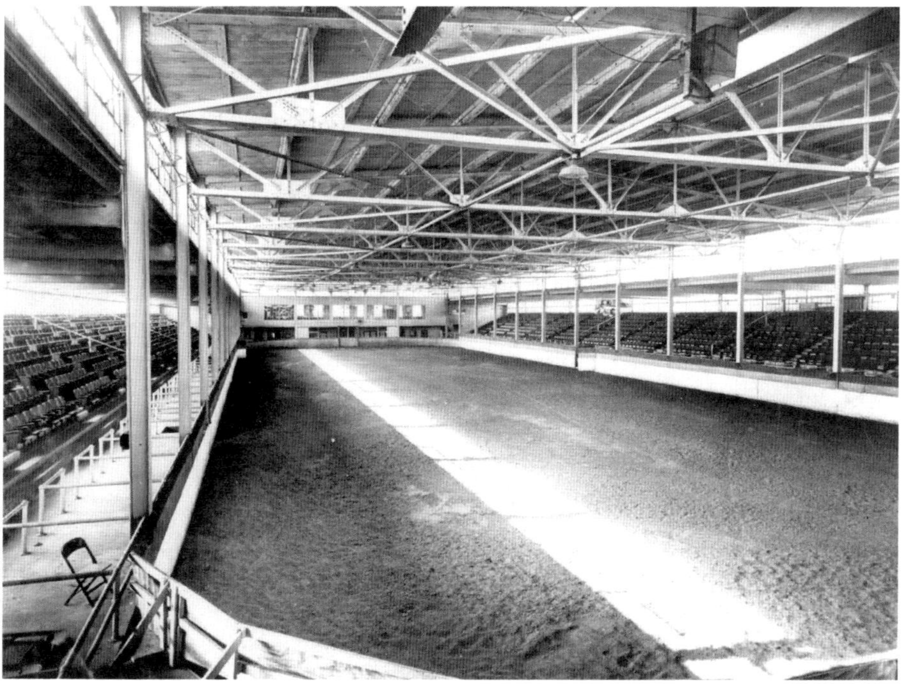

The Equistrium, circa 1929, before conversion to the Rollercade in 1941. Note the dirt floor and bleacher stands on both side of the building. *Cleveland Press Collection, Cleveland State University Library, Michael Schwartz Library Special Collection.*

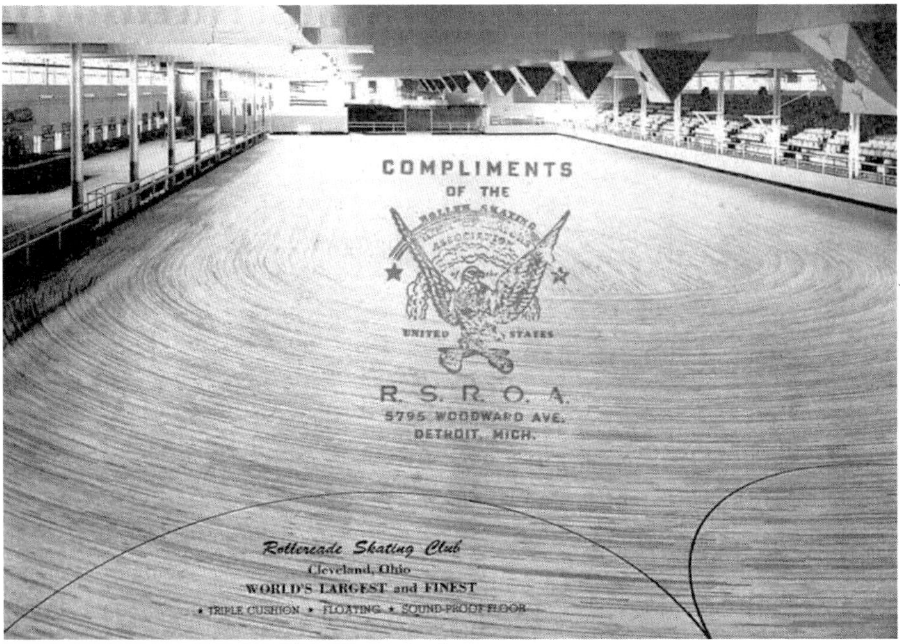

The Cleveland Rollercade in 1948 as it prepared to host the RSROA National Roller Skating Championship. Note the bleacher stands on the left that were removed to accommodate skaters; the bleacher stands on the right for spectators; the ceilings lowered, with acoustic treatments to deaden sound; and the huge speakers overhead on the right. *National Museum of Roller Skating.*

and another 1,500 turned away.[203] Afterward, it hosted the 1951, 1953, 1955 and 1958 U.S. Roller Skating National Championships. The Cleveland Rollercade closed in 1968.

The Cleveland Rollercade illustrates the conversion that took place to repurpose facilities from ballrooms, armories and livestock barns to roller rinks during the 1940s. In 1929, it had a dirt floor and spectator stands on both sides. Roll forward to 1940 to see the barn modified into a massive roller rink with a floor surface of 31,200 square feet; the left side spectator stands were removed and outfitted with skater benches, lockers and other amenities. Huge speakers were hung from the ceiling and served the dual purpose of blasting music throughout the facility along with speaker program announcements. Music had to be loud enough to overwhelm the sound that came from wood wheels on a wood floor along with the enthusiastic chatter that took place on the floor as well as off.

If there is any doubt about the enthusiasm toward roller skating, note that the Cleveland Roller Club hosted a forty-mile marathon in Ohio to commemorate National Roller Skate Week, with the race concluding at the Rollercade. Not far behind the Rollercade in terms of size and prestige was the Akron Rollercade, with a huge 100- by 200-foot (20,000 square feet) plastic floor rink and a seating capacity of five thousand spectators. In 1953, it hosed the USARSA National Championship.[204]

Empire Rollerdrome (1941–2007)

200 Empire Boulevard, Brooklyn
Tagline: Home of the "Miracle Maple"
Multiple owners/operators: Swanson family (1941–56);
Henry and Hector Abrami (1956–80); Gloria Abrami McCarthy (1980–98);
United Skates of America (1998–2007)

The Empire Rollerdrome was the heart of the roller disco craze in the late 1970s. In addition to installing a twenty-thousand-watt stereo system, Empire installed a disco lighting system and fog machines, all of which exalted roller disco fever. Roller disco is credited with a revival of roller skating during the short-lived roller disco era (1977–83).[205] The Empire may well have been the epitome of an old-school roller rink that adapted to generational musical whims and dance styles, one that would transform the pop culture of the twenty-first century—on rollers!

It was announced when the Empire opened in 1941 that it was the forty-first roller rink operating in the New York Metropolitan Area.[206] The rink opened in a one-story retrofitted parking garage by the Swanson family, who, coincidentally, owned a flooring business. The J.T. Swanson Floor Company produced the "miracle floating floor," known as the Swanson floor and used by large rinks across the country.[207] The garage was located across from world-famous Ebbets Field.[208] A feature of the new rink was the speaker system from the 1939 New York World's Fair, along with a state-of-the-art 31,000-square-foot maple wood floor along with restrooms, a lounge and a skate rental area. In 1956, the rink floor was reduced to 20,944 square feet, with 30 square feet set aside to accommodate a beginners' rink. Years later, the spacious floor was referred to as the "Miracle Maple Flooting Floor" due to its feel by skaters being as "smooth as satin."[209]

In 1949, Empire hosted the largest and most glamorous beauty contest on rollers in the United States, called the "Empire Rollerdrome Skate

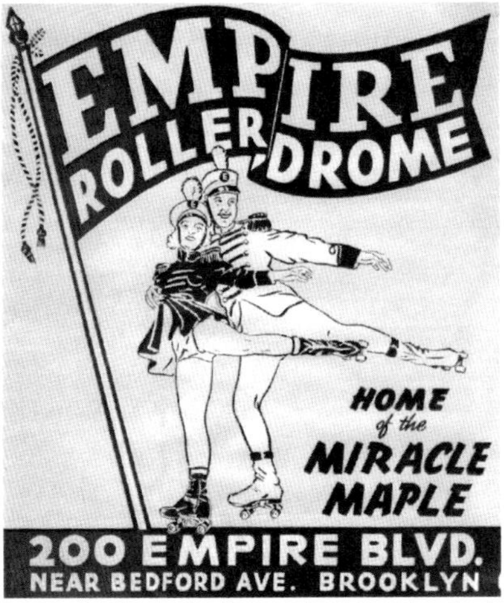

Empire Rollerdrome, "Home of the Miracle Maple," at 200 Empire Boulevard, New York. *Author's collection.*

Queen Contest."[210] More than three hundred entries participated in the contest. The first-place prize was a vacation to the paradise of Bermuda aboard a luxury liner.

During the golden age, Empire was one of twenty-eight rinks that formed a circuit in New York City to compete, provide lessons or just skate. Ownership of the Empire illustrates the transitional nature of rink ownership—how it stayed in families but also among rink skaters. During the Abrami ownership, Gloria, daughter of Henry Abrami, was a roller skate dancer along with her brothers Henry Jr. and Ronald. The last lace-up for the Empire Roller Skating Center came on April 22, 2007, for the sixty-six-year-old rink among the last roller rinks in New York City.[211] The Empire served as the last large-scale roller rink in Brooklyn.

Gay Blades Rollerdrome (1943–56)

239 West 52nd Street, west of Broadway, New York
Tagline: "America's Most Magnificent Roller Skating Rink"
Louis J. Brecker, Owner/Operator

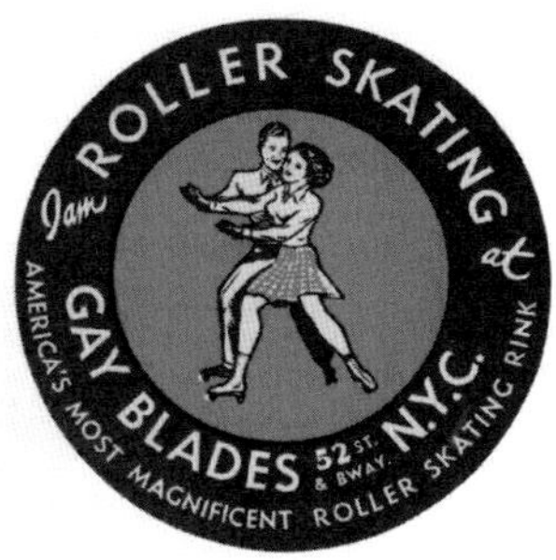

Gay Blades Rollerdrome, "America's Most Magnificent Roller Skating Rink," at 239 West 29th Street, New York City. *Author's collection.*

Opened as the Gay Blades Rink but renamed the Gay Blades Rollerdrome,[212] this site was among a handful of roller rinks scattered around Brooklyn, including the Empire Rollerdrome, Bay Ridge, Eastern Parkway and Park Circle. As Long Island's largest and most beautiful rink, Gay Blades shifted from ice skating to roller skating as early as 1939 but was in continuous operation by 1943.[213] Gay Blades was introduced as a mammoth roller skating palace[214] and was the only rink in the Times Square area of Manhattan.

Gay Blades was the scene of the RSROA nationals in 1946, described as the "greatest in the organization's 11-year history."[215] It also hosted northeastern regionals in 1948.[216] In 1948, Gay Blades hosted the New York State Roller Skating Championships, with more than five hundred skaters attending the event.[217] Competitions included figure skating, skate dancing, pairs, fours and speed skating, divided into five divisions (Juvenile, Junior, Novice, Intermediate and Senior).

Gay Blades was originally built in 1922 as an 80- by 200-foot (16,000 square feet) ice skating rink by the Iceland franchise operation. In 1932, Iceland went bankrupt, at which time the site opened as the Gay Blades Ice Rink.[218] Louis J. Brecker acquired Gay Blades when it operated as a roller rink with the intent to convert it to a dance ballroom. Initial reports revealed that conversion began in 1948.[219] Brecker simultaneously bid for RSROA regionals but denied rumors that Gay Blade operations as a roller rink were ending.[220] But by 1956, the rink had become the Roseland Ballroom, replacing the former Roseland located at 1658 Broadway at 51st Street. Roseland was called the "World's Most Famous Ballroom" since 1957. Gay Blades represented the eighth roller rink shuttered in Manhattan in the 1950s. Brecker was known for marathon dance contests before they were banned. Roseland closed in April 7, 2014, after Lady Gaga headlined six shows from March 29 through April 6.

Levittown Roller Rink (1955–86)

East Meadow, Long Island, New York
Tagline: "The Rink of World Champions"
George Petrone, Owner/Operator

Levittown Arena/Roller Rink achieved a reputation as "The Rink of World Champions" during its three decades of operations. The building included a 100- by 200-foot (20,000 square feet) maple wood skate floor, an exotic lobby, a large refreshment area, a sports shop, check and skate rooms and a stage where the organ was perched.[221]

Levittown was part of the America on Wheels, a network of rinks in the Northeast, primarily New York and New Jersey, that hosted competitions within the circuit for its skaters.[222] It is best described as a "franchise" network

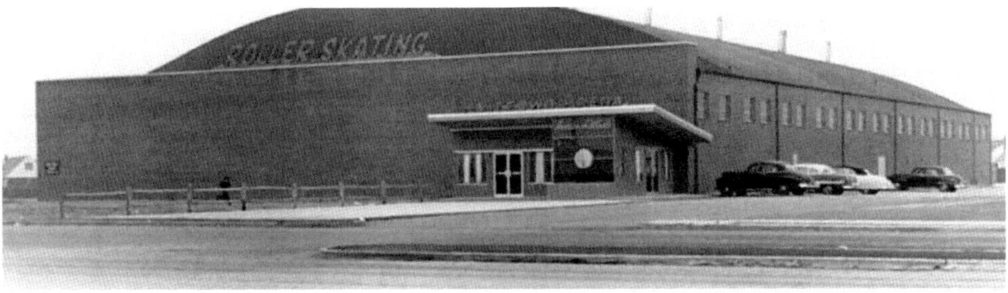

Levittown Arena, "The Rink of World Champions," at East Meadow, Long Island. *USA Roller Skaters.*

of rinks that served to host localized competitions to develop a corps of national competitors.

In 1986, the Levittown Arena was the most profitable of the America on Wheels chain of rinks when the decision was made to close and sell the 3.7-acre lot.[223] The closing of Levittown Arena after thirty years of operation resulted from "real estate that must be used to its highest and best value," according to Marvin Facher, owner of America on Wheels.[224]

The closing of Levittown, a rink located in the suburbs, came about as skate numbers dwindled and insurance rates climbed rather dramatically.[225] The economics of continued operations worked against Levittown, as the real estate value required a better choice despite the decades of loyal followers, memories created and the nostalgia that persisted.[226]

Mammoth Garden Roller Skating Rink (1935–62)

1540 Clarkson Street
Denver, Colorado
Irving Jacobs (1935–62), Owner and Operator
Mammoth Garden Roller Club[227] *(1935–62)*

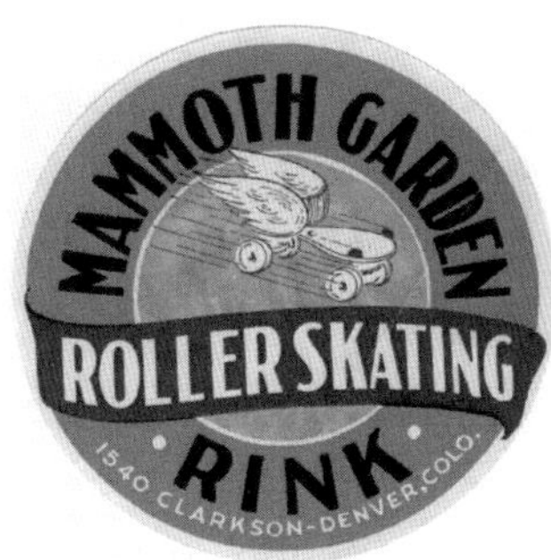

Mammoth Garden Roller Skating Rink, at 1540 Clarkson Street, Denver. *Author's collection.*

To Denver skaters, it was known as Mammoth Gardens, but its history dates to 1905; it resisted cultural shifts and sporting transitions. Today, the venue has become a prominent force in Denver's music scene and is known as the Fillmore Auditorium. Built in 1905 and completed in 1907, the sports arena operated as the Mammoth Roller Skating Rink until 1910. By 1911, roller skating had faded, and it had become a factory for Fritchle Automobile & Battery Company, with the plant closing in 1917.

In 1935, the venue opened for a variety of first-class sporting events. It simultaneously operated as the Mammoth Garden Roller Club from 1935 to 1962 as a first-rate, high-class rink when roller skating was the rage. Its rink floor measured 195 by 90 feet (17,550 square feet). Its four-thousand-spectator capacity made it a popular venue for hosting several national championships. In 1950, Mammoth hosted the RSROA National Championships. Traditional speed skating tracks were twelve laps to the mile, while Mammoth was fourteen laps to the mile, with long straightaways sought by speedsters. This made it ideal for speed skate events, both roller and ice skating.

By 1999, the Mammoth skating rink had become an entertainment venue, the Fillmore Auditorium.[228] Once the Denver Coliseum opened, sporting venues gradually moved to the Coliseum, and by 1967, Mammoth had closed. In 1999, the venue was purchased and, after multimillion-dollar renovations, opened as the Fillmore Auditorium, which it remains today.

Mineola Roller Rink (1934–60)

Mineola, New York
Tagline and Legacy: "Home of Dance Skaters"
Earl Van Horn and Inez Van Horn, Owners and Operators

Once a cattle exhibition barn, Mineola Roller Rink in Long Island was opened in 1934 by Earl Van Horn and his wife, Inez. Once established, Mineola claimed the title "Home of Dance Skaters" when its doors opened, establishing both its tagline and a legacy. Previously, Earl Van Horn was a professional skater and rink manager at the Oaks Roller in Portland, where he met Inez and fell in love. The couple married in 1918.[229] They toured Europe as "Van and Inez," performing on roller skates for royalty and appearing in New York's famous Palace Theatre twenty-two times.

The Mineola was located on the fairgrounds in Mineola and was only the fourth rink in the metro area. The rink was established with the intent to create a family-oriented roller skating rink. As showman and promoter, Van Horn understood that the environment needed to transform roller skating from its rowdy past to the class of roller sports. He was among the

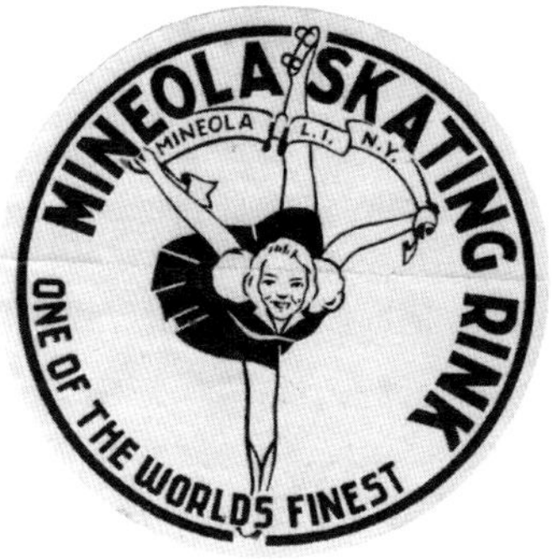

Mineola Roller Rink, "Home of Dance Skaters," Mineola, Long Island. *Author's collection.*

first to recognize that rink fundamentals required a quality floor, skate-oriented music and the best skates possible.[230] In 1937–38, the Van Horns invested $80,000 for improvements to create special effects; a silver ceiling was also installed. When the rink floor lights were lowered and the colored lighting system faded in, it created an enchanting, shimmering iridescence that made skate dancing romantic. Initially, the rink floor was 80 by 204 feet (16,320 square feet). It was enlarged twice over the years to accommodate the popularity of roller skating in Long Island.

They called it "dancing on wheels" when Mineola introduced skate dancing on roller skates. The new roller craze caught the attention of sports pages across America as the story moved westward. For example, in 1940, Ohio's *Evening Review* described the revival of roller skating as being due to the new roller dances that swept through the nation's modern rinks.[231] Mineola formalized skate dancing with instruction in all types of dance routines, including the Chicago hop, two-step, chicken scratch, open- and closed-circle waltzes and even the Mineola swing. Not only Chicago rinks but also rinks around the country were quick to sense this trend and adopt skate dancing, scrambling to become the next skate dancing rink offering instruction, programs and competitions.

Mineola Skate Club hosted the first RSROA roller skate dance and figure skating championships at the Mineola rink in 1939. Twenty-one contestants from a dozen states competed for the title of national champion in that first event. Earl Van Horn announced the quest to achieve Olympic sport status, and that quest would result in skate dance competition being included in the 1944 Olympics.[232] The Mineola Skate Club grew to become among the most active in the country. It boasted seven thousand paid members, many of whom traveled from fifty miles away to exercise and have fun.

It the 1940s, Van Horn became disenchanted with RSROA and resisted joining its ranks, instead operating as an ARSA-style rink. The dispute seemed to be about the clash of personalities and dance competition rules. As a result, it was big news in the roller world when in November 1957 the Van Horn Mineola Skating Rink filed application for RSROA affiliation.[233]

Earl Van Horn died tragically at the age of sixty-two on October 20, 1959, shot by his wife with a shotgun. He died of his wounds.[234] As the interest in roller skating faded, the rink closed. It was later demolished and today hosts a municipal parking lot.

Oaks Skating Rink[235] *(1906–present)*

7805 Oaks Park Way
Portland, Oregon, 97202
Tagline: "Skaters Paradise"

The Oaks Skating Rink presents the longest and richest story of a roller skating rink that survived civil strife, development overtures and the musical whims of generations to become a rink gifted for perpetuity. Today, the rink remains America's largest and oldest under the umbrella of the Oaks Park Association, a nonprofit organization that manages both the rink and park attractions. Originally built by the Oregon Water Power Railroad Company in 1905, Robert Bollinger entrusted the park to Oaks Park Association in 1985.

Built in 1905 as Oaks Amusement Park, the mammoth roller skating rink was but one of eighteen attractions in the forty-four-acre park. Among its features, the park included an auditorium, a Japanese tea garden, an ostrich farm and a walking path called the Merry Maze. With its buildings painted white, Oaks Park quickly became known as the "White City" of the West, nicknamed for the White City in Chicago.[236]

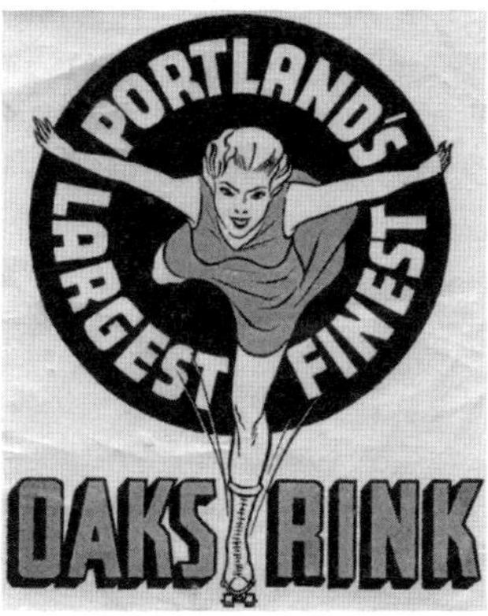

Oaks Skating Rink, "Skaters Paradise," at 7805 Oaks Park Way, Portland. *Author's collection.*

The grande dame of its day due to size, rules, dress and style of management, Oaks Rink remains the oldest continuously operating rink in the United States west of the Mississippi. It sported 29,125 square feet of skating surface and included two separate beginners' floors when it opened for the 1940 season. The Oaks rink features the only floating rink floor in the nation. Built in a floodplain, the rink flooded in 1948, at which time the floor was installed to float above the floodplain. Since then, the floor has survived two major floods.

At the outbreak of World War II, the Oaks Rink conducted a "rubber night" for skaters, offering an evening's skate for each auto rubber tire or two tubes turned in. The campaign was a special arrangement between an oil company and rink management. More than 1,020 pounds of rubber were collected. The pile was displayed in the lobby throughout the campaign.[237]

The Oaks Rink thrives today and carries the tagline "Skaters Paradise" to accompany its 100- by 200-foot Michigan maple floor and the last live Wurlitzer pipe organ[238] to operate in a U.S. roller rink.[239] The Wurlitzer's pipes hang on a platform above the rink floor and deliver an authentic look and feel, harkening back to those roller rinks of the 1940s when pipe organs were the standard form of skate music. The organ was originally used in Portland's Broadway Theatre for the silent films of the 1920s but then moved to the Oaks in 1955.[240] The Oaks hosted the 1963 RSROA nationals, the first time a national roller skate convention was held in the West.

Sefferino Rollerdrome (1937–56)

2827 Gilbert Avenue, Cincinnati, Ohio
Tagline: "Skaters' Paradise"
William F. Sefferino, Owner/Operator

The Sefferino Rollerdrome opened in March 1937 and hosted the first RSROA-sanctioned national speed skating championship in 1938.[241] Cincinnati was the center of speed skating, hosting both national and regional speed events. As early as 1940, *Billboard* magazine reported that speed skaters, a temperamental lot, demanded so much powder to help with floor grip that female patrons left the rink gray-haired, looking like they had aged in just a few hours.[242]

The Rollerdrome was built as a flagship venue, with its huge floor, patron amenities and capacity to handle three thousand skaters. It opened with a massive skate surface that measured 248 by 135 feet (33,480 square feet).[243] Over the next two decades, with renovations and amenities, the floor surface was reduced to 90 by 250 (22,500 square feet).[244]

At one point, membership in the Rollerdrome Club made it one of the largest clubs in the skating world, but a study of surrounding circumstances leaves the reasons for such growth suspect.[245] In 1946, it was reported

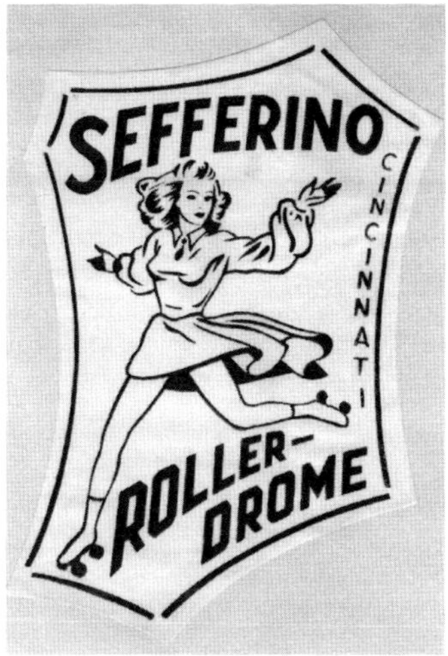

Sefferino Rollerdrome, "Skaters' Paradise," at 2827 Gilbert Avenue, Cincinnati. *Author's collection.*

that the Sefferino Rollerdrome reorganized under Ohio law as a private skate club with more than twelve thousand skaters.[246] By April 1947, club membership had grown to twenty-five thousand skaters.[247] This chapter of the Rollerdrome's life occurred in the context of desegregation actions that targeted recreation and amusement public accommodations. Prior to reorganization as a private club, a group of sixteen African Americans sought entrance to the Rollerdrome. They were turned away on the basis that the rink was closed for a private party. In court, Sefferino was acquitted of the charges.[248]

Desegregation activities targeting Cincinnati and Coney Island persisted from the late 1940s through the 1960s. Roller skating rinks remained in the line of fire, as protestors went after urban big-city attractions such as Coney Island. Just as civil strife in Chicago led to the 1968 riots and brought its oldest and best-known rink to ashes, so did civil strife result in the revelation of the Rollerdrome's sudden closure. In 1956, Sefferino announced that the Rollerdrome would not open for its fall season after two decades of operation, without offering a reason for its closing.

The end of the Sefferino Rollerdrome is probably not unlike the closing chapter of many roller rinks during the golden age. Numerous recreational facilities simply disappeared from the landscape in response to recreational desegregation.[249] The clashes of hostile protestors who sought equal rights to public accommodations created an environment where attending a roller skating rink became a dangerous adventure. Roller rinks had established reputations for being family-centered, safe and moral, places for social recreation and decorum. The clash between races undermined that reputation. Contested recreational spaces became dangerous for both youth and adults. In the end, rinks were abandoned by white skaters, and in the 1960s, urban rebellion closed many parks, pools and rinks.

A series of encounters at the Skateland Roller Rink in Cleveland describes the dependency by white owners/managers to permit white patrons in smaller rinks to police the rink against "unwanted" patrons. Small rinks did not have the security personnel or contracts with security firms.[250] Thus, the aggression of white patrons to police unwanted patrons became a permitted practice by white management at small rinks and served as a rationale for business reasons. Small rinks with limited resources avoided hiring security personnel to police patron activity. As a result, their actions avoided the call to law enforcement for intervention, along with unwanted publicity.

PART III

CHICAGO RINK RATS

In the 1900s, Chicago city kids started with sidewalk skates on the streets and grew up to shoe skates in the rink. This was a period when modern city streets were asphalt instead of the packed-dirt streets that had preceded city streets just a few decades earlier. This meant that clamp-on skates gave kids wheels and introduced tremendous mobility for city youth. This mix of wheels and improved skate surface also produced the best skaters. It is not unlike how kids who played baseball or football in the sandlots eventually became among the best ball players—or kids anywhere who started a sport at a young age became a new class of Olympians.

They adapted to rinks easily to become graceful skaters whose movements were quite natural and fluid and illustrated a considerable amount of innate, artistic form. Movements of the most famous skaters were likened to those trained in ballet or stars of ice skating turned rollers. These were the attributes of kids from the neighborhoods who spent their adolescent years in the roller rinks and became Chicago rinks rats.

Clamp-on style skates served as the manufacturer's promotional vehicle for city kids to transition from street skating to those supercharged rollerdrome rinks with their rosin-prepped all-maple wooden floors. The clamp-on style was perfect for first-time learners. Kids could slip them on, adjust for foot size and then clamp and secure the strap over the ankle. In Chicago, kids sported either Richardson or Chicago sidewalk skates and later moved up to the one-piece boot skate. During the later years of World War II, rink operators faulted an insufficient supply of sidewalk skates for kids, due to

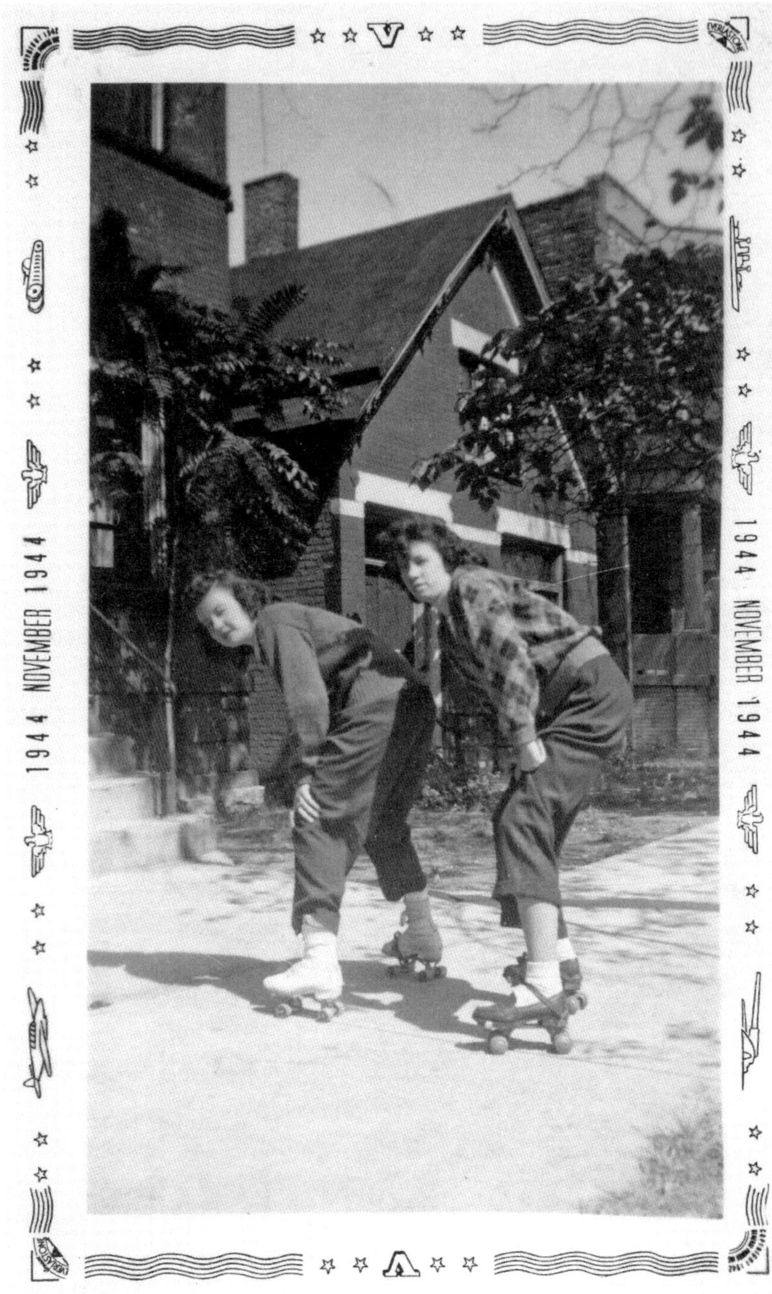

Westside skaters pose in race-ready position with boot skates and clamp-on skates. *Author's collection.*

war requirements, as being what reduced the number of pre-trained skaters ready for big-time neighborhood rinks. By the end of World War II, manufacturers were reporting that they had not built new skates in nearly three years.

If teens learned skate fundamentals on the street, Mohawks, Choctaws, lifts, spins, dance routines and backward skating were learned at the rink. The West Side Madison Gardens Rink typified one neighborhood story among many not only in the Chicagoland area but also throughout the nation during this golden age. Chicago had its North Side, South Side and, of course, West Side. Kids connected by learning who street skated, who was good and where they lived. As they learned to skate, kids got mobile and formed informal skate social networks, many of which persisted for a lifetime. Even today, old-time skaters reacquaint at the few remaining rinks in the suburbs. Gone are the roller rinks of yesterday that defined the neighborhood social skate scenes of Chicago.

FROM SIDEWALK TO RINK, 1938–1941

For the United States, World War II had yet to break out when a thirteen-year-old teenager walked into the neighborhood roller rink for the first time in 1940. Marion Smith had made friends with Liz and Allen on the streets of the West Side, hanging around places like Hensell's Drugstore, Andie Candies and Hamburger Haven. Their eager curiosity grew to see what went on in this huge building where loud organ music would seep through its walls and young people would come and go, skates draped over their shoulder with boot laces used as a skate leash, laughing, smoking cigarettes and having fun. They had learned that the kids who went to the rink jitterbugged on skates, popular among young people. When parents went to the dance ballrooms, they danced to the Lindy Hop, but the jitterbug was a new dance for young people. The excitement of learning to jitterbug on skates competed for floor time with speed skating for many of the new skaters.

A big man at the door collected tickets. The girls learned that was Big Bill, a longtime Madison Gardens employee. Other men were security guards, while still others skated on the floor. They were floor guards and helped with pileups. Inside Madison Gardens Rink on Chicago's West Side at 2560 Madison Avenue, neon glass signs glowed from one end of the rink, cascading the mix of neon colors over the snack bar area while a mirrored ball hung in the center of the rink. The ball was twenty feet above the floor, rotating and reflecting the multicolored but dimmed lights over the rink floor. The rink floor was separated from the snack bar by those diner-style booths, with couples occupying most of them. Behind the larger rink was a smaller beginners' rink, near the area where skates were rented by the snack bar.[251] On the second story was a Wurlitzer organ, which had the appearance that it grew up from the first floor and required a second story to host the massive instrument. It consumed one side of the rink, while the other three sides had a balcony with three rows of seating. The organist sat in a position of command in front of the Wurlitzer, with the gaggle of pipes to its backside. The music resonated from the Wurlitzer throughout the building, leaching through its wall to the outside and escaping past the double doors with each patron's entry and exit.

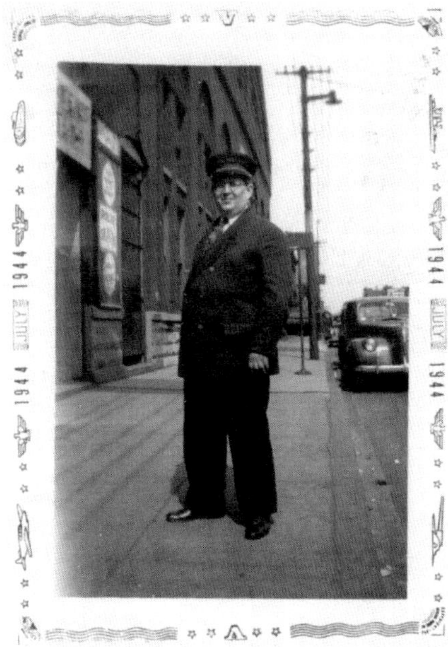

Madison Gardens' Big Bill, in rink uniform, stands at the front entrance of 2560 West Madison Street. The signage to the left reads, "Roller Skating" and "Matinee." *Author's collection.*

Skaters whirled around the rink, while couples whizzed along, with boys leading by skating backward in a fog of cigarette smoke and rink surface rosin. They noticed other skaters hanging on to a rail along the rink wall, kind of walking step by step, carefully, while others scooted away from the wall but close enough to reach out and catch their balance in the event their feet rolled out from underneath them. Several did spill, and guys dressed up in uniforms and hats blew whistles to stop the action and caution oncoming traffic while another helped them up. The girls learned later that these were floor guards and would stop the action when skaters tripped, fell and ended up in a pile, called pileups. Other guards watched for others skating too fast, weaving, playing tag or pulling a girl's hair as they passed by.[252] It seemed like whistles were blowing all the time for one infraction or another. As the younger kids fell, they laughed, rolled over and then jumped back up and scooted some more.

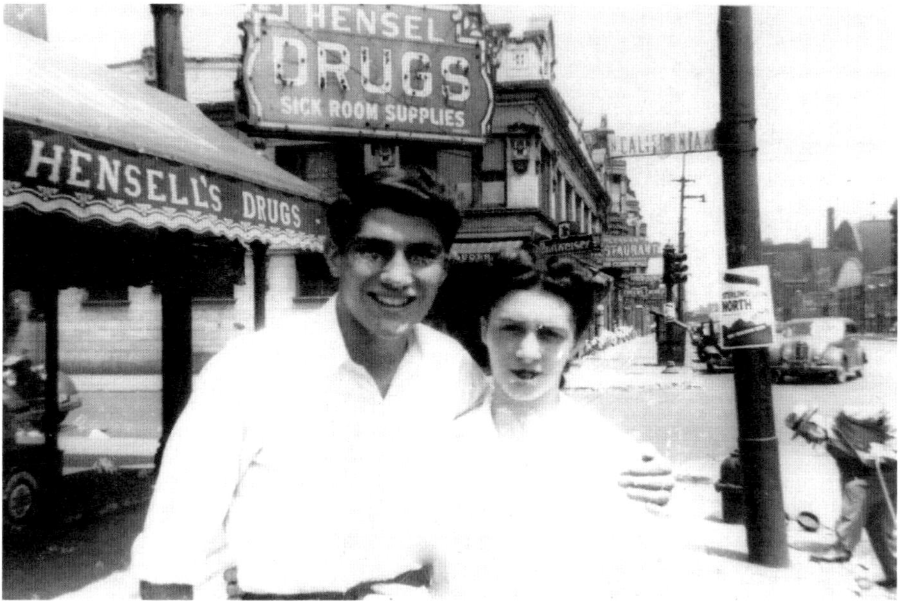

Hensell's Drugstore, at California and Madison, where west side kids hung out. Pictured here are Marion Smith and neighborhood friend. Marion wears a popular 1940s "victory" rolls hairstyle. *Author's collection.*

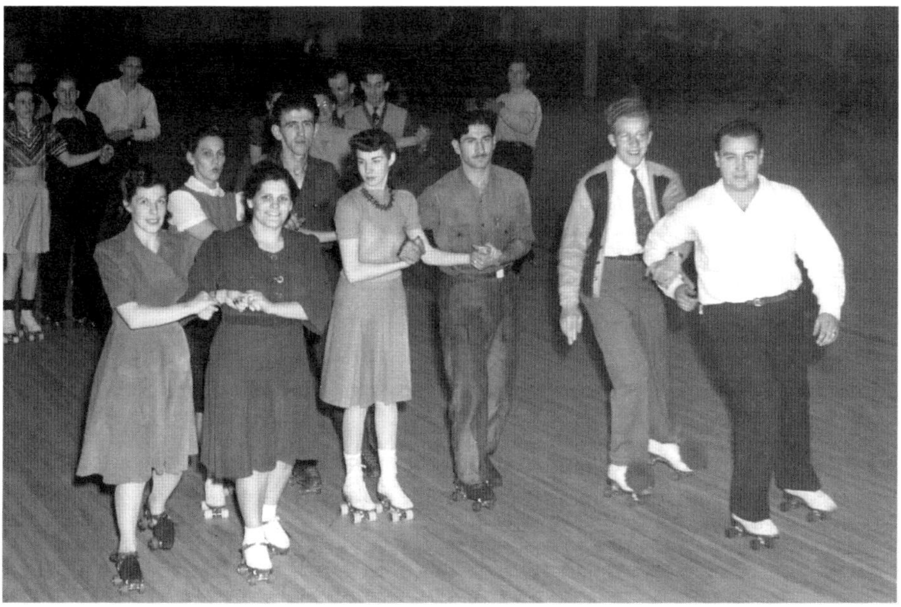

Cleveland Rollercade Fellowship Defense Skate Club. Couples are shown in traditional graceful skating form on November 8, 1941. *Cleveland Press Collection, Cleveland State University Library, Michael Schwartz Library Special Collection.*

Marion and Liz noticed that the older girls would go to the ladies' room and come out with dark-red lipstick and fixed hair—their first social introduction to hair and makeup. They watched other kids on the rink to measure how they would fit in before the two girls got onto the floor. Most kids had a hard time keeping their balance when crossing their feet, one over the other, to turn at each end of the rink. Sidewalk skating did not require a whole lot of turns, and this would require practice. Older girls completed the crossover with ease by gracefully moving their right skate over the left and then lifting the left to the front of the right and repeating the move. Something to work on!

The most memorable recollection was the music, which skaters said was the best in town. Skaters kept rhythm to the tempo banged out by the organist on the huge Wurlitzer as skaters bounced to each metronome beat. Not only did their feet move to the beat, but the best skaters also flaunted a shuffle or bounce with each skate-step that set them apart from first-timers. For Marion and her friends, the excitement built as they worked to lace up those rented boot skates and take the floor for the first time. In the city, this is where teens learned about dating, having fun and making friends for life. The rink scene for many would become like family and keep them close in the war years.

Believe it or not, music was debated during the golden age, with the most sought-after being from pipe organs. Rink operators differentiated between "feet music" and "listening music," with roller skating requiring the former.[253] Feet music was mostly staccato with a definite beat and rhythm and required organists to know how to rewrite music to accommodate skaters and move feet. When skate dancing, beats had to be distinct enough so that partners could hear them and know when to step—and step in unison.

In 1940, Madison Gardens Rink was the oldest and best known and promoted itself with the tagline, "Chicago's Favorite Rink." The talk wasn't just about the skate dancing, the new sensation, but also about the many speed skaters who were members of the Madison Gardens Speed Club. The club had established that reputation by its success with training the skaters who represented Chicago in speed events around the country. The view in the early 1940s was that Madison would produce the decade's next corps of speed skaters.[254] For example, Leroy Junge had won the 1940 Illinois state speed skating championship and set his sights on the national title.[255] At his heels were Bill Hay and Russell Brown, both having competed at the 1941 nationals in Cleveland. Hay trained at Madison Gardens Rink, but his home rink was the Hollywood Rink up at 4825 North Kedzie Avenue. At that same meet, Russell Brown set a new U.S. record for the one-mile speed event with a 2:53.4 time. But Bill Hay walked away with the Rodney R. Peters Senior Men's Speed Skating Trophy.[256] But there was also mention of women speed skaters, such as Maxine Rosser, a junior girl who won the 1940 speed championship.

In the late 1930s, Marion Smith was one of thousands of kids with sidewalk skates rolling around neighborhood streets. She learned to skate at the age of eleven on the sidewalks between California and Sacramento on the West Side, and then she'd hang out at Hensell's Drugstore on California. In 1938, she heard about Gloria Nord, a teen roller skater who at the age of eighteen traveled the nation and roller skated. Chicago was among Gloria Nord's Midwest tour stops for skate exhibitions at the Chicago Coliseum in 1941 promoting a new roller magazine, *Skating Review*.[257]

Harold Steinman caught Nord's 1941 Coliseum performance at the same time he was organizing his roller skate revue, similar to the ice skating Ice Follies.[258] Steinman was in search of roller talent, but talented amateurs did not want to give up their amateur status with RSROA until they had completed their championship campaign. In fact, *Skating Review*, in its coverage of the Roller Follies premiere in January 1942, called for "more good skating talent."[259] By the second season, September 1942–43, Roller Follies had become Skating Vanities.[260] With new talent and a new name, the roller skating extravaganza was described by *Billboard* as the "fastest two-and-a-half hours of spectacle, novelty and comedy skating and a general mélange of strong vaudeville novelty acts that played across the country."[261] Young girls learned from Gloria Nord, and her visits to Chicago, that the teen star never had a lesson but rather taught herself to skate.

The West Side of Chicago was a tough neighborhood, and the young learned to defend themselves. Madison Gardens Rink anchored the West Side neighborhood. Converted from a retired Rockwell cable car powerhouse in 1906, it survived World War I, Prohibition, the Depression and the decline of roller skating during the 1920s and 1930s and emerged in the 1940s as the oldest and best-known rink in Chicago. Young people would meet, congregate and skate at Madison Gardens. Friendships formed among members of the roller skate gang that lasted a lifetime.

Madison Gardens Rink is a microcosm of the roller skate scene typical of not only other Chicago rinks but also other rinks across the nation during the Golden Age of Roller Skating. But Madison Gardens, with its West Side location, occupied a centralized location for skaters throughout the city.

Skaters could travel to any other Chicago rink in fifteen to twenty minutes whether it was north, west or south using public transportation.

In those days, kids got permission from their parents before they were allowed to go to the rink. In fact, kids were expected to tell their parents where they were going when they left the house. It was not uncommon for a group to head downtown on the Green Hornet, Chicago's first electric trolley system, replacing both cable cars and horse-drawn streetcars.

Marion's mother did not like her going to the roller rink. Her mother grew up at a time when rinks were gang hangouts and frequented by juvenile delinquents. They had a bad reputation for mischief, including being pickup places. By the 1940s, rink operators had organized and fought back against this dated reputation by instituting dress codes, using male floor guards to stop aggressive skate behavior and so forth. The roller skate industry had also instituted new styles of roller skating, such as skate dancing and figure skating, that tamped down excess behavior in an attempt to create an upscale form of recreation. But the mothers of the West Side, including Marion's, did not know that roller skating was going through a transformation and was about to embark on its golden age. What they recalled were the roughhouse rinks around since the 1920s when they were West Side youths.

Skate racing in the 1920s and 1930s contributed to the demise of roller skating and resulted in the bias against speed skating by rink operators during the early 1940s. Operators were faulted for permitting "a bunch of roughnecks in overalls and sweat shirts to take over the rink in the belief that it would give patrons a thrill."[262] Roughnecks came to race, knock people down and instigate fights and arguments. Those rink operators who saw the benefit of skate racing felt that if it were managed, it would add to the box office. The public loved skate racing. But it was the rink skate clubs that brought order to racing as one of three competitive divisions that included both figure and dance. Uniforms were required by competitors in all divisions, and events were managed by a rink race manager. The first national speed championship was held in 1938, and by 1940, both figure and dance competitions had been established. But it would be 1947 before operators across the nation began to see the positive response by the public to speed competitions.[263]

In 1939, Marion was not allowed to go to that roller rink. She asked her mother if she could go, but her mother would not approve of such activity. In those days, Madison Gardens scheduled afternoon skates for kids younger than eighteen, while evenings were reserved for adult skates. The girls could usually get in on the evening skate if they looked old enough and if their parents were not looking for them. But for Marion, the request to go to the rink went on for some time.

But that Saturday afternoon in the fall of 1940, Liz asked Marion if she wanted to go with her to the rink. She had a friend, a boy who would get them in. Marion said sure but did not have her skates. Liz said that was probably better, as then her mother would not notice where she had gone, plus skate rental was only twenty-five cents. The girls continued to go to the rink for some time, well into the winter, without Marion's mother knowing. However, Marion had to confront her mother's displeasure with her continued rink visits when she failed to stop in time to avoid a pileup at the rink, fell and sprained her arm. Boys were clowning around and skating in the wrong direction when Marion ran into a group of skaters and fell. She had yet to learn how to stop in time to avoid fallen skaters. Rinks in those days had arrangements with doctor's offices and sent Marion to a Madison Street doctor's office. Friends went with her. Marion left with her arm wrapped. When she got home, Marion told her mother that she had fallen outside on the ice.

Other neighborhood kids also street skated, inspired by Gloria Nord, and found their way to local rinks as well. Young skaters, new to the rink, met other young skaters at Madison Gardens. Marion Smith met Louise Audie and her sister, Deloris; the Knight brothers, Elmer and Earl; Jack Smith; Norma Carroll; Wanda Hoffman; Irv Gianneschi; Lorraine Freis; and Doris Raines. In 1940–41, their ages ranged from fourteen to sixteen. Generally, the boys were a few years older, but the Madison Gardens Rink was a neighborhood icon, a lure and the next step in the social scene. Louise, Marion and Earl were fourteen, while Bud, Jack and Allen were sixteen in 1941. Others in the gang fell somewhere in between. Over time, they formed a rather tightknit group, joining the rinks at about the same time, age range and skate skill level. All of them grew up on sidewalk skates, learning fundamentals and visiting the neighborhood roller rink with friends.

The rumblings of war persisted in the late 1930s, with Japan striking first in China and Hitler's Germany rolling through Poland two years later in 1939. By 1940, Italy had entered the war alongside Germany. But the bombing of Pearl Harbor was the call to action for the United States. On December 7, 1941, President Roosevelt asked Congress for a declaration of war against Germany, Italy and Japan.

SKATING THE WAR YEARS, 1941–1945

The West Side gang gathered early on a bright, clear Sunday afternoon at Madison Gardens to warm up for the late afternoon's special event. Speed racing and graceful skating finals had been planned for months, and the day had finally arrived. As they entered the doorway, the huge 1941 national speed roller championship trophy won by Bill Hay[264] was proudly displayed in the trophy cabinet. Big Bill was collecting the admission tickets, while Happy Johnson, organist with well-pressed clothes and neatly combed hair, sat atop his new golden throne at the Wurlitzer's keyboard and played dance music for the warm-up session before the contests later that afternoon. It was the first Sunday in December 1941, and Madison Gardens was hosting Chicago's Old Timers' Roller Skating Club of Chicago with race competitions, waltz-skate contests, prizes and trophies. Everyone had been invited.

Madison Gardens Rink's new season opened in September, hosting dance classes Sunday mornings. Jitterbug skate dancing was the craze among teens, but skaters in their twenties preferred the traditional dances. Thus, Madison taught dance classes Sunday mornings featuring the fourteen-step, the collegiate, spread-eagle waltzes, mohawk waltz, Keat's fox trot, barn dance and the blues.[265] Couples could learn the basic dance steps in three sessions. Charlie Tyler's November column "Rollin' Round Roller Rinks" in the *Herald-American*[266] reported that Roller Skating Club of Chicago's President George Corbeil and Mrs. Corbeil learned the straight waltz in one session. The couple mastered the collegiate in three sessions. Most members of the West Side gang loved the skate dances but had little patience with organized classes. Members like Jack and Louise, Marion, Earl, Wanda, Liz and Bud watched the experienced skaters and picked up the basic steps in a session or two.

Few rinks could afford air conditioning, so many rinks operated seasonally. The lack of air conditioning made summers in the rink stifling hot. The mix of rosin and cigarette smoke, coupled with the need for repairs and renovations, made summer the perfect time to shut down and ready for a new season. Summer was also used to plan special events for the coming season. Madison Gardens, in cooperation with Arcadia Gardens Rink on the North Side at 4444 North Broadway and the Roller Bowl at 1058 West Washington Street, worked to ready its competitors for the state and national champion contests. Event dates and host cities were made during the summer by the Roller Skate Rink Operators Association (RSROA).

Usually, Arcadia or the Roller Bowl would host the state competitions. As a result, these special events required extensive planning to ready local competitors for a successful run at those championships and required contests that lead up to the event. The time was used to plan events, including contests of all sorts, and set the rink schedule for speed skating, dance classes and other figure skate events. Thus, the finals on this day had been set since September, when the new seasoned opened.

The Wurlitzer suddenly went silent from the all-skate warmups. Skaters stopped immediately or slowed, twisting to look back at the Wurlitzer. Happy Johnson was leaning over, and Charles McCormack (the Madison rink owner) was whispering in his ear. From the rink floor, it appeared that McCormack was attempting to check to see if all was okay with Johnson when he took the microphone and announced that Japan had attacked Pearl Harbor. America was at war! McCormack heard it on the radio and had passed the news to Johnson. A moment of silence was held for the boys and America. After this, the Wurlitzer belted out "America the Beautiful." Skaters joined Johnson and sang along.

President Roosevelt was in his study at the White House, waiting to meet with advisor Harry Hopkins, when he learned of the attack. Secretary of the Navy Frank Knox burst into his office at 1:30 p.m. (EST) and announced that Pearl Harbor had been attacked by Japan.[267] Major radio networks began to interrupt regular programming at 2:30 p.m. after confirming a 1:07 p.m. Associated Press bulletin reporting the attack to news organizations and radio networks.[268] In Chicago, it was 2:46 p.m. when word reached the rink, the city and the nation.

At that moment, few understood the impact that war would have on citizens, the economy and the nation. The boys were eager to sign up for the armed services, but the administration had been reluctant to ready the nation for war. Little mobilization of industry had occurred. It would be another year before the Selective Service expanded the age range for males from twenty-one to forty to eighteen to forty-three. At that moment, Britain was under siege by Germany, the nation's naval Pacific shield lay on the ocean floor after the Japanese surprise attack and the nation's weapon stores were nearly empty.[269]

National hostilities before World War I were always one between armies and rarely affected citizenry. Even though World War I required the industrial base of the nation to defeat Germany and the Axis powers, the United States was officially at war only from April 1917 to November 1918, or eighteen months. What most Americans learned was that the nation goes to war and wins in eighteen months, the boys come home and normalcy returns. Few were ready for the protracted war this conflict would bring to the routine of American life nor the many sacrifices each citizen would bear.

Skaters and rink operators quickly learned that skate manufacturers would be issued requirements by the War Production Board (WPB) for equipment and supplies that would be directed to support the armed services for training stateside and those serving overseas. Roller skates were among those supplies requisitioned for the troops, while ball bearing industries like Richardson Ballbearing Skate Company shifted from roller skates to ball bearings for artillery, tanks, planes and trucks. Metal of all sorts was needed to not only meet the army's needs but also build navy ships. One tank required eighteen tons of metal, while a single ship required nine hundred tons.[270] But that was not all that would change. Roller skating rinks under lease with states for national guard armories got word that state national guards would be mobilized—the 202nd Armory on Broadway would be taken over by the Illinois National Guard. Word got out that the Rollerdrome in Gary had been taken over by the Indiana National Guard as well and roller skating suspended there.

Over the course of the war, roller skate rinks created incentives for current and former skaters (those who gave it up) to return broken skates, parts and unused skates so those could be recycled or used as parts to repair old skates. This became the new norm, but skaters continued to skate, rinks continued to operate and the entire industry supported the war effort from day one through 1945. Food rationing began in 1942 with sugar and progressed to include all sorts of basic food types, including flour, meat, grease, canned goods, rubber and gasoline. Few commodities were exempt from rationing.

But for now, with a war declaration imminent, weekly skates continued, and those who had grown up around the roller rinks of Chicago would keep rolling. That particular December 7, 1941 afternoon crowd at Madison Gardens had arrived and readied for the finals after weeks of classes, training and semifinal competitions. Finals were held that afternoon, but the next four years would not be the same.

More than three hundred couples had begun the preliminary competitions on October 18, and now nine couples remained for the grand finals. Silver and bronze medals had been awarded each week to preliminary finalists who moved on to the grand finals. Judges were represented by members of the Madison Gardens skate clubs, and the Madison Gardens trophy would be awarded by owner Virginia McCormack.

Marion and the girls were upstairs in the balcony watching. Some were talking to boys. The floor downstairs was always crowded, especially with the skaters and their friends. Upstairs, they could see some of the couples warming up over on the beginners' rink and watch all the action. Everyone called it the beginners' rink, but couples used it all the time to practice turns, spins and other fancy moves.

The contest came down to a duel between two very graceful skating couples, Yvonne LaMoore and Elmer Klos and Audrey Brabec and Kenneth Foley. Honors and trophy went to Brabec and Foley. As the evening came to a close, Happy Johnson announced that Madison Gardens would celebrate its thirty-fifth anniversary sometime in March 1942 as "Chicago's Favorite Rink." Competitions, prizes and a featured skate revue were in the making.

1942

Chicago rinks brought in the New Year with grand celebrations, and despite the war, rink operators were optimistic that 1942 would be a growth year. Admission was waived for the boys showing up in uniforms. Flyers announced that dance classes were being offered, training schedules set for state and national competitors and parties planned for servicemen headed out for either basic training or with orders for overseas duty. Madison Gardens opened the New Year with a Waltz contest that started on Tuesday, January 14; Arcadia had the Illinois state championships set for late February; and another new rink would open in the summer.

Arcadia was preparing for the Illinois dance, speed and figure championships at the end of February. Russell Brown from Madison Gardens, who competed well at nationals in 1941, and Conway Manahan were in training and expected to challenge Bill Hay, U.S. and Illinois state champion. All were expected to represent Chicago well at the nationals given five race events, but Hay was expected to retain his title. Roy Sopper, a newcomer and 1941 state junior champion, provided a worthy training opponent as well. For the first time in a few years, the ladies were stepping out onto the speed side of roller skating. Anita Newquist from the South Side Planet Roller Rink would take on Madison Gardens' Lorraine Fries and Jackie Melsen from Arcadia.

Juanita Williams and Tommy (Dominik) DeCicco of Madison Gardens would make another run at freestyle pairs. In 1941, Williams and DeCicco competed in novice freestyle as first-timers. Ten-year-old Caroline Buchanan of Madison Gardens, a local darling and favorite, entered with Roller Skating Club of Chicago (RSCC) and took junior girls' figures and junior dance state titles in 1941. Buchanan was expected to represent Chicago well at the nationals.

The dominance of Chicago male speedsters in recent years sparked interest among the lady skaters at Chicago rinks, especially among the young crowd coming of rink age in the fall of 1941 and 1942. Speed skating had been dominated by males well before the early 1900s and throughout the first decades of the twentieth century. And Midwest states like Ohio and Detroit, as well as Chicago, were consistently represented. Perhaps all the antics that accompanied the sport of speed skating kept respectful women distant from the delinquency that accompanied roller skating until roller derby demonstrated a skill role for women.

But many rinks outside the Chicago area and the Midwest resisted speed skating as a roller style, insisting it was "rough stuff" especially for women, even as late as the mid-1940s.[271] Some described speed skating as the brawl of wrestling with the speed of racing and a touch of football—on roller skates. The perception held by operators is that by promoting racing, they would be inviting rowdyism, while others objected to the dust created by the necessity of powdering the surface for races. Rink managers found that speed skating added nothing to box office revenues, while others found that business was good and there was no need to warrant speed skate promotion. Too often, rinks failed to use floor guards along with a defined skate session program to manage the floor, allowing unsupervised youth to exploit the frenzy that resulted from the lack of oversight. For example, James J. "Sonny" McCannon was barred by an attendant for fast skating in Rialto Rink, Springfield, Massachusetts. He was found guilty in the district court of beating George Walkley, the attendant, who called him to order. McCannon was given a suspended sentence of two months in the detention center and charged with assault and battery by Associate Justice Ralph S. Spooner, who warned him to stay away from the rink.[272] But in Chicago, speed skating was a tradition and was managed.

Even as roller skating organized for competition skating before 1941, women had not participated much in those structured speed events, with the exception of the rough-and-tumble roller derby scene. In 1938, at the first national roller speed skating championship, only fourteen women participated compared to the forty-five men who competed. Most came from Detroit, Cincinnati and Chicago's 202nd Armory Rink, now relegated for guard duty with the 1942 skate season. Interestingly enough, Russell Brown and

LeRoy Junge were among those first thirty-eight entries.[273] Beatrice Ederer was the sole female Chicago contestant in that 1938 national championship series representing Chicago's 202nd Armory, while Maxine Rosser took the junior girls' title in 1940. But the early 1940s were a new day for women, as much more was being expected on the homefront or working in the defense industry. Women's entry into this once male-dominated skate style seemed inevitable, and young women felt that their time had come.

Skate clubs were instrumental in closing this rowdyism and reputation gap, coaching the new corps of speed skaters and supporting their competitive climb to success. Those urban areas with established clubs maintained an advantage over rinks without the benefit of skate clubs throughout the 1940s. Those rinks that sought to compete organized skate clubs in the skate style that fit their theme, whether it was dance, figure, artistic or speed.

Chicago was among the first urban areas to establish citywide clubs. In fact, Chicago had two citywide clubs: the Roller Skating Club of Chicago (RSCC) and the Old Timers' Roller Skating Club of Chicago, organized in 1939 and first hosted by the 202nd Armory Rink. The Roller Skating Club of Chicago (registered at 3241 Broadway, Chicago) was among the few independent clubs registered with the U.S. Federation of Amateur Roller Skaters of RSROA, which meant that the club was not affiliated with any single rink. As a result, skaters who wished to compete but stuck with their non-RSROA member home rink could be a member of the club and compete at RSROA-sanctioned competitions.[274] But there were others that formed along the way as well, like the Chicago Figure Skating Club. Their purpose, in essence, was to support and send skaters to sanctioned contests (ARSA or RSROA) who wished to compete but whose host rink did not support a particular skate style. Madison Gardens had the Madison Gardens Speed Club, while Riverview Roller Rink hosted the Riverview Speed Club.

All clubs contributed quite a lot to the success of Chicago-area skate competitions. The Old Timers' Roller Skating Club of Chicago club members organized special skate events and provided trainers, judges and fundraisers on behalf of promising competitors. Its members tended to be the old-timers of roller skating who not only worked to coach, promote and encourage Chicago-area skaters but also frequently organized field trips to other state or Midwest rinks and showed up when a new rink opened up, such as the Rinkydink Rink in downstate Illinois. Skate clubs would visit other cities and their rinks.

In May 1942, the Roller Skating Club of Chicago organized a bus trip to the national convention at the Philadelphia Convention Hall to

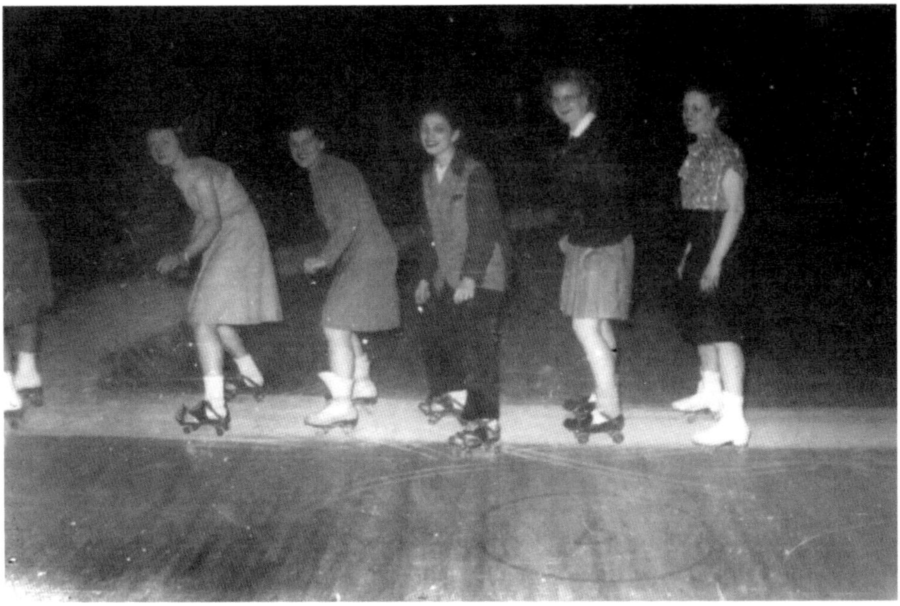

Lady rink rats line up for the circa 1943 Madison Gardens race with boot skates and clampons. Note the rosin powder ring on the wood floor in the shape of an oval. *Author's collection.*

support the new crop of Chicago skaters.[275] Given gas rationing and the cost of pleasure driving, they secured funding and a means to get Chicago skaters to the convention. This story is not unique to Chicago but rather represents the role roller skate clubs across the nation took on by their club members whose passion for the sport inspired them to help new skaters enjoy, compete and achieve the art of artistic, dance, figure or speed roller skating. Thus, skaters were supported in many ways whether through skate clubs or magazines such as *Skate* magazine that offered many tips for the new skater.[276]

Chicago figure skaters and skate dancers did well in their first national event with the new skate styles at the nationals, but the speedsters of Chicago did not fare as well. Chicago speedsters failed to make top three in either men's or ladies' divisions. Lorraine Freis represented the women well but was unable to grab a top-three finish against the speedsters coming out of the Midwest and the East. Ten-year-old Caroline Buchanan finished twelfth in junior girls' figures, while DeCicco-Williams finished eleventh in novice pairs skating. Mary Bragg and Conway Manahan finished twenty-fifth in novice pairs skate dancing but took time with RSROA Dance Committee chair Perry Rawson to pick up the differences between dance and figures, planning to add those to their routine.

Skaters from around the city knew of the strong tradition of speed skaters that was coming out of the North and West Sides. It was not unusual to see South Siders travel north to Madison Gardens and Arcadia to skate at the larger rinks, join skate clubs and compete. In fact, at Madison Gardens' April race series, Lorraine Freis of Madison Gardens raced against Anita Newquist, 1941 Illinois state champ and a South Sider from New Planet. Freis took the series and the trophy, with Newquist as runner-up. Freis's performance demonstrated the West Side dominance of speed skating events. They had battled earlier at Arcadia, where Freis took top honors and state title for ladies' speed champion.

Esther Swiat was among those from the South Side who followed Newquist to Madison Gardens but also frequented Arcadia for the speed events, including training sessions. The two were a few years apart in age and competed in different divisions. But the rivalry on the floor in local competitions was intense and provided great training. Eventually, Esther got to know Lorraine from Madison, as well as the other girls in her age group like Louise, Marion, Deloris, Doris, Wanda and others. In fact, Doris had been working out in speed events but had yet to make a commitment to racing. In Esther, she found a training partner for speed work. Esther fit in with the group, and as she hung out, earned the nickname "Shorty" due to her four-foot-eleven stature. You knew she would become a Madison regular. In fact, getting a nickname was the badge of acceptance for the group. Louise was "Lou," Marion "Mare," Jack "Smithy" and Elmer "Bud."

It was rumored that the new rink on the near West Side, at 1058 Washington Avenue, would open in July with a "soft" grand opening. Named the Roller Bowl, it became the sixth full-time roller rink to open in the Chicago area. It featured a 100- by 200-foot rink floor with a practice and figure skating rink that measured 50 by 100 feet. Knotty pine on the walls helped with acoustics, and there was carpet on the lounge floor. Al Beckwith played both the organ and the Novachord. The Roller Bowl owners had gone all out with skater amenities to attract national events and was expected to submit proposals to host national events, such as the 1944 National Amateur Roller Skating meet.

In early March, the news was announced that the Madison Gardens' thirty-fifth anniversary was set for March 24 and gold skate pins would be given out to all who showed up. When the Tuesday came, the crowd was huge, and the West Side gang showed up with skates en masse. Owners Charles and Virginia McCormack welcomed each guest, thanked them for their patronage and handed out the pins. Each pin was gold-colored brass and featured the winged sandal and foot of Mercury/Hermes, the fleet-footed messengers of the gods who symbolized skate speed. They were quite the novelty. If you were a Chicago rink rat, you wanted one, regardless of rink affiliation. The Chicago Roller Skate Company logo was embossed across the front of the boot.

Madison Gardens had gone all out to decorate with balloons, special lighting and new music. Happy Johnson was rolling out a special music program that included an organ adaption of what was a trending instrumental by Benny Goodman and His Orchestra, the "Jersey Bounce." Many orchestras were playing their own version, but it was the Benny Goodman instrumental that took it to the top of the charts as the number one song in America. It was played at USO events, defense recreation centers, on the ships, overseas and anywhere where there were Americans. It was the top song around the world.

But it was those rink organists like Happy Johnson who adapted it to roller skating, popularized for rink music and made the "Jersey Bounce" memorable. Madison Gardens seems to have been the origins of where skaters began a bounce-shuffle to the beat while skating. With each beat, skaters bounced and shuffled while shifting smoothly from one foot to the other. Marion Smith recalled that Madison Gardens skaters called it the "Jersey Bounce." When it played, skaters jumped to the skate floor, bounced and shuffled. Whether the "Jersey Bounce" originated in Chicago is unknown. Marianne Pepitone years later recalled that the bounce was so characteristic of Madison skaters.[277] Virginia Monforte, who skated at Madison Gardens as early as 1938, told *Chicago Tribune* reporter Barbara Iehl that she ran into her current skating partner in 1991 because his skate style was the same as hers. It was that Madison Gardens bounce.[278] Virginia added that "all Madison Gardens skaters bounced because the organist played that way!"

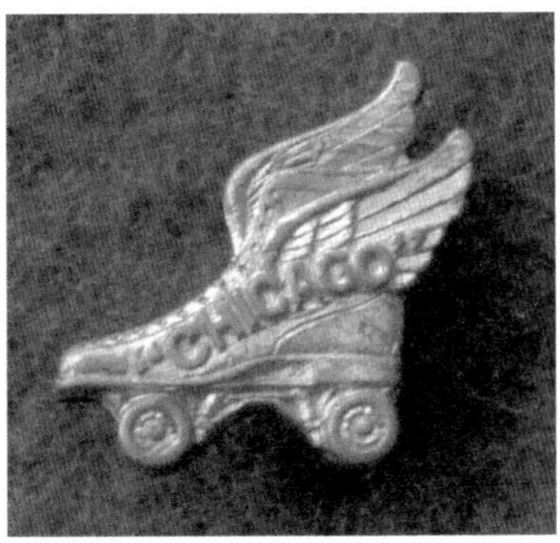

Chicago Roller Skate Company's gold-colored brass skate pin, circa 1942. *Author's collection.*

Other skaters in the Chicago area showed off their own version of the "Jersey Bounce"

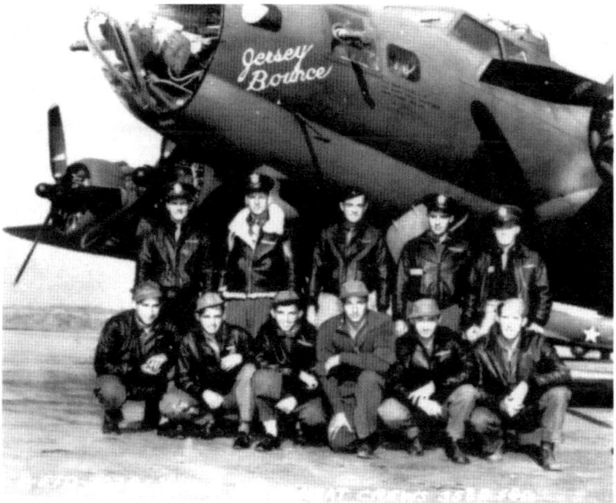

A B-17 Flying Fortress, with "Jersey Bounce" nose art, flown by Robert J. Nolan Crew, 358th Bombardment Squad, Prestwick, Scotland, October 13, 1942. *303rd Bomb Group Association.*

by skating in reverse with the backward strut. These skaters, skating backward, raised a leg in an exaggerated crossover move and landed with a soft bounce. The exaggerated backward crossover move looks awkward, but the move was deliberate to avoid catching your skates and tripping. Not surprisingly, adults still shuffle skate to organ music, while many younger skaters shuffle skate to pop culture's favorite "Jersey Bounce"–style music.

To listen to Benny Goodman's version now, skaters would conclude that there was no way a skater could skate to the "Jersey Bounce." This is where the skill of the rink organist, such as Happy Johnson, could take a popular song and make it rink ready for skaters. Not all organists had this ability, which is why those organists were sought out most by rink operators. Many of the rinks in Chicago had great organists who contributed to the popularity of Chicago skating. While Madison Gardens had Happy, Arcadia had Leon Berry and the Roller Bowl featured Al Beckwith and William Backman. So songs like "Jersey Bounce" were made popular by the organists throughout the country. Rinks often gained reputations for the best music and best rink due solely to the organist.

Skaters were not the only group inspired by the "Jersey Bounce." The crew of the naval battleship USS *New Jersey* claimed that when the sixteen-inch guns went off, the ship would heel from the force, causing a "Jersey Bounce." Not to be outdone, all sorts of JB nose art forms adorned many U.S. aircraft that saw duty overseas. The first aircraft to sport the name "Jersey Bounce" was a B-24D Liberator that served in the 8th Air Force with the 93rd Bomb Group out of Alconbury, England, in 1942 and 1943. Later, other aircraft wore the popular namesake.

With new rinks opening in the 1940s, rinks rats were always headed out to explore new sites. Madison had just held its "getaway party" the last Sunday of May with the slogan "Keep 'em Rolling" as everyone said goodbye for the summer.[279] In June 1942, the gang gathered to head east to the Roller Bowl at 1058 West Washington Street to check out the new "air-cooled" rink and soundproof floor. Inside the rink floor was huge at 24,000 square feet, especially compared to Madison Gardens' 11,000 square feet or even Arcadia's 15,000. Overhead at rink center hung a large ball that turned slowly, with lights reflecting from the mirrored glass surface. The 7-foot-diameter ball rotated with 2,500 individual mirrors. When it came time for couples skate, the lights were dimmed, and reflected light rays from spotlights would circulate onto and across skaters while simultaneously spinning around walls and spectators.

The Roller Bowl claimed the "Largest Rink in Chicago" and had introduced the international style of skate dancing that had swept westward from the East Coast. Not just the Roller Bowl but rinks all over the city were drawing big crowds of soldiers, sailors and marines, who showed up day or night. Wearing a uniform was a "get in free" card. Uniforms were also required for civilian males. The Roller Bowl dress code called for ties. When Jack, Elmer and Earl showed up without ties, the doorman offered them some from the counter to wear for the evening.

The Roller Bowl, while hosting speed and figure events, sought to become the skate dance center of Chicago. It was only ten minutes east of Madison on the streetcar. As they traveled, the whole gang—Marion, Louise, Deloris, Wanda, Esther, Irv, Bud, Earl, Jack and the other West Siders—came to prefer skate dancing, finding its emphasis on dance versus other styles much more enjoyable. It was easy to learn a new skate dance, described as a "sport-art" that you did not have to be a first-class skater to learn and enjoy.[280] It was not uncommon for skate dancers to learn half a dozen dances. Teens preferred the faster-paced dances like the jitterbug or two-step, while adults would venture into the waltzes. Rinks that specialized in skate dancing also offered regular classes on specific dances—or, for those who preferred, private lessons. That summer, Chicago rinks with air conditioning, especially the Roller Bowl, took advantage by staying open and featuring weekly dance lessons. One night a week was set aside for teaching beginners roller waltzing, among other popular dance steps.[281]

Skate dancing had taken the nation by storm and added to the growing popularity of roller skating, especially for servicemen stationed overseas. The guys, when asking for news, always wanted to know about the new

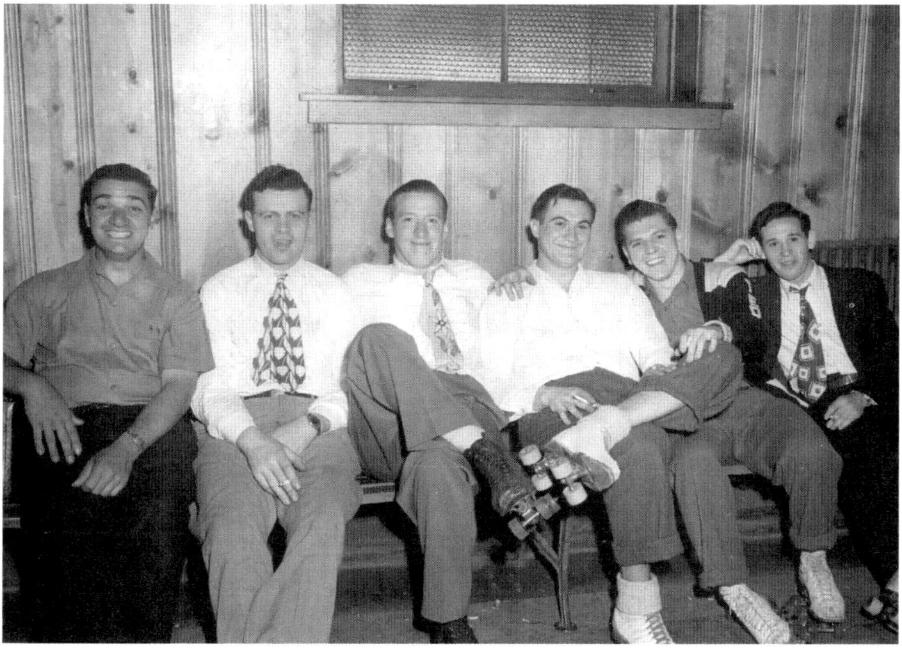

Young men relaxing with skates at the newly opened Roller Bowl in 1942. In the background is the new knotty pine paneled wall and "blackout" shades over the windows. Note Ted, who is second from end with skate club sweater (club unknown). Peter Russo, the author's father, sits on the far right end. *Author's collection.*

dances. Sometimes the girls, before they wrote their letters, would have to get out to the rink and see who was up on the new dances and learn them before they wrote back. It was easy to make friends at the rink because experienced skaters were always willing to share their knowledge and techniques with those who were eager to learn. For example, when West Siders wanted to know "what's new?" they asked Juanita or Tommy to show them the new stuff. They were considered the young pros.

One tip they got from Juanita and Tommy (they learned from Perry Rawson at the nationals) was that to maintain balance when skate dancing, use the ball of the foot and stay off the heel. Too much heel throws the skater's balance off. Those skaters who worked off figure skating books learned that figure skating required more use of the heel.[282] So, for those skaters transitioning from figure to dance and who continued to rely on the use of heel to turn, pivot and so on, it threw their balance off. They also learned that posture and poses are adopted from ballroom dancing versus from figure skating, either ice or wood. The point is: skate dancers dance!

They don't skate, a lesson that sat well with the gang and made it much easier for most of them to pick up dances.

Good skate dancers, as with any dance routine, demonstrated a disciplined body posture, with such characteristics as an upright, erect carriage, natural motion and no visible stiffness no limpness. Body posture is also accompanied by dance position that is locked by both partners. This locking assists the pair or team to track the dance routine, rotate together and remain parallel at all times. The woman locks her partner's hand positions by placing her hand over his to ensure the bond whether the body position is face to face, side by side or with the lead partner guiding his partner from behind.

While many roller establishments around the country claim to have first introduced skate dancing, the general consensus is that it started in the East and moved west. The first roller skate dance championship was held in 1939 at the Mineola Skating Rink, New York, by two early 1930s skaters, Inez Sibley and Earl Van Horn.[283] When the couple wrapped up their tour of Europe, they took over a large building on the Mineola fairgrounds that had been used to show cattle, establishing Mineola as "Home of Dance Skaters." By the later 1950s, the West Coast had become a dance stronghold, with competitors taking honors in either ARSA or RSROA.

On rink nights, the gang would gather at the drugstore or hamburger place and figure out which rink to visit, depending on special events or friends competing in dance or speed. If they had not been at a particular rink they liked in a while, they would head out to it to check out other skaters, what they were doing and the music. They had learned that different rinks catered to different dances or skate styles. But setting up meeting times was not difficult since they met regularly at Madison three to four times per week. Louise was the ringleader and would get a few of the girls, like Marion and Deloris, to gather the others and pass along information over the week.

The girls would let the guys know where they were headed as well so there would be some good male skaters they could depend on. But the best male skate dancer turned out to be Jack "Smithy" Smith. He was a natural, with a keen ability to watch others, learn the sequence of steps and then apply those to learn any particular dance step. At Madison Gardens, and whatever rink the gang visited, Smithy was as smooth as those competing amateurs. Smithy was not only a great skater but also a great athlete, one who never smoked—recognizing it simply as not good for one's fitness or health. Over the years, he skied and ran marathons, and once his knees gave out, he continued to be active into his seventies by using rollerblades. In later years, he and Elmer raced the asphalt pathways around Busse Park in Mount Prospect. Earl Knight, Elmer's brother, was another great skate dancer. He was tall, which was a challenge for partners, according to Marion. When the male was skating backward, his female partner's role was to watch for other skating pairs, but she found herself straining to peer over his shoulders to spot oncoming collisions.

The number of people taking up roller skating was, at times, overwhelming to rink operators. Complaints were common about scooters and a-rounders, new skaters who would either scoot or just go around and around while hugging the rails. Rink rats would also comment on the new skaters and their reluctance to learn new stuff. Too often they would cluster up into herds that moved slowly, skated in the wrong direction, fell backward and just became a cluster of people in the way. Accomplished skaters avoided the herds and the pileups they knew would come. But RSROA officers and skate instructors would remind rink operators that scooters and a-rounders presented opportunities for developing their potential as skaters, people who could become dedicated to the rink and increase box office receipts. They were encouraged to transition the novice skaters to what was described as plain forward skating—rolling gracefully in rhythm with the great organ skate music.[284]

With the year ending, the balance of power in the war was shifting in favor of the Allied coalition. Men were enlisting or being drafted at incredible rates, and the drain on rink operations became apparent. Russell Brown had joined the army and was among those who would head out in May. By the end of January 1943, the tide had turned on many fronts. The Soviets' counteroffensive in November 1942 stopped the German advance on Stalingrad. And by the end of January, German troops had surrendered there. With the victory at Midway in June 1942, the U.S. Pacific Fleet, in cooperation with Allied naval forces, began its island-hopping strategy and retook territories that Japan had occupied since 1941 and 1942. By mid-year, the Allied invasion of Sicily and Italy had dismantled Mussolini's government. As positive as the war's progress looked, government officials also knew that they could not allow complacency to settle in. Labor disputes were abundant, absenteeism was rising and the incidence of low morale was increasing, not only in war plants but across the country as well. But the nation kept 'em rolling.

1943

Early in 1943, rinks across the nation reported that numbers were down and attributed this to both the fuel shortage and a pleasure driving ban imposed by gas rationing. Rinks with poor public transportation access often stated that box office receipts were down. But not all: Chicago rinks reported that business had held up well and was on par with past seasons.[285] This is credited to those rinks being located near public transportation centers, streetcar and bus lines where gas restrictions had not affected attendance. Riverview Rink, located in Riverview Park, reported good business with large crowds on weekends. Arcadia Gardens, Madison Gardens and the Roller Bowl all attracted satisfactory crowds throughout the week and on weekends. However, driving bans did affect contests and championship series, both state and national. For example, in other urban areas, like Philadelphia, the driving ban made it impossible for many rinks in nearby communities to join competitions, like the annual roller skating contest where eight rinks were entered.[286]

In Chicago, the "Green Hornet," as it was affectionately called by rink rats, ran routes throughout the city connecting major suburban transit lines with downtown Chicago and provided great mobility for the gangs of skaters that traversed the city. The Madison Street line ran down the middle of Madison, connecting the far West Side to State Street. Anyone living along these transportation corridors knew the clang of the trolley bell and the *clickity-clack* of iron wheels bumping over rail joints. Horse cars were first drawn by horse in 1859. Horse-drawn streetcars followed. These forms of public transportation were replaced by cable and cable cars and then by electric trolleys or the Green Hornet. At the turn of the twentieth century, Chicago was the most connected city in the nation, running an estimated three thousand cars. The public bus system would begin to replace streetcars after World War II. The few remaining Green Hornets were retired to Chicago museums.

With the arrival of 1943, President Roosevelt's military draft executive order went into full effect. The executive order changed the age range from twenty-one to forty-five to eighteen to thirty-eight years of age. Male skaters noted plans to depart for basic training camps daily, announced regularly in local newspapers. Male rink rats were among those who joined one branch or another of the armed services. Some waited to be drafted, while others enlisted in the service branch of their choice. For example, Paul Lukach, employee of Madison Gardens, was inducted into the army in January. Fritz

Huber, former professional skater at Arcadia Gardens (Chicago), was with the U.S. armed forces headed to Australia.[287]

The boys from the West Side were turning eighteen in 1942 and 1943. They enlisted rather than waiting to be drafted, recognizing that patriotism was doing the right thing and serving the country. Bud Knight turned eighteen in November 1942 and joined the Army Air Corps (the future U.S. Air Force). He wrangled out an enlisted date that would fall after the upcoming Illinois state championship so he could compete in the speed event before heading out to become an aircraft mechanic. Jack Smith enlisted in the army, while others enlisted in the navy.

But it was not only the boys who enlisted. Women were being recruited for the newly formed Women's Army Corps and would serve in noncombat roles. Wanda Hoffman joined the WACs, enlisting at the age of eighteen in 1943. Wanda was a five-foot-two blonde with blue eyes. Louise would always say of Wanda that she was the only girl who could wash her hair and leave it and, once dried, it looked great naturally. Her enlistment surprised the entire gang, but it revealed the sense of duty and patriotism felt by women as well as men.

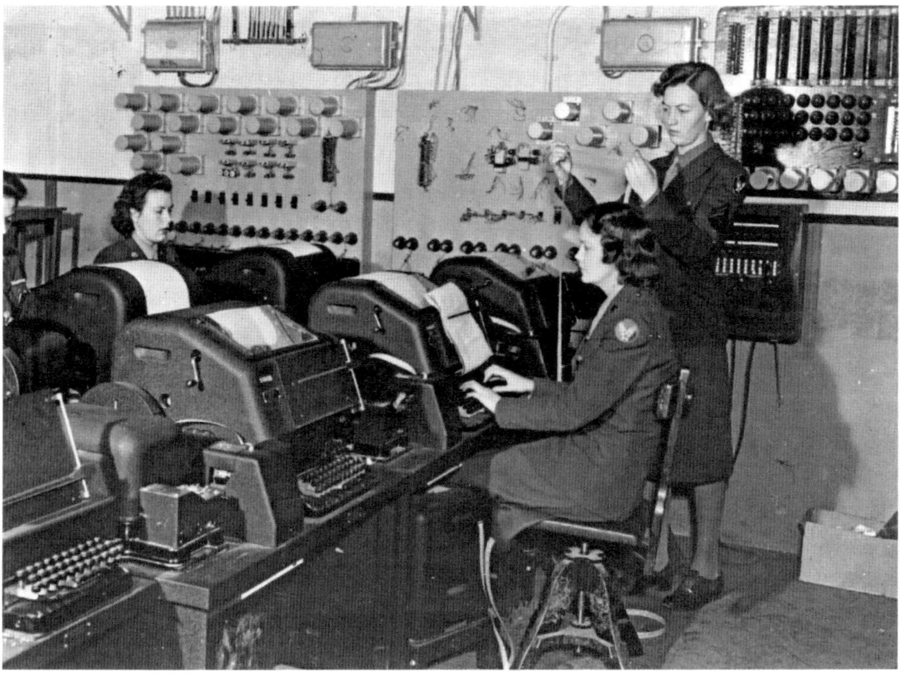

Members of the Women's Army Corps (WAC) assigned to the 8th Air Force in England operate Model 19 teletype machines. *Courtesy of U.S. Army Center of Military History.*

Another skate dancer, Claire Miller, professional with the Mineola rink since 1937, had been sworn into the Women's Army Auxiliary Corps and was awaiting active duty when her full-page article in *Billboard* magazine made the case that there was no shortcut to skate dancing. In her teaching, she found that amateurs were eager and ambitious but were taking the time to learn skate dance fundamentals. Miller made the case for learning the fundamentals by study, practice and use of skate edges to master skate dancing.[288]

First named an auxiliary in 1942 by Public Law 554, the Women's Army Auxiliary Corps (WAAC) became known officially as the Women's Army Corps (WAC) in 1943 and recognized as a branch of the U.S. Army. Public Law 78-110, signed on July 3, 1943, established the WAAC as a full branch of the army before the name change. Due to manpower shortages, women were recruited for all sorts of roles, including as an adjunct to the boys on the front line. The politics of assimilating women into the army were considered dangerous by many constituent groups, but the generals loved them for the work they did. Women became a critical manpower source for the defense industry whether on the front line or in war production factories. General Douglas MacArthur called the WACs "my best soldiers," adding that they worked harder, complained less and were better disciplined than men.[289]

The new year was shaping up to be a big one for Chicago-area roller skate rinks. Arcadia Gardens would host the March 1943 Illinois RSROA championships, and owner-manager Phil Hayes was pulling out all the stops to make it a success. Other Chicago rinks would support events in the lead-up to the March championship to ready their corps of racers, dancers and artistic skaters. Waltz contests were underway at Madison Gardens and attracted large crowds for the trophies and medals that would be awarded at the February finals. Madison also announced that it would host a series of speed-skating races that would follow the state championships at Arcadia. Both events would keep Chicago's speedsters at a high level of training for the national championships to be held at Detroit's Arena Gardens in early May.[290]

Contests were open to Illinois amateur skaters who held an amateur card issued by RSROA, the sanctioning governing body that would manage the state event. Entries had been received from all over the state, and among those included former title holders. The matchup that promised to bring on the drama was the one between Russell Brown and Bill Hay. The rivalry that persisted between ARSA and RSROA would play out in a friendly but competitive way between the state's best speedsters. Brown's title was under the jurisdiction of the Amateur Rolling Skating Association (ARSA), while Hay's title came from the RSROA National Championships. But Russell Brown, 1942 speed champion, though stationed at Glenview Air Base, would defend his state title. Bill Hay was expected to show up as challenger for the state title, while newcomer Ray Sopper would show what the future of Chicago looked like. Tommy DeCicco, the preceding year's champion in the novice men's figure and novice pairs, wrote to the Chicago Roller Skating Club, asking that it let others know he was recovering from a spinal injury in the Fort Taylor, Key West army hospital and would not be competing this year.

The March 8 Illinois state speed roller skating championship contests, held at Arcadia Gardens, proved to be a real barn burner, as a new corps of women speedster stole the spotlight from the guys.[291] Anita Newquist swept the seniors' ladies speed event that included the 440-yard, 880-yard and 1-mile events. Esther Swiat took the intermediate girls' title, while Beverly Luft of Riverview Rink took junior ladies' honors. But the star everyone was talking about was two-time state junior figures champion Caroline Buchanan, who was expected to represent the state well at the Detroit nationals. Charlie Tyler, Chicago's *Skating Review* representative, referred to Caroline as "Red" Buchanan. Red was featured on the cover of the April 1943 issue of *Skating Review*.

In the Arcadia men's speed events, Conway Manahan (Arcadia Gardens) and Russell Brown (Madison Gardens) tied for the senior men's state title, a near repeat of 1942, when Brown took the title.[292] The championship would be decided a week later when both would skate three races to decide the 1943 state title. The races would include 440-yard, 880-yard and 1-mile events. Given the 1942 outcome the year before, this made for one great spectator contest.[293] Manahan was self-taught (or "book-taught"), moving from speed to figure skating, and was featured in *Skating Review*.[294] In his first year, Conway competed in men's novice figures and finished first in the 1943 Illinois state novice figure skating event. As a newcomer to speed skating, Elmer Knight made a statement as well, finishing third in the 2-mile event and second in the 5-mile event.

The following week, Russell Brown took the title after winning two of three events. He and Anita Newquist, both representing Madison Gardens, were "once again the class of the speed field in Illinois," representing the state in Detroit, according to Charlie Tyler's column in the *Chicago American-Herald*. Charlie also revealed that Phil Hayes, manager of Arcadia, was opening up Chicago's largest rink at a North Side armory, 16th and Michigan. The new armory would feature a huge 34,500-square-foot rink floor. This would not only rival the Roller Bowl's 24,000-square-foot floor but also match the rink floor size at the former 202nd Armory Rink, which closed in late 1941. It was set to open on June 17, 1943, with a big show. The Armory rink would make the twelfth rink that operated in Chicagoland.

With the wrap-up of the state championships, Madison Gardens' series of speed-skating races got underway Saturday night, March 20, and continued for six weeks through the end of April.[295] Winners would earn gold, silver or bronze medals. Those headed to the nationals used the series to train for the competition. Esther Swiat would also train with Newquist and Raines at Arcadia, working on speed. The gang would travel with Esther and Doris over to Arcadia and, between speed events, skate during the all-skate sessions. Esther and Anita learned that Dorothy Law, due to age, would compete against Beverly. Anita would be up against former national champ in the intermediate girls' division Jeanette Killoren, from St. Louis, who was moving up to senior ladies' division. Anita knew what to expect at the nationals and had watched both Killoren and Law the preceding year. Law was a tough competitor and competed in not only speed but also figures. She had won the 1941, 1942 and 1943 junior girls' national speed championships.[296]

Madison's speed-skating sessions every Tuesday night had drawn large crowds—both competitors and spectators—with the women's speed events becoming the new speed spectacle for rink spectators.[297] The women who won the semifinals and were moving on to the finals were Anita Newquist, Esther Swiat, Doris Raines and Rose Mary Campaign. On the men's side were Richard Manahan, Irv Gianneschi, Irv Lurie, Jay Trenadue and Anthony Domback.

Many called the Madison Gardens speed series winner the city speed champ. So there was a lot of talk and title grabbing given that there were no age divisions and no advantage—just who was the fastest! Both men and women would race three heats, the 440-yard, the 880-yard and the 1-mile. Win two of three and you carry home both the city title and the trophy. Both Swiat and Newquist had qualified for the national events in Detroit representing Madison Gardens but would compete in their respective age divisions, the former in intermediate girls' and the latter in senior ladies'. But on this day, in the final heat, Swiat won in a thriller by seconds over Newquist and carried home a nice trophy.

New skaters learned that the rink was not just a social scene where they met other skaters—there was also a skate club, and the best skaters belonged to that club. Just about every rink had a club, and then there was the Old

Timers' Roller Skating Club of Chicago, whose members traveled to all the rinks to socialize, skate and support not only the rinks but also the skaters who competed for trophies and the title of skate champion. Madison Gardens was full of skate champions. Russell Brown was the newest national champ, having set speed skate records to win the male speed skate championship in 1941, months before the war broke out.[298] He won the national title in 1942 and in 1943, tying with Conway Manahan for the Illinois state title. There was also Teddy Rosdahl, who not only won the figure skating championship but also pairs with his future partner Betty Rosdahl.

Once again, the Old Timers' club arranged transportation to get Chicago's competitors to Detroit. And the girls did not disappoint. In fact, it was the girls who held up Chicago's speed skate image. Esther Swiat placed second at the nationals in intermediate girls' in speed skating, while Anita Newquist took second in senior ladies' division. Beverly Luft placed third in the junior girls' division. The men were nearly shut out of the top slots throughout the speed divisions, but Russell Brown squeaked out a third in senior men's, while Harry Tinesella made his mark in junior boys' with a third-place finish. Madison Gardens skaters were at the forefront of Chicago's contingency, but it was apparent that other sections of the roller nation had stepped up.

At the conclusion of the 1943 Detroit nationals, it was announced that Chicago's Roller Bowl would host the 1944 RSROA National Championships.[299] The Roller Bowl's skater amenities, like a clubroom, impressed the national leadership, and with the support of Arcadia and Madison Gardens, the roller capital knew that it would deliver a first-class national event. Meanwhile, Arcadia manager Phil Hayes called for a statewide meeting of rink operators at the Chicago Sherman Hotel to plan for the 1943–44 season and set dates and events that would lead up to the Roller Bowl's national contest.[300]

After a year or two of regular skating, kids pretty much mastered the fundamentals, and if they had not specialized in a style, most learned to skate dance. It was what all the skaters were doing. The young, really good skaters mastered turns early on that resulted in backward skating. Marion Smith skated backward most of the time but had to watch for the pileups and avoid those. In fact, skating backward smoothly was an important first milestone toward becoming an advanced skater. She could also dance the Russian Cossack, but those were the kind of tricks skaters would only perform in the middle floor. Oftentimes, the older men would ask the girls to skate, and most of them were pretty good. They would teach the girls how to swirl, skate backward and even master a dip or two. The girls knew they were probably 4f'ers.

The second important marker is the three-turn and, from there, learning dance steps.[301] Usually, the RSROA members like Tommy and Juanita, or even Conway, would share their copy of *Skating Review* that described these turns. One of the West Side skaters would look at it and, with some study, watch the amateur pros and catch on pretty quick. The three-turn transitioned the skater 180 degrees to backward skating and was quite smooth, so much so that if you wanted to look good on the skate floor, the three-turn needed to be mastered.

Rink skaters fell into several groups, and while never formalized, a skating hierarchy was clear to rink rats. There were the professionals, the serious students of skating style, session skaters and then the roll-arounders. The real challenge to rink operators was ensuring that their skate program accommodated all skate styles—dance, figure and speed as well as the roll-arounders. Roll-arounders[302] were those who had not learned any specialized routines, specific steps or dance moves and just rolled around the rink. They were the novices or beginners and scooted around and around in a rink, doing what regulars portrayed as straight skating. The rink officials referred to roll-arounders as "scooters" and worked judiciously to teach them to skate. Session skaters were practice skaters and moved around the rink rather well but reserved their skating for the public session skates.

Good skaters spent more time at the rink, not unlike any other sport, and could be found in the center of the rink. In fact, skating in the center of the rink was a rite of passage, signaling that a skater had arrived among the "inner circle" of advanced skaters. Beginners and novices typically skated around the perimeter. Rink rats were there three to four times a week and eventually acquired boot skates. They realized that to learn footwork required skates with flexibility so the edges could be used. They became serious students of skating, watched the good skaters and worked to master a particular routine or skate dance style that mimicked the professionals. They not only showed up during peak times, like Friday and Saturday, but also spent a few other days either for lessons or designated skate programs (speed or dance) or just to skate. Many rink rats became advanced skaters who worked to become amateur competitors and put in serious time to master their trade. They were all in!

As noted earlier, those with great skate skill went on to become instructors and coaches and were hired as a professional by a rink. As the rink's pro, they provided instruction and classes and managed rink operations. Russell Brown

(Madison Gardens), Teddy Rosdahl (Arcadia) and Jaci Zimmerman (North Avenue) were among those Chicago skaters who became professionals and continued to teach and coach.

Over the summer of 1943, Madison Gardens renovated for the next season and its thirty-seventh anniversary.[303] The makeover was done in gay, bright colors, with hundreds of flags hung from the ceiling. Its plan for Chicago's West Side was to operate nightly except Mondays, with matinees on Sundays. In addition to the regular rink, Madison Gardens featured its beginners' rink with instructors to assist and supervise skaters. The regulars liked this since it kept beginners out of the way on the main floor. Happy Johnson, one of the country's top rink organists, would return at the Wurlitzer. Happy was a veteran organist of the day who played electric organs but learned to play pipe organs in theaters during the old silent movie days. For Happy, emceeing the skate floor was like theatrical organ work all over again.

1944

The roller capital was rocking in the new year with roller action for the next six months. The newly opened Armory rink on Michigan Boulevard was hosting the state RSROA speed championships and Arcadia the state RSROA, dance, figure and pairs contests, while Madison would hold its six-week series. The Roller Bowl had secured the 1944 ARSA nationals. Rink organizers were putting a full press on city officials to step up and put Chicago's best foot forward. Newspapers' sports columns were full of details, while competitors had to decide early whether they were to stay at home with the ARSA competition track or follow RSROA rules to the Arena Gardens in Detroit. What excited the skate managers was not only the buzz around town for the attention contests were bringing to town but also the young Chicago-area skaters coming of age and experience. While the seasoned pros and amateurs were headed off to service, competitive skaters were coming to the forefront to compete for those titles.

Skeptics claimed back in 1941 that Pearl Harbor would sink the roller industry, given the requirements of war whether in the civilian sacrifices, men headed overseas or raw materials consumed by the war industry.[304] Yet rinks across the nation reported that rink participation had shown a steady increase over the past few years. To explain, rink organizers pointed to competitive skating, which had been a major boost to the growth of roller skating. They admitted that teams suffered as men left for service. At the same time, young stars seeking the laurels of competitive skating were coming forward. Chicagoans had seen this transition on the West Side, as longtime speed champion Russell Brown left for service. Nonetheless, along came Teddy Rosdahl in dance and figures, while a young "Red" Buchanan from the West Side became a citywide favorite. Young female speedsters had also made their mark, like Beverly Luft, Anita Newquist and Esther Swiat. Many other youngsters from Chicago-area rinks were rising to the top as well.

But not all the West Siders competed. In fact, most did not. Skate dancing was the predominant skate style that locals did because it was the social recreation of roller skating that attracted most, like the rink rats of the West Side. When Roller Bowl held dance classes, like for the Chicago hop, instructors asked why they were taking the class. They were told, "Because all my friends are doing it."[305] Most classes during the war years consisted entirely of girls. The girls would tell the instructors that dancing together without boys was a war hardship. Rink owners tapped into this perceived hardship by running ads for classes: "Roller Skate Dancing is your Passport to Social Independence."[306] Even amateur competitors worked to learn what local skaters were doing so that, when socializing, they met the expectation of "regular" skaters and how they skated. Skaters hung out by skate style and got to know other skaters who skated the same way. Only perhaps 20 percent of a rink's membership were competition skaters.

Bill Henning, veteran Chicago skater, traveled to the various rinks, skated and gave instruction to both competitors and the serious students of skating who had no interest in competing but wanted to master a particular skate style. He wrote columns for newspapers that also were printed in *Skating News*.[307] For example, he taught that the two most elementary skills in figure skating are balance and maintaining momentum—but balance is primary. He offered young skaters a cute saying remembered years later: "Learn to skate and move your shoulder east and your hip west, The Twain Must Meet." His point was that balance is considered the art of roller skating, but a delicate balance must be taught first. Momentum comes naturally and automatically as balance is mastered.[308] Fundamentals include coordination, proper posture, body control and foot and leg placement, as well as correct use of arms and hands. As the novice improves his or her poise, grace and firm footing, it instills confidence. Once fundamentals are mastered, the skater will show a ballet style that delivers rhythm and graceful movement.

Henning also worked with rink managers who saw teen jitterbugs as a nuisance on the skate floor. Standing back to back, locking their arms, teenage jitterbugs would throw one another over their head and away. One rink operator described teenage jitterbugs as "crazy."[309] Skate jitterbugs grew out of the jitterbug dance popular in the late 1930s. First popular in the Savoy Ballroom,[310] the jitterbug migrated to white dance floors and onto skates. The dance involved pelvic motion with a sway of the body, forward and backward, with controlled hip movement, steady shoulders and feet that glide along the floor; the man's right hand is held low on the girl's back, with his left hand down at her side, enclosing her hand. Teenagers who jitterbugged conflicted with the decorum rink owners strived for. Dress codes and rules of conduct were attempts to establish a respectful establishment that attracted families, adults, church and school groups. Rink managers saw teenagers who jitterbugged as presenting a distasteful dance that might offend adult clientele and, along with roughnecks and speed skaters, disrupt rink order.

Rink managers were shrewd promoters and served as national leaders for the roller industry. They were also the most ambitious. For example, this group selected the National Foundation for Infantile Paralysis (today's March of Dimes) as its national charity program. In 1944, RSROA hosted a huge roller spectacle on February 16 at Madison Square Garden, with proceeds donated to this foundation.[311] Interestingly enough, February 16 was President Roosevelt's birthday. The spectacle included nearly 750 skaters. Final estimates placed an amount of $10,000 raised and donated to the president's personal charity, NFIP. The 1944 success called for a repeat, and in 1945, RSROA raised and donated $20,000 to NFIP.

Ozzie Nelson, president of the ARSA, officiated the April Illinois state championships in Chicago at the Roller Bowl in preparation for the ARSA nationals to be held in Chicago May 1–5, 1944.[312] Officials unfamiliar with a state operation preferred to work a state contest to ready for the national competition. Nelson was expecting a record turnout, especially from the eastern states, with many state contests having already wrapped up. Chicago speed club competitors dominated the event, representing Madison Gardens Speed Club (MGSC) and the Riverview Roller Club. Russell Brown and James Falada of MGSC were headed to the nationals along with senior ladies' division winners Lillian Muza, Norma Nelson and Adaline Roeder. The Riverview women dominated the women's speed races, with Muza first, Nelson second and Roeder third.

Simultaneously, many of Chicago's top speedsters were preparing to head to the Arena Gardens rink in Detroit for the RSROA National Championships. Reports coming out of Detroit showed that turnout expectations were the highest ever, with hotel reservations and train reservations at record levels. Madison Gardens' Irv Gianneschi, senior men's speed; Esther Swiat, senior ladies' speed; and Marilyn Julian, competing in junior girls' (also MGSC), had qualified under RSROA rules and were headed out to Detroit. For figures, Teddy Rosdahl had teamed up with Lorraine Mazzuca, and the team won junior dance. Representing the Arcadia club, the Rosdahl/Mazzuca team headed to Detroit as well. Tommy DeCicco had returned to form, winning the state title in senior men's figures, and would compete at nationals as well. Rosdahl and Mazzuca would go on and place third in junior dance, while Rosdahl won the national junior boys' figure skate championship, claiming the Joseph P. Seifert Challenge Trophy.

Once the girls reached sixteen, they looked for work, and most employers were eager to hire them. It also meant teenage girls had discretionary income. Among their many entertainment choices were the Skating Vanities with Gloria Nord. Regular skaters knew that Nord returned to Chicago in the fall to develop new routines, using Arcadia Rink as her Chicago-based home rink.[313] During the next year, she played at more than two hundred rinks throughout the country, where teenagers from across the nation watched her skate. Ironically, *Seventeen* magazine was founded in 1944, illustrating the increase in discretionary income available to teens and the target customer base advertisers wished to reach with consumer products. For example, Marion Smith, who turned seventeen in March, bought her first pair of boot skates, previously limited to professional skaters. She also picked up a Madison Gardens Skate Club sweater; both items of skate gear cost significant amounts of money. Shoe skates, with case, could be bought for twenty dollars. If purchased from a rink, a skater could put a couple bucks down and pay fifty cents per week. But purchases of this nature were common among Chicago's rink rats.

Women's fashion was dramatically affected by war requirements. The government's War Production Board published mandates for the garment industry called the L-85 Regulation ("L" stood for "Limitation Order") for all sorts of restrictions.[314] For example, women's wear, if made with a tuck or pleat, could not include a ruffle. Skirts had set lengths, cuffs were banned, color selection was more limited and drastic style changes were prohibited. Likewise, skating skirts could not be made at all. The restrictions led to the emergence of the synthetics industry, where natural materials were replaced with fabrics like Rayon and Teflon.

Japan's control of the silk market restricted the availability of silk stockings for women. All silk went to meet military demands for parachutes. Once the

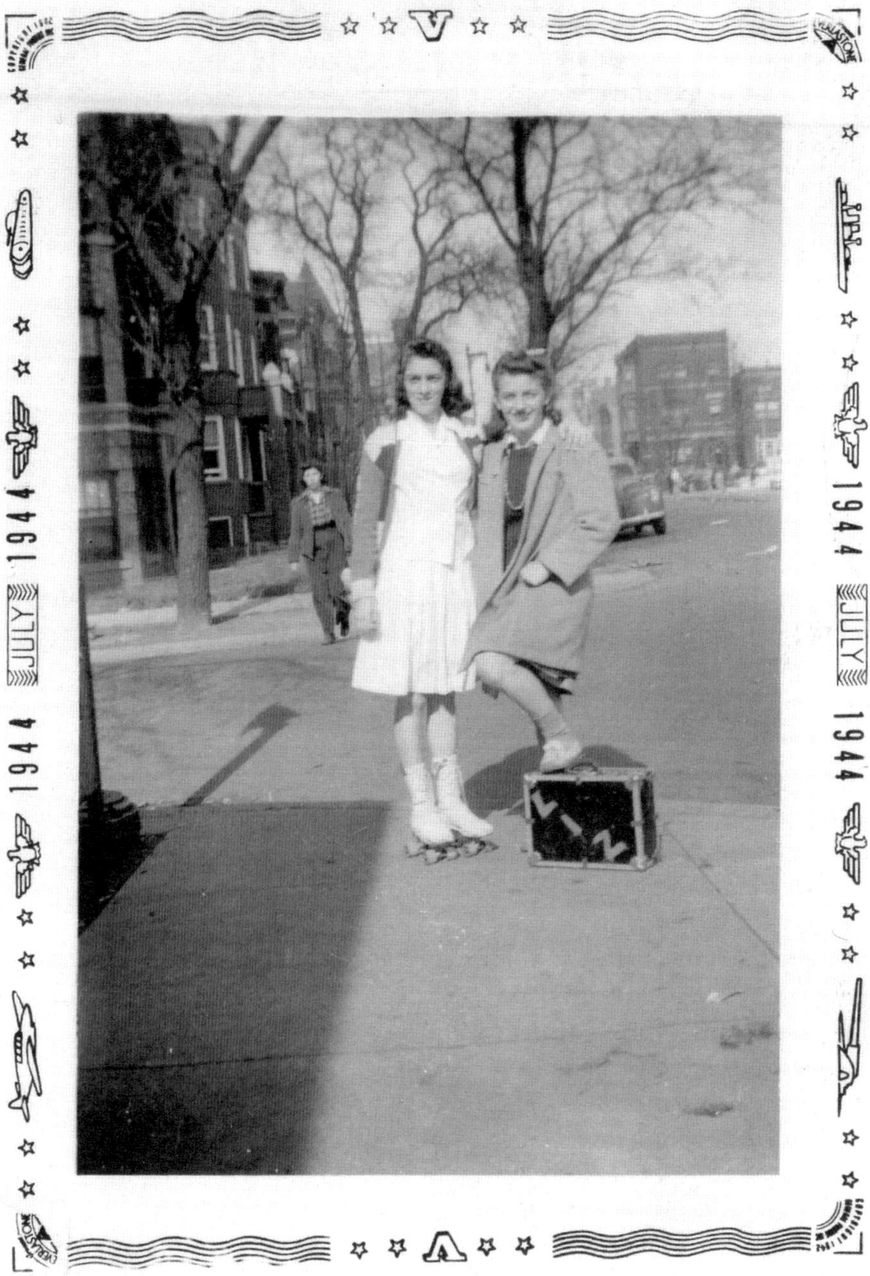

Marion Smith with boot skates and Madison Gardens Skate Club sweater. *Author's collection.*

United States entered the war, even nylon, silk's replacement for women's stockings, became restricted. Leg makeup and various gadgets to paint stocking seams led to the surging acceptance of trousers for women, as such gadgets were marketed as painting stocking seams on the backs of legs to simulate the presence of silk stockings.

Before the war, trousers on women were socially unacceptable and viewed with disdain. This view persisted initially, but once women's military uniforms showed trousers as one uniform option, along with women's fashion for war industry work, this attitude changed. Young women who wished to look fashionable were quick to adopt the new fashion style, with its "equal to men" statement and the newfound independence that accompanied the look. Meghann Mason, in her thesis, described how the styles became modest, masculine and militaristic.[315] The Federal Security Agency's "Jenny on the Job" poster campaign promoted the new look, with Jenny in work overalls. But fashion restrictions did not stop women from feminizing the new look, and the cosmetic industry was quick to offer products themed with patriotism. Not only was makeup, like eyeliner, used for simulating silk stocking seams, but lipstick colors also reflected patriotic themes, such as "Victory Red" and "Jeep Red."[316] Cutex marketed a red nail polish called "Alert!" Hairstyles included "victory rolls" to keep hair out of the way while at work yet also showcase feminine patriotism after hours.

The national skate organization, RSROA, was quick to capitalize on fashion restrictions by establishing a Fashion Department at *Skating Review*, and it began selling patterns in 1942. These patterns offered a basic design with few frills. In January 1944, the organization announced a trophy for the best homemade fashion design. It offered a "basic" skate dress pattern that skaters could request for one dollar that included contest entry. The best-looking and most original entry, at the lowest cost, would win. Contestants only had to send a picture to the office along with an itemized list of material costs. But skaters had known that for years, Gloria Nord's mother had made all of her skate outfits and even gave classes at rinks around the country. It resulted in a surge of Singer sewing machines humming in the homes of skaters.

With skate skirts ready, RSROA's national championship proceeded with great anticipation, as the festivities began on May 1, 1944. This year was the first Esther Swiat would compete as a senior, and she found herself pitted against Dorothy Mae Law of Detroit, who would be described by *Skating News* as the "U.S. Queen of Rollers" due to her impressive athletic ability to cross over and compete successfully in either speed, dance or

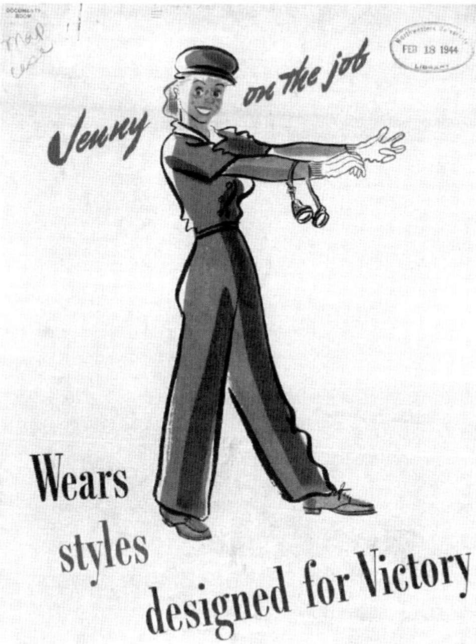

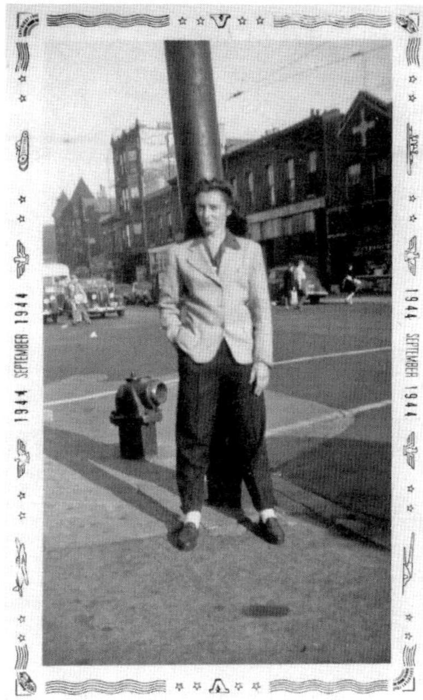

Left: "Jenny on the Job: Wears Styles Designed for Victory." Jenny models work coveralls, cap and gloves. *Federal Security Agency, U.S. Public Health Service, World War II poster collection, 1943, Northwestern University Library [FS2.25:10].*

Right: The austere women's fashion look of the 1940s. Women dressed in trousers, bobby socks and basic jackets with squared shoulders. Pictured is Marion Smith. *Author's collection.*

figure competitions.[317] The women ran three events, including the 440-yard, 880-yard and the 1-mile. Swiat's strength was distance, and she beat Law in the 1-mile event, while Law beat Swiat, taking second place in both the 440 and the 880. But then there was Ruth Jones from the Cincinnati Sefferino rink, who took first place in all three events and went on to win the senior ladies' championship. Swiat took third. Law grabbed second in speed and proceeded to win the senior ladies' figure skating championship and the M.H. Hinchcliffe Challenge Trophy.[318] In senior men's speed, Irving Gianneschi (MGSC) placed third.

Back in Chicago, ARSA's national championships attracted the attention of Chicago sportswriters, as a number of Chicago speedsters were among the nation's top competitors. Russell Brown was a dominant figure in speed skating, and his affiliation with Madison Gardens brought attention to the speed club. At the Illinois meet, Russell Brown, wearing Madison Gardens Speed Club colors (red, white and blue) and insignia, completed a grand slam sweep of the five speed events, with wins in the 440, 880, 1-mile and 2-mile events. The speed event made the *Tribune*'s May 5, 1944 sports page highlighting "Roller Speed Titles Won by 3 Chicagoans."[319] It took the last 20 yards, but Brown took the 5-mile speed event and completed the sweep.[320] Chicago's Riverview Speed Club swept the women's events, with Lillian Musa taking first place in all three senior ladies' events, the 440, 880 and 1-mile. Irving Benchik, another Madison Gardens speedster, took the intermediate boys' title. Even in the midget's division, Larry Richter tied for a title with Michigan's Lawrence Wells. The *Tribune*'s report added that it looked like the eastern skaters would rout the rest of the field in the dance and figure skating events, with Earl Van Horn's dance and figure skating club playing well represented.

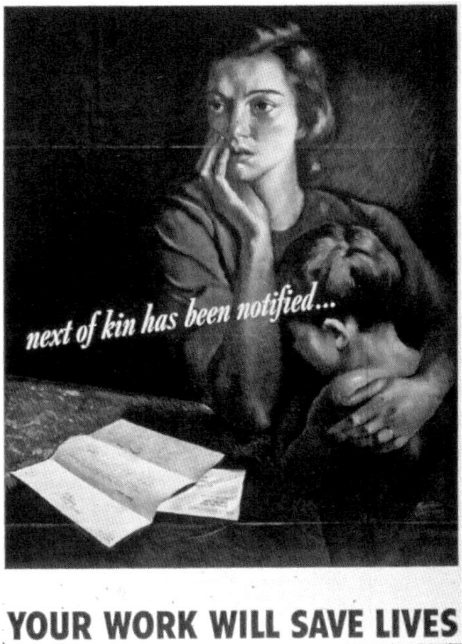

"Next of kin has been notified. Your work will save lives." World War II poster, 1943–45. *U.S. National Archives and Records Administration [NWDNS-44-PA-1403].*

It was February 1944 when Marion and Liz stopped in at Hensell's Drugstore and learned of Allen DeLisle's death from one of Allen's friends. Learning by word of mouth was typical of the way neighborhood friends learned of the wartime death of a close friend who was serving. Servicemen's deaths were too frequent and always received with subdued emotion. The notices to letter writers and close friends were not direct. Letter writers would simply get a returned letter stating it was undeliverable. Death notices were sent directly to "next of kin." The initial death notice was a Western Union telegram delivered to the serviceman's home by a messenger. Later, letters would arrive from the secretary of war, conveying condolences along with the circumstances of death, its cause and place of burial. It would be decades before Hensell regulars learned what happened to Allen DeLisle. Following is one result of retrieving military records from World War II and the whereabouts of the USS *President Adams* at the time of Allen's death through research of digital records seventy-two years later. This circumstance was not unusual:

Allen DeLisle, U.S. Navy (USNR), Seaman 2nd Class, served on the U.S.S. President Adams, died in pacific February 16, 1944 (cause unknown). The U.S.S. Adams played an active role in the Pacific theater to drive the Japanese up the Solomon Island chain toward Rabaul. The USS President Adams was a 16,175-ton transport ship retrofitted from a civilian passenger-cargo ship taken over by the Navy in June 1941, commissioned in November 1941 as attack transport. The ship supported amphibious assaults and later was part of Marianas invasion forces, landing troops on Guam in July and taking casualties back to Hawaii and the U.S. west coast. During 1945, President Adams took part in combat landings at Iwo Jima and spent the remainder of the Pacific War on logistics duties, supporting occupation activities and bringing veterans home from the former Pacific war zone.

It was not until the Vietnam War that the Department of Defense adopted a more respectful and sensitive approach to the delivery of bad news by having military personnel deliver the news personally to the family at their home.

1945

The war in Europe continued to grind out as it entered its seventh year in 1945. The United States' entry marked the fourth year. President Roosevelt requested the cooperation of citizens and the nation in an all-out effort to win the war and also requested that all conventions involving the use of transportation be canceled. The drain of the nation's raw materials such as wood and newsprint, as well as oil and gasoline, continued to require severe rationing. For example, in February the War Production Board announced that by April 1, the national stockpile of coal would be down to a twenty-two-day supply.[321] If supplies were below thirty days, it was considered serious. The WPB was authorized to fine and issue jail time to utilities that failed to cooperate with the national war interest. During brownouts, electricity could not be used for advertising, outdoor decorative or ornamental lighting, show windows or outdoor signs. The exception were traffic lights and street identification signs.

As a result, RSROA's President Brown sent a letter to President Roosevelt noting that, in support of the "win the war" effort, RSROA would cancel the 1945 roller skate national championship. The meet had been awarded

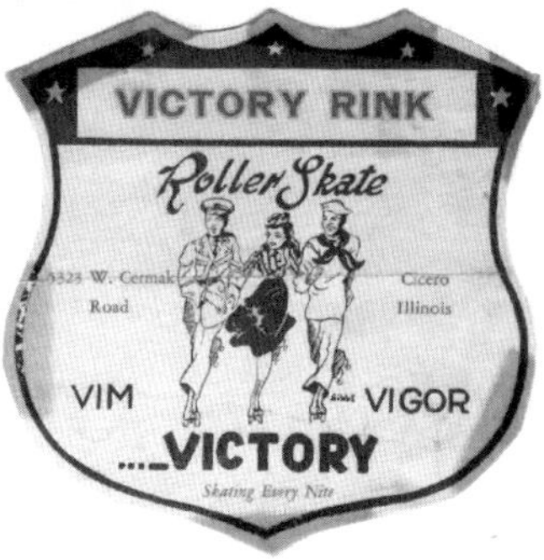

Victory Rink, at 5323 West Cermak Road, Cicero, captured the spirit of the roller industry with "Vim, Vigor...Victory & Skating Every Nite." *Author's collection.*

to Mammoth Gardens, in Denver, in December 1944 and was tentatively set for July 9–16, 1945. States were encouraged to hold their state meets. The Illinois state meet was awarded to Chicago's Arcadia.

However, the nation was soon shocked upon notification that its four-term president, Franklin D. Roosevelt, had died of a cerebral hemorrhage on April 12, 1945. Americans loved and hated Roosevelt. The New Deal rallied opponents, including longtime southern Democrats, while his repeal of Prohibition renewed liberty for all Americans. His policies, actions and work to keep America safe won him popularity that persisted through four terms.[322] He had guided America through World War I as assistant secretary of the navy, a role that served him well as a future commander in chief. Roosevelt came to power as the thirty-second president during the Great Depression and guided the nation throughout the world's most destructive war. While he was quite private about a personal illness, citizens were energized by the president's personal victory over polio, while his persistent optimism and activism renewed the national spirit through tough times.

Harry S Truman was sworn in as the thirty-third president of the United States. His courageous but controversial decision to use mankind's most destructive weapon ever built, the atomic bomb, saved tens of thousands of American servicemen's lives. Celebrations erupted worldwide with the announcement of Germany's surrender on May 8, 1945, and victory in Europe. Massive, spontaneous celebrations were held throughout Chicago, Los Angeles, Miami and New York's Times Square. President Truman, celebrating his birthday, delayed a formal proclamation, waiting for a coordinated announcement with Moscow and London. There persisted widespread skepticism over the authenticity of the end of hostilities. The delay was to avoid premature celebrations, as had happened at the conclusion of World War I and a false armistice in 1918.[323] Truman dedicated the victory to the memory of President Franklin D. Roosevelt, who had died one month earlier.

Ironically, as war in Europe ended, RSROA announced in the May 1945 edition of *Skating News*[324] that in keeping with its support to reduce unnecessary travel, it had canceled the 1945 national championship, but nationwide sectionals would be held across the nation. States were assigned to one of seven sectionals that would be held in June and July. The RSROA, whether insightfully or coincidentally, had positioned its state organizations, local rinks and competitors for a national meet later in the year and delivered a note of optimism that peace and prosperity were around the corner. The roller skate industry signaled plans to move forward with future activities for all sorts of events. The end of war was in sight, and the industry was rolling into the future with a reality that roller skating would become the top recreational sport in the nation.

By the end of the summer of 1945, skate manufacturing companies had announced plans for reconversion from war supplies to producing skates. Chicago Roller Skate Company and Richardson Ballbearing Skate Company both announced that backorders for rink clamp skates would be filled, followed by rink shoe skates.[325] For years, leather and ball bearings had been in short supply for the civilian sector, as the needs of armed services were filled first.

However by July 1945, times had remained restrictive for not only civilians but the roller industry as well. New skates had not been sold in years. Rinks showed the signs of wear with years of heavy use and were ready for the promises of new features and materials like air conditioning and plastic floors. Also, new materials for race outfits had been in short supply during the war years. Skaters had to scratch around to put together a race costume.

One particular story that illustrated the hard times (but did not dissuade one determined skater) made *Billboard*'s "Rinks and Skaters" column. The story was about Tony Belyea, a speed skater from West St. John, New Brunswick, who dyed a set of long johns (actually a union suit of woolen underwear) blue. A union suit buttons up the front, with a flap in the back secured with buttons. It worked well initially, but given a five-mile race on an indoor rink without air conditioning, his perspiration weighed heavily, seeped through and began to drip. As his lap count increased, the water drained from his body and drenched the union suit. Depending on the size of the rink floor, lap counts could have been anywhere from twelve to sixteen laps per mile, or sixty to eighty laps! Perspiration was running faster than he could skate, and a blue stream followed as he cranked out laps around the rink. Finally, the back flap broke open as the button holes stretched from the weight of sweat. They could no longer hold the buttons. Belyea battled the blue dye drip, but it was that union suit flapping in the wake of his speed that ended his race day. Tony finally skated into the dressing room with embarrassment and a wounded ego—he had failed to complete the race. A speed skate race of endurance had concluded with a light moment for spectators.[326]

Mobilizing for Competition, 1946–1959

Demobilization of 7.6 million U.S. armed force troops stationed abroad began in May 1945 and continued throughout 1946. A point system was used by the War Department and promised that all servicemen stationed in Europe eligible for demobilization would be home by February 1946, while those in the Pacific would be home by June 1946. The War Department was heavily criticized by both servicemen and citizens back at home for a slow bureaucratic process. General Eisenhower found ways to expedite demobilization. Aircraft carriers, destroyers and merchant vessels were retrofitted as troop carriers, and the boys came home to victory celebrations across the country.

For skaters, demobilizing from military service also meant mobilizing for a run at skate championships. As they arrived home from overseas bases, a skate fever swept through Chicago's rinks that rivaled the zeal among speed skaters during the early 1900s, when the city's speedsters dominated the sport. Bud Knight wasted no time in readying for the Illinois state championship with his return after his November 18, 1945 army discharge. Like many soldiers overseas, he trained on-base, at makeshift rinks or off-base rinks such as university gymnasiums. Never having taken up smoking and avoiding peer pressure while serving overseas, Bud came back nearly race ready. The state championship was set for March at Arcadia in 1946. The boys were home, and competition was expected to be intense.

Speed skating required constant practice, building on skate fundamentals. Fundamentals included timing, rhythm, drive, grace, stamina, pacing and equilibrium or balance.[327] After the initial spring from the start line, a conditioned skater set a pace that worked to tire opponents, with sufficient reserve for the final sprint. Stamina comes from constant exercise and practice, as with any sport endeavor with cross training essential to build stamina. Speed skaters were encouraged to bicycle or take long walks in addition to speed work. Coaches challenged athletes that if they wished to excel, smoking, drinking and staying out late should be avoided. Coaches

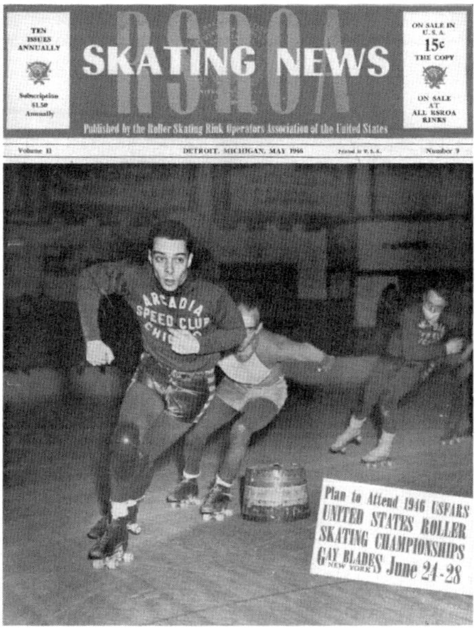

The "Thrill of Flying Rollers," captured on the May 1946 RSROA cover of *Skating News* from the Illinois State Roller Skating Championship, held at Arcadia Rink, Chicago. Ray Sopper leads, with Vic Tramkian and Charles Fuertsch at his heels, with Elmer (Bud) Knight just off the edge of the photo. *National Museum of Roller Skating.*

understood, without the benefit of today's scientific data, that these habits took the competitive edge off an athlete's effectiveness. It was common sense then as well as today.

Building a training schedule was challenging, and skaters worked around the speed skate schedule of the area's rinks. Skaters traveled to each rink's scheduled speed skate session to log sufficient training hours. For example, Madison Gardens held its speed-skating sessions that continued to draw large crowds on Tuesday nights. Arcadia scheduled its speed skating for Monday nights, while the Armory set speed skating for Wednesday nights. But speed skating competed with rink time for other skate styles such as skate dancing. At Madison Gardens, the rink's waltz contests attracted large attendances where trophies and medals were awarded to winners.[328] To be profitable, rink operators worked and catered to the many interests of their patrons by scheduling rink time for basic skate classes, discipline-specific training sessions for competition skaters, family skate sessions and so forth. Weekend evenings were scheduled for public skates, and organists worked to offer a buffet of the rink's best music to attract skaters of all skill levels and interest.

The turnout at Arcadia for the state contests was always huge, with four hundred amateur skaters registered for the meet—the most ever. Competitors represented ten of the fourteen Illinois rinks (RSROA member rinks), and competitions were held for all divisions—artistic, dance and speed. The Madison Gardens rink rats showed up to watch the competition, but loyalties played on individuals' emotions. The senior men's competition had Bud; his brother, Earl; Ray Sopper; Chase Fuerthsch; Vic Trankina; and Carl Combeck. While Bud and Earl were Madison Gardens skaters, they were also members of the Arcadia Speed Club along with Sopper, and all of them wore Arcadia colors for the state meet. Not only were competitors in place, but former speed champions such as Russell Brown, Connie Manahan and Bill Hay were also in the audience.

While official RSROA race classes (age groups), for senior men, meant competing in five events—440-yard, 880-yard, 1-mile, 2-mile and 5-mile events, with points assigned based on finish—local race events were usually limited to a 440 or 880 sprint. Even the disqualification (DQ) was somewhat relaxed at a local event. At an RSROA-sanctioned event, touching another racer resulted in a DQ.

The race for the state title each year was incredibly close, and the intensity was captured among the faces of racers on the 1946 *Skating News* cover, with Ray Sopper in the lead of the final event, the 880-yard. Vic Trankina was at his heels, with Fuerthsch following and Bud Knight in fourth. Sopper had to finish first to move into second in the overall quest for the title. Knight needed fourth place or higher to maintain his point lead over the pack for the title. In the end and after place, finish and points were added up, Bud Knight took first in Illinois state senior men's, earning the 1946 senior men's speed skating championship. Ray Sopper and Chase Fuerthsch tied for second, while Earl Knight took third.[329]

Due to the growth in numbers of rinks and competitors, RSROA instituted a regional competition system in 1946. States were structured into regions where 200 to 400 competitors would be reduced to 120 who were eligible for nationals. To illustrate the growth in the Great Lakes region, some 600 competitors would compete in the Sefferino Rollerdrome regional contest for one of those 120 coveted qualifying slots. State contest winners would advance to the regional events.[330] Regional competitors who placed first, second and third qualified for the nationals. Just as rinks renovated and changed to accommodate skaters, so did the national organizations adapt to the growth of roller skating. Roller skating was popular, and the mass availability of TVs increased rink attendance. Once TVs became a basic household entertainment appliance, audiences watched roller derby matches at home with friends and screamed for their darlings and hissed the bad boys or bad girls. And the big cities that hosted seated venues, either derby matches or Skating Vanities, were standing room only. Afterward, TV spectators sought out their local rinks.

By 1949, the ranks of competitive rinks had grown significantly, as RSROA reported five thousand rinks across the country, and not all were RSROA member rinks. In fact, the U.S. Amateur Roller Skate Association had expanded its ranks among rinks that elected to be ARSA-style rinks. The ARSA competitions closely followed the competition rules that had regulated ice skating over many decades, but now those rules had evolved for roller skating. In many areas of the country, competitors would ice skate in the winter months and then roller skate in summer months to maintain their competitive edge. Thus for ice skaters, the styles and requirements were more closely aligned with ARSA than with the RSROA competition rules. The North Avenue Rollerway became an ARSA-style rink, while a number of the downtown rinks remained RSROA member rinks.

But rinks were not always focused on competitive skating contests. Most had become neighborhood recreation centers and hosted all sorts of community events, whether birthday parties, fundraisers for community groups or skate clubs traveling to neighbor rinks and putting on shows. Probably one set of events that drew more attention than most others was the outreach to blind skaters. A project of Chicago Skate Clubs, its members got involved by encouraging rinks to work with local skate clubs to mentor blind skaters. Two Chicago rinks followed the lead of a New York rink and inaugurated special

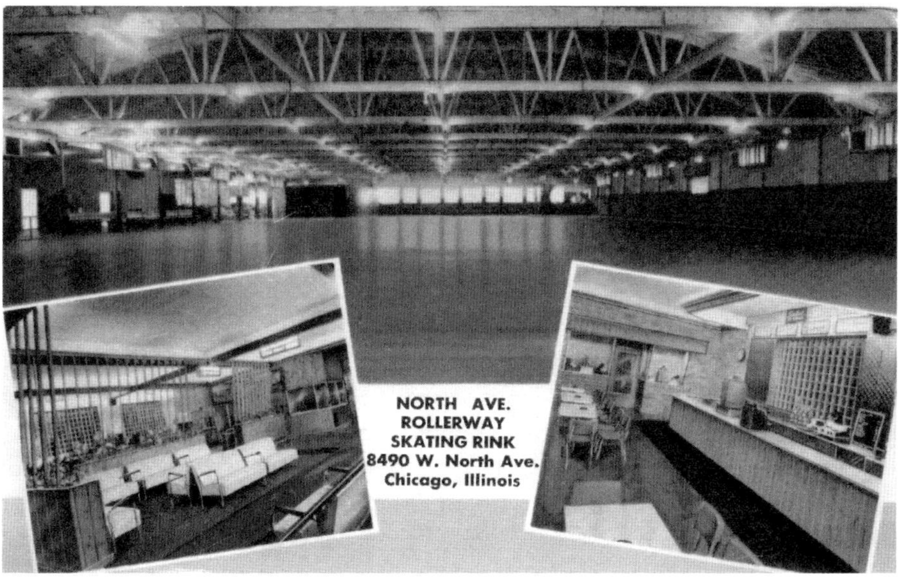

North Avenue Rollerway Skating Rink, "Largest and Most Modern Roller Rink in the Country." *Jaci Zimmerman Charbonneau.*

nights for blind skaters, sponsored by the RSCC. Sessions got started at the Roller Bowl and Arcadia rinks.[331] The South Side Swank Roller Rink joined the group, offering its rink for the blind and other physically handicapped skaters. They skated with no charge for admission.

Competing was a thrill for World War II warriors who had seen the worst, returning home with few fears remaining. It also meant that contests were red-hot, as *Skating News* noted after the April 20–22, 1949 Illinois state meet held at Arcadia. Downstate winners made a statement to their northern neighbors as they claimed many top titles. But Chicago speedsters continued to dominate speed events. In senior men's contests, Conway Manahan took first and won the state speed skate championship, while Bud (Elmer) Knight placed second, with Ray Sopper and Jerry Kroeckel on their tails.[332]

The end of war also created a phenomenon that years later would earn the title of the "baby boomer" generation. The war generation was entering the state of matrimony in such a way that would affect pop culture for generations to come. Full Roller Romance was in the making. Skaters found the company of other skaters to be the perfect match for marriage. GIs returned home and married their rink-mate sweethearts. Other GIs and sailors came home in search of the girls they met at the local rink, left behind and with whom they wrote letters while overseas. One particular sailor sought the help of the rink manager at the Oaks Rink to see if a girl he met in the early 1940s was still single. Classified ads went into the newspaper asking for information. The girl had quit skating but was still single. In the end, the two reunited and were married. Others found new love on the old, dusty wooden floor. Teddy Rosdahl of Arcadia married Betty Lou Henderson and Jack "Smithy" Smith married Louise, while Bud fell in love with a Hollywood Rink gal, Deloris. Marion would find love with a goofy sailor who was the life of the party, Petey Boy. She admitted later that he was not a very good skater, though.

However, the origins of Roller Romance grew from roller skating's popularity that dated to the 1870s during the Victorian era.[333] London's fifty rinks improved opportunities for supervised venues where boys met girls in the 1870s. One particular story credited James L. Plimpton with a four-wheel skate design for healthy exercise that could be taken to the pathways to speed up the strolls around London. The healthy exercise Plimpton had in mind was flirting, equipping couples with a method to evade the watchful eyes of Victorian elders in London, who followed courting couples on foot. Once couples sported Plimpton's "nimble wheels," they could speedily steal away—along with a stolen kiss or two. This Victorian "rink-o-mania" was

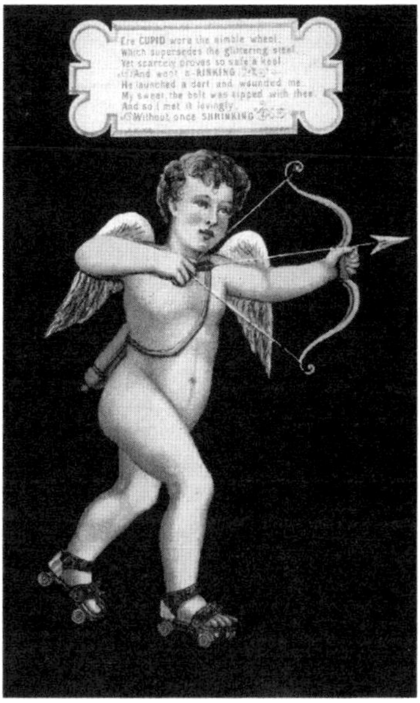

Roller skating Cupid, postcard from England's Victorian era, circa 1870s. *Museum of London.*

captured in London's roller skating Cupid, featured in Victorian Valentine cards.

For the Knight brothers, marriage was a brief interlude to a national championship speed title. In 1952, Bud Knight was pushing twenty-seven and Earl Knight was twenty-five as they readied for another run at a national title. Earl and Bud may well have been inspired by the thirty-one-year-old 1951 national men's senior speed champion Harold Slack from Ohio. Slack first entered the senior division in 1941, placing third in the 5-mile event before Uncle Sam interrupted his run to a title. After the war and honorable discharge, it took until 1949 before Slack had regained his prewar form, taking third the next year. In 1950, Slack took fourth in Denver. Slack's physician told him that he shouldn't pursue another push in 1951, but his drive and determination overruled doctor's orders and compelled him to go for another run.[334] The result was that Harold Slack, father and husband, won the 1951 men's senior speed championship.

Brothers Earl and Bud had been around long enough and knew that the best plan of action was to build a team for training but one that could also push members to the nationals, to the front and a final trophy run. The Knights had to get through the state championships in April and the regionals at the end of June to qualify for the nationals in July. Knowing the speedsters in Chicago, they pulled together a competitive team from both current and promising speed skaters. The 1952 Chicago speed team included the Knight brothers, Raymond Sopper (future champ), Edward Hagan, Bernie Gustafson and Jerry Kroeckel, all from Arcadia Speed Club.[335]

At the Roller Bowl state contests in April 1952, results placed Earl Knight, Kroeckel and Sopper first, second and third, respectively, while Hagan and Gustafson finished first and second in the intermediate men's speed event. Knight took first in the 440 with a time of 48.6 seconds, as well as first in the 2-mile race.[336] Raymond Sopper took the 880-yard contest. This group, along with Bud, would make up the Arcadia men's relay team as they prepared for the regionals at Palomar in Milwaukee. In the same event, a newcomer caught the attention of coaches with his speed and style in junior boys. George Heist, or "Whitey," competed for the first time and took the number one junior boys' spot. Heist was from the southwest side but was inspired by those televised derby matches and found his way to Arcadia to quench his derby speed skate thirst. Arcadia had a junior derby team, but the skate dance enthusiasts had their favorites as well. In dance, Betty and Ted Rosdahl finished second, while Ted Rosdahl took first in men's figures.

The Great Lakes Regionals were set for the end of May in Milwaukee at the Palomar Roller Rink. For the regional, states sent their first-, second- and third-place finishers from Indiana, Illinois, Michigan, Ohio and Wisconsin. Historically, this region produced speed event champions in both men's and women's events. The event's date gave competitors a few months to train for the contest.

The Arcadia senior men's speed team dominated the regional events, with Earl Knight taking first and Ray Sopper finishing third, both moving on to the nationals. Earl Knight and Ray Sopper had qualified to compete in senior men's speed, while Edward Hagen would compete in intermediate men's division. Also, the Arcadia men's relay team took first and would compete at Denver's Mammoth Roller Rink for the national title. Arcadia newcomer Heist finished third in junior boys' speed and was also headed to Denver. The relay speed events did not break out by age such as in the other events. There were the men's relay, ladies' relay and mixed relay. The mixed relay required two men and two women. Teddy Rosdahl took first in men's figures and, along with his wife, Betty, won dance, earning qualifying trips to the nationals.

The 1952 RSROA national roller skating championships at Denver's Mammoth Gardens were promoted as the largest in roller skate's history, exceeding the thirty-eight thousand spectators who witnessed the 1950 championships in Cleveland.[337] Promoters promised that America would see the best young athletes that America's top participatory sport had to offer, in terms of both thrilling speed and graceful artistic skate performances.

The men's speed events proved to be the thriller promoters promised, as Burton Speed from Texas battled Earl Knight in every event over the five-day series, with teammate Sopper right in the middle of the action. But racers had to get through the first-round heats to qualify for the finals. On the first day of the races, Tuesday morning, Knight took the 440, with Burton right on his heels, just missing a top-three finish. Tuesday afternoon was qualifying heats for the 2-mile event, and Burton, Knight and Sopper qualified for the finals on Wednesday. Knight took first in the 2-mile on

Wednesday afternoon. Thursday was qualifying heats for the 880 event and was a repeat of the 2-mile qualifying event with Burton, Knight and Sopper. The 880 finals were set for Saturday. On Friday, Burton inched past Knight, taking the 1-mile event. Sopper did not place. However, on Saturday morning, Sopper took the 880, with neither Burton nor Knight placing. All of this presented a showdown between Knight and Speed, with only Saturday evening's 5-mile race remaining.

Denver's Mammoth Gardens' rink floor was ideal for race events, with fourteen laps to the mile and being built with long straightaways desired by speed skaters; traditional speed skating tracks were twelve laps to the mile. It also meant that speed racers had to be adept at taking the corners at high rates of speed. The 1952 championship title came down to the 5-mile event. Earl Knight needed a top-three finish to win the title. He had the point total advantage, but Burton Speed only needed to take first in the event to take the speed title and the championship trophy. He also knew there were only two ways to win: take the front and lead at the end or master the technique of passing on any lap.

The starter gun went off as six speedsters sprinted from the starting line at the scheduled time of 10:00 p.m. central standard time. The lap count began at seventy, with signs flashing the counts regularly. After the first five laps, skaters began to settle down into long strides, working to keep within the pack and not allow any single skater to get a significant lead. As the pack completed the first five laps, Sopper was in the lead, followed by Burton Speed and Knight. Charles Wahlig of New York City and Chase Gray of Phoenix were followed by Richard Remley of Pontiac, Michigan, and Ed Mailo of Denver. By lap fifty, a lead group had pulled away from the pack.

Skaters knew the race résumés of their competitors, and whatever they had not known they picked up over the five days of races. Gray of the Arizona Speed Club had taken first in both the Southwest Pacific Regional and the state title. Mammoth was Mailo's home rink, where he qualified with third place in the Mid-West Regional. His relay team took first place in that same meet. Burton Speed paced Mailo around the Mid-West Regional racetrack and paced both Sopper and Knight throughout these national contests. Remley of the Rolladium Speed Club of Pontiac tailed Knight at the Great Lakes Regionals. Wahlig had placed second coming out of the Northeast Regional and placed second in state senior's men. He had also followed Knight in the 440 sprint event, finishing second, followed by Remley. Both Gray and Remley had finished behind Sopper in the 880, while Speed took first in the 1-mile and Mailo took third behind Knight's second. Both Speed and Gray followed Knight in the twenty-eight laps of the 2-mile event.

For the next fifty-five laps, skaters worked to stay in the pack by synchronizing their stride with those in front, with some passing but most holding their lane and position, drafting behind the leaders. As the heat moved into the last ten laps, Sopper continued to lead, with Speed in second and Knight in third. Suddenly and expectedly, the real race began with three laps to go. Speed made a move to pass Sopper on the outside along the straightaway on the backside of lap two. Gray came around Knight, working to get behind Speed, who was overtaking Sopper as they came into the corner. Knight knew that he had to finish top three but had always held his own in the 5-mile endurance event. As Gray passed, Knight moved behind Gray, drafting as they closed the gap with Sopper and Speed.

The lead pack came around the corner with one lap to go. Knight had to pass Sopper to stay in the lead pack and pushed hard to tail Gray. As they came around the backside stretch, Gray and Knight picked off Sopper by passing on the inside and simultaneously closed the gap with Speed.[338] The threesome came into the final corner of lap seventy, and as they rounded the corner into the final stretch, they sprinted to the finish line. As they crossed the finish line, it was Speed in first, Gray second and Knight third. However, now it was the final point tally that would determine the national championship, to be announced at the awards ceremony. Scores were announced, with first place being ninety points, second eighty and third fifty. With ninety points, Earl Knight was awarded the 1952 Rodney R. Peters Senior Men's Speed Skating Trophy.[339]

The excitement at Denver did not end with speed. Chicago's Arcadia Skate Club was proud to have supported another winner at the 1952 national championships, when Teddy Rosdahl won first place in men's figure skating. The twenty-two-year-old had won the 1944 junior figures as well as both senior men's figures and freestyle at the 1949 national meet. With his wife, Betty, Teddy had won first place in senior dance at the Great Lakes Regionals the previous May. Teddy turned pro and headed to the Pallomar Rink in Milwaukee. Later, he returned as professional at the North Avenue Rollerway.

The 1940s youth generation had come of age. Most had moved on from roller skating into raising families and building careers, while others turned pro and began mentoring the next crop of Chicago champions. For example, another upcoming Arcadia speedster in the early 1950s was George "Whitey" Heist. His banked track antics got the attention of league

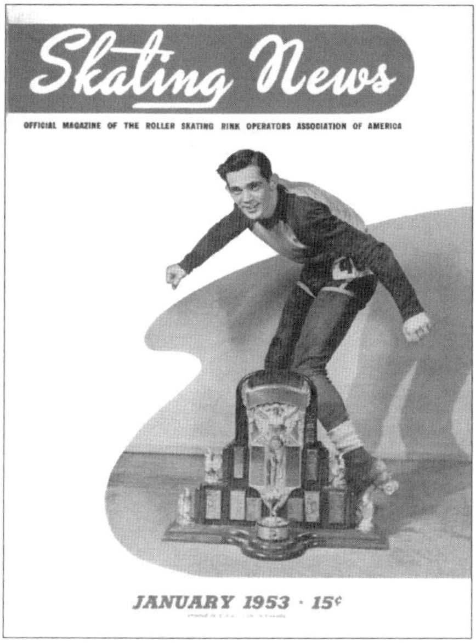

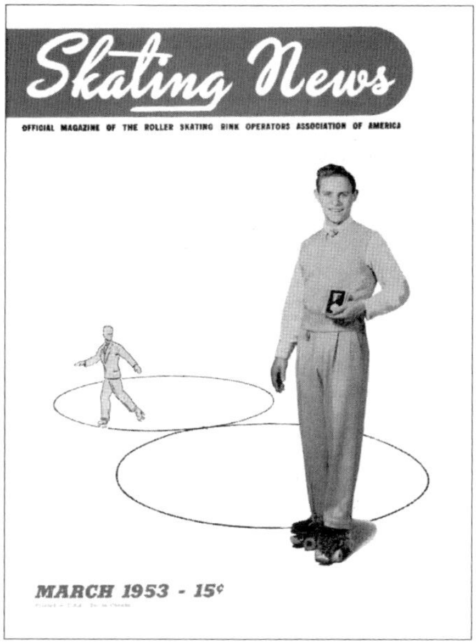

Left: Earl Knight of Chicago, 1952 senior men's speed skating champion, from the January 1953 RSROA cover of *Skating News*. *National Museum of Roller Skating.*

Right: Teddy Rosdahl of Chicago, 1952 senior men's figure skating champion, from the March 1953 RSROA cover of *Skating News*. *National Museum of Roller Skating.*

coaches, as he demonstrated an ability to bend low on the inside, his fingers barely touching the floor as he took the corners.

In 1952, Whitey was selected for the first national all-star junior derby team along with teammate Mickey Martin, both from Arcadia. Heist would go on to win the 1954 Illinois state speed skating championship in the intermediate division and place third at the Great Lakes Regionals. He was disqualified at the nationals for brushing against another skater as he passed to gain the lead. Heist joined the Arcadia men's relay with Ray Sopper, Jason Deligianis, Jerry Kroekel and Bernie Gustafson and the mixed relay with James Deligianis, Beverly Wilson, Ranee Gauli and Ray Sopper—both teams placing first. Beverly Wilson took first in senior ladies' speed, and Raneei Gaull took first in junior girls' speed. Beverly placed second in senior ladies' speed.

By the mid-1950s, cultural and demographic shifts were occurring across the nation and throughout the Chicago area. West Side families were migrating to the western suburbs, and along with those shifts, recreational interests were changing. Simultaneously, rinks were closing in Chicago while new single-purpose rinks were being built in the suburbs with state-of-the-art amenities, such as the Elm Rink in Elmhurst.

Along with demographic and cultural changes came the closing of rinks. In 1958, the Roller Bowl and New Planet closed, followed by the loss of Arcadia, destroyed by fire in 1959. Also in 1959, the end of White City Roller Rink concluded with a fire that destroyed the last structure of the White City Amusement Park. Park City Rink, the former White City, closed in 1949. Even a name change to Park City in 1947 could not prevent the inevitable when races clashed over public accommodations. Small rinks had closed earlier, including the Hollywood, Savoy and Roseland. By the end of the 1960s, four more golden age rinks in Chicago had ended operations.

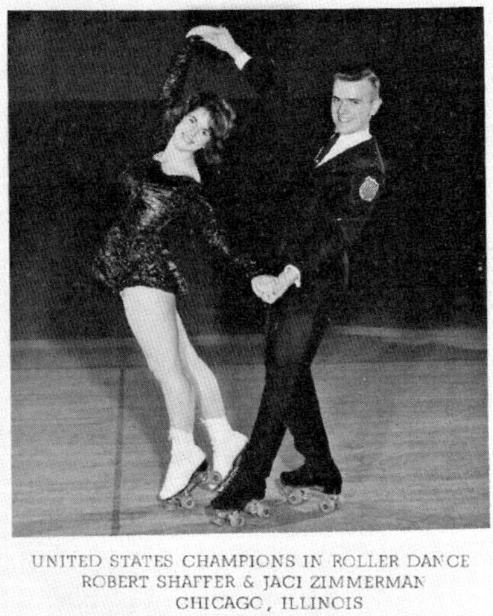

Robert Shaffer and Jaci Zimmerman, U.S. ARSA champions in roller dance, 1962. *U.S. Amateur Roller Skating Association.*

Roller fervor continued to spread outward into the suburbs, tracking the arteries of development that began with Chicago's cable car system in the late 1800s. Today, that public transportation system has morphed into the massive Chicago Regional Transportation System (RTA), with its integrated CTA, Pace and Metra Lines. New rinks in the suburbs accepted the mantle of roller capital, producing champions in those skate styles established in 1937. Champions represented the new rinks, while old-school rinks continued in their traditions. For example, Tom and Carol Seipp of the North Avenue Rollerway were ARSA national intermediate dance champs in 1953. Later, Robert Shaffer and Jacqueline (Jaci) Zimmerman represented North Avenue at the 1962 ARSA National Championships, won dance and were awarded the Gladys and George Werner Senior Dance Challenge Trophy. The couple would go on to take a bronze at the world championships that same year. By the 1960s, roller skating had grown to an international event, and Chicago skaters marched to the front of international competition to represent their home rink.

For the rink rats of the 1940s who endured the war years, roller skating was recreation that provided normalcy during conditions when the homefront was on a war footing. The federal government worked its levers of power to influence mass media and deliver messages and campaigns that called for caution from its citizens but expected full support for the requirements of a war that would bring victory to the Allies, this nation and its people. In 1942, Roosevelt established the Office of War Information and the Bureau of Propaganda to oversee, and direct, a deliberate campaign of keeping the home fires burning.

PART IV

THEY KEPT THE HOME FIRES BURNING

United States government war agencies were quick to identify campaigns that sought civilian support for winning the war. There were no cable stations or social media, and television for the masses had yet to arrive. Americans got their news from either newspapers, radio or the movie theater, where war clips would serve as the prelude to the second feature. In those days, theatergoers saw two movies for a dime. Interspersed with news and entertainment were the civilian-coined "propaganda" campaigns. In the 1940s, government agencies could direct a multimedia campaign without the interference and distractions that are commonplace with twenty-first-century U.S. government public relations efforts. The Office of War Information was established in 1942 and immediately enlisted Hollywood to incorporate messages that were favorable to the war effort.[340]

Posters were one component of World War II multimedia campaigns and offer a historical perspective and snapshot of overt public relations by the nation's federal agencies focused on domestic communication campaigns.[341] War message themes filled the newspapers, movie theaters, trade journals and posters and were day-to-day reminders displayed in both public places and war industry workplaces. The messages were frequent and repetitive, such as "Be Productive," "Exercise Is Duty," "Stay Healthy," "Don't Squeal," "Keep 'em Rolling," "Don't Tell Secrets" and "Write the Boys," to mention a few. And these campaigns were not only directed to the civilian population but also specifically targeted the duties of women. The rationale was simple: give the boys everything they need

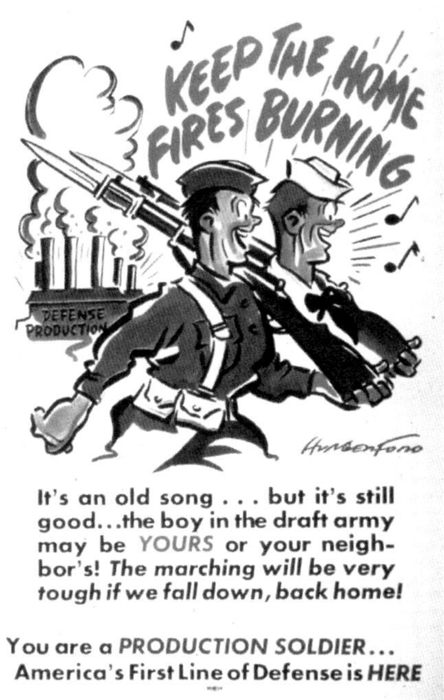

Left: "Keep the Home Fires Burning." Office of War Information's World War II series poster. Note the message at the bottom of the poster reminding civilians, "You are a Production Soldier…America's First Line of Defense is Here." *National Archives and Records Administration [LC 44-PA-1209].*

Below: "Keep the Home Fires Burning." Chicago Roller Skate Company ad, 1942. The ad illustrates the industry support for war bonds and duty as a production solider. *National Sports Company.*

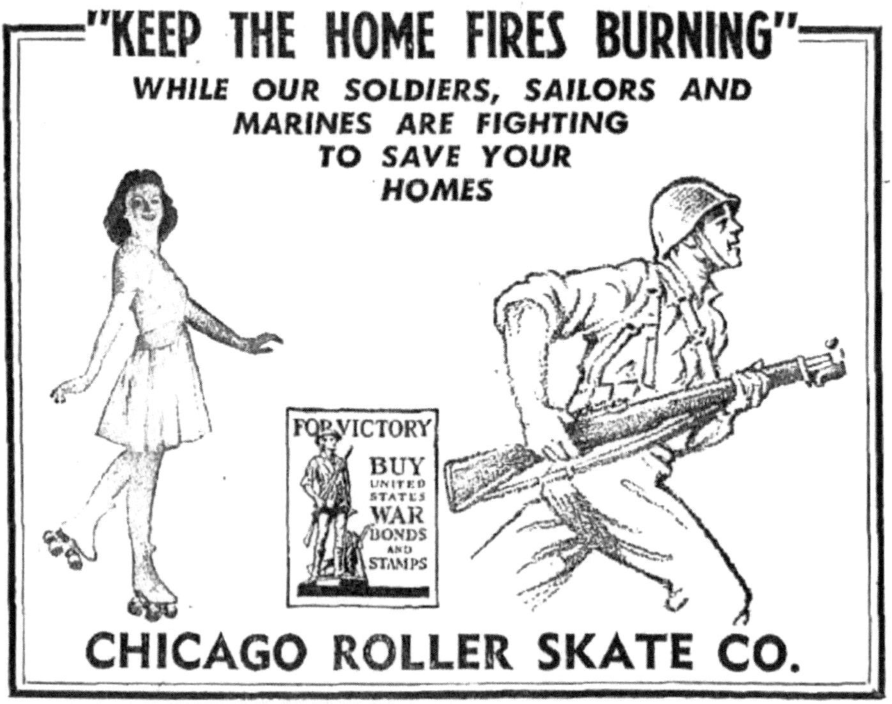

to fight the war, even if it means personal sacrifice, and let them know we have not forgotten them by staying in touch with letters. Campaign themes were quickly adopted by national organizations and industries and pushed down to business or industrial members, demonstrating that all were on board with the national goal.

Preservation of the "American way of life" was the foremost guiding principle and led to targeted campaigns, such as the "Keep the Home Fires Burning" ad. They also shaped the role expected of women to support the war effort.[342] Ads like those of the Chicago Roller Skate Company were representative of the themed efforts directed toward female roller skaters to remind women that their duty was to maintain the social scene that connected the boys to the homefront. Themed ads were used by skate companies and rinks. They appeared in trade journals, newspapers and skating news and skate programs. To win the war meant full mobilization, and every citizen had a role and a duty.

Mobilization

Mobilization of the homefront for full war industrialization was a massive undertaking, given the lack of preparedness by the Roosevelt administration and by Congress. Once undertaken, mobilization took over various fronts, from agriculture, industrial, manpower and construction of government buildings to conversion of existing private sector plants for artillery, tanks, jeeps, aircraft, ships and weapons of all sorts. Mobilization included building military bases here and abroad. It included training camps and the extensive use of trains to transport troops from training camps to bases and to ports. At one point, the government threatened to "federalize" the railroad system if it did not prioritize and fulfill military transport requirements. A similar message was delivered to the auto sector. Thousands of buildings had to be constructed to meet production requirements.

Not to be forgotten in weapon mobilization and production was the application of science and technology. For example, natural rubber sources were controlled by imperial Japan, and a rubber report revealed that the United States had not kept pace with synthetic production, either plants or technology. That same report revealed that 90 percent of the nation's rubber supply had been cut off once Japan entered the war in 1939.[343] When the United States entered the war, the nation was consuming 750,000 tons

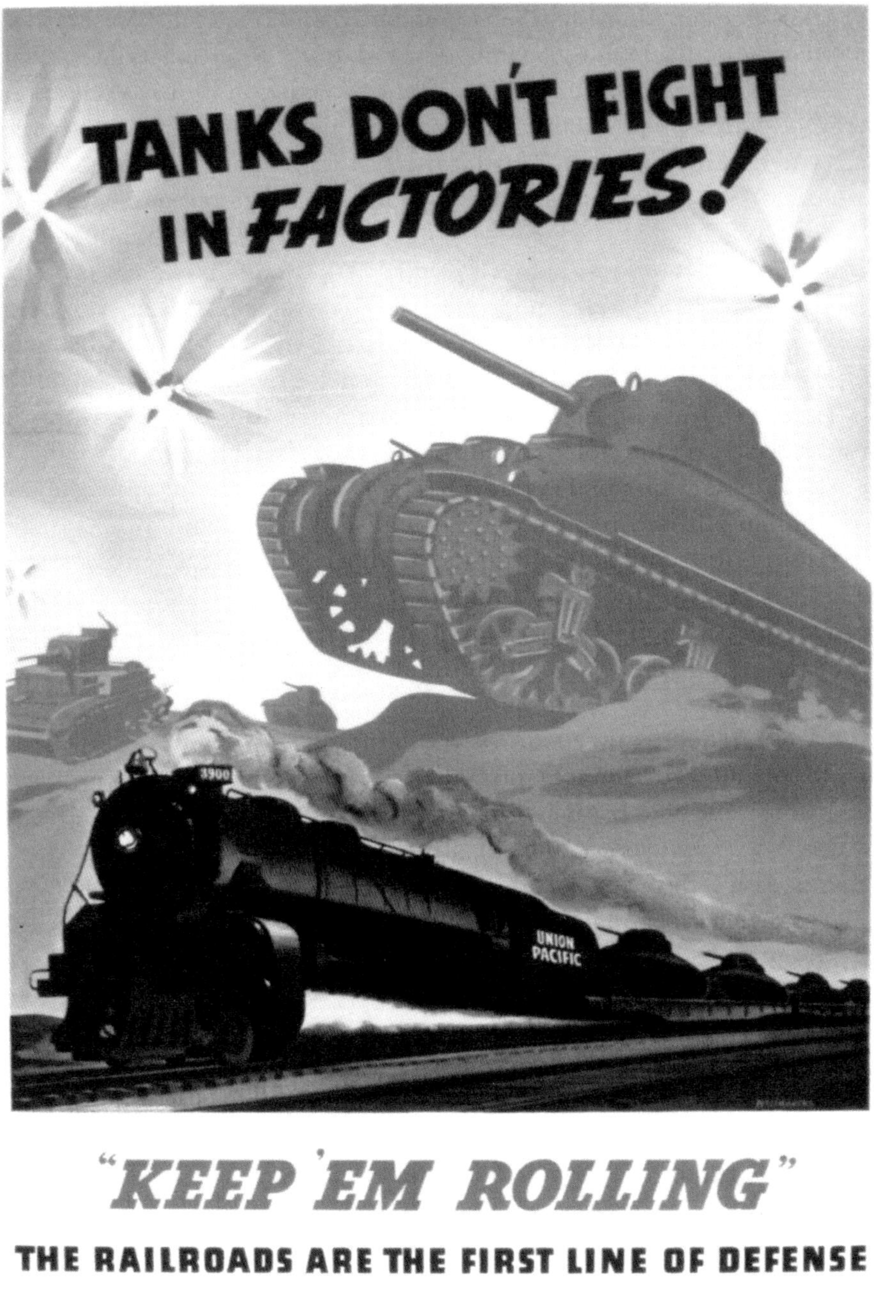

"Keep 'em Rolling!" Propaganda poster from the U.S. Office of War Information, War Production Board, productivity campaign. *National Archives and Records Administration [NWDNS-44-PA-1403].*

of rubber annually, of which only 8,000 tons were synthetic. It would take until 1944 before the U.S. synthetic sources could match the 750,000-ton requirements. And of course, there was also the Manhattan Project, which developed the atom bomb, ending the war.

The demand on workers was grueling. Not everyone could manage the mechanization of industrial-based wartime industry, where plants operated 24/7 six to seven days a week, calling on employees to work double shifts. Regions responsible for war production and with a dearth of entertainment were blamed for lowered war production. To counter this trend, the Division of Recreation of the Federal Security Agency published a report titled *Spare Time: A War Asset for War Workers* to encourage increased leisure-time entertainment activities for war workers.[344] Military commanders, supportive of the agency's work, made similar observations. Commander R.E. Davenport, personnel officer of the Norfolk Navy Yard, reported that about 30 percent of the yard's 42,800 workers were on the swing shift, which worked from 3:30 p.m. to 11:20 p.m. The second shift was only 70 percent as efficient as the day shift, believed attributable, at least in part, to the fact that employees on the night shifts worked while others played. Bowling alleys, dance spots, skating rinks and other forms of amusement closed early, and with early curfew on sales of beer and wine, few places were open when the workers left their jobs. The FSA report concluded that the lack of adequate entertainment and recreation for war workers was a threat to war production.

This connection between low production and lack of entertainment opportunities was further linked to low morale. The demands of the military were unprecedented, and no stockpiling of armaments had taken place. By the fall of 1942, full war production had yet to be achieved.[345] The government worked to balance civilian needs with those of the military as industry worked toward full production. The imbalance perceived by the public and experienced in daily living resulted in low morale that had to be addressed. Recreation and entertainment were viewed as a war resource—as the solution.

U.S. government agencies understood that recreation was a resource of war and not to be taken for granted. Massive federal agency structures were created to administer the consultation and technical assistance that war-based industrial communities required. Improve recreational facilities and morale would increase, along with the efficiency of war production.[346] By mid-1943, the entertainment industry had organized itself through the National Entertainment Industry Council to support the government's request to improve and increase both morale and entertainment opportunities throughout war industry communities.[347]

Communities with a high density of war production industries experienced the impact on defense workers as well as social and recreation programs and facilities. The federal government stepped in with both funding sources and personnel through the Division of Recreation of the Federal Security Agency.[348] Its regional offices provided consulting services and assisted communities with the applications for securing funding to support or expand recreational facilities. Governmental assistance, such as the Community Facilities Act of 1940 (the Lanham Act), provided federal funds to defense-affected communities to help with construction of new facilities that could meet these needs while furnishing workers with recreational outlets.[349] The Portland-based Oaks Rink was renovated using Lanham funds.

With the outbreak of war, the roller skate industry, organized and structured since 1937, jumped on board early in 1942 with support for the national wartime publicity campaigns. RSROA reported in *Billboard* that 12 million skaters were called on to support the Office of Civilian Defense's nationwide physical fitness program.[350] The effort was headed up by James G. Morton, who wrote a skating column in the *New York Journal-American* newspaper. The roller skate industry was quick and adept at leveraging war needs and identifying how it could use its collective influence in support of war efforts. It used the Office of War Information's campaign themes, adopting them via industry advertisers for inclusion into its promotional campaigns, always linking the roller skate industry to war aims.

Recognizing that rinks with flexible schedules could accommodate night-shift workers, especially on the East and West Coasts, motivated rinks to offer morning sessions, but transportation limitations prevented workers from getting to the rinks. The Office of Defense Transportation (ODT) recognized the value of rinks in maintaining morale of soldiers, sailors and war workers and authorized use of a free bus service. Generally, these rinks were located in industrial centers, near army camps and naval bases. The view was that if rink access was denied, defense workers might develop harmful habits and engage in idleness conducive to juvenile delinquency.[351]

With war declared, the boys eagerly enlisted in the armed forces. A new draft policy waited a year for President Roosevelt's December 5, 1942 executive order to change the age range from twenty-one to forty-five to eighteen to thirty-eight years of age. By 1943, the War Manpower Commission was drafting 200,000 men per month for the length of the war. As they left for military service, skating rinks saw the pool of male skaters decrease. Rink operators wrote new rules that would not only keep rink activity alive during the war but also show support for the boys, as well as the girls, who once danced and skated around their rink. Rinks watched as employees answered the call of duty by joining the army, navy or Marine Corps. The demands of war resulted in women migrating into numerous roles once dominated by men, not only in the workplace but also in amusement and recreation industries.[352]

As the war drained the nation of healthy, fit men of military age, what remained were those too young, too old or too unfit for military service.[353] Newspaper headlines reported that America had become a nation of 4-F status. (A 4-F deferment was issued when a man was determined unfit for military service due to medical or psychological reasons. It was estimated that only 50 percent of men qualified for military service.) Couple this with the discretionary income workers had and the purchase of available automobiles and fitness advocates argued that the nation's workforce was getting soft physically. They pushed for fitness programs. It was argued that it was time the 50 million homefront workers got fit to meet the requirements for maximum industry production and support those fighting the war.

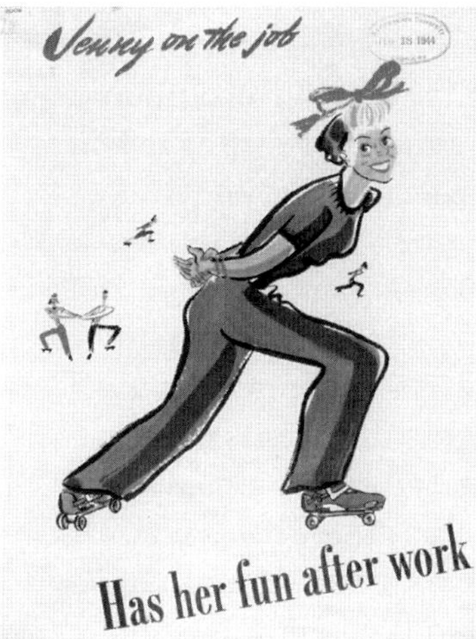

"Jenny on the Job: Has Her Fun After Work." After work, "Jenny" changes out of work coveralls to trousers and roller skates. *Federal Security Agency, U.S. Public Health Service, World War II poster collection, 1943, Northwestern University Library [FS2.25:14].*

At the outset of the war, the fitness program was met with Congressional outcry. The director of the Office of Civilian Defense agreed and threatened to resign if the fitness initiative were set up within OCD. He argued that it should be moved to the Federal Security Agency's committee. Subsequently, in 1943, it was moved out of OCD and into FSA's Division of Recreation. This division pushed for on-site entertainment and recreation programs. If a facility were large enough, FSA encouraged the industry to build a roller rink. The program was rolled out into war plants and factories, and the "Jenny on the Job" series of health and safety posters reminded workers that whether on or off the job, war duties did not stop—workers should also engage in exercise and remain ready for work.

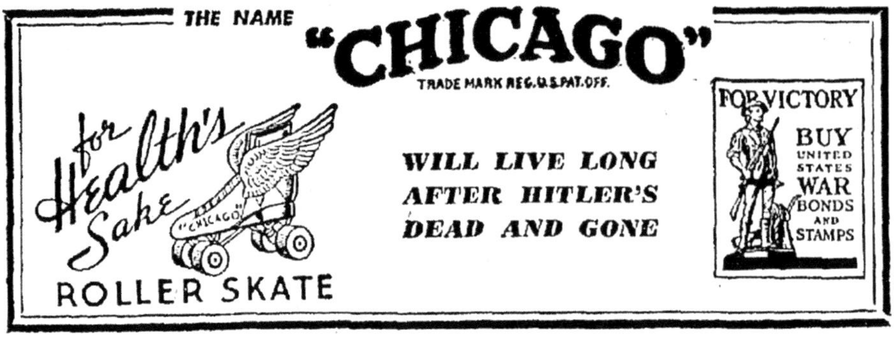

"For Health's Sake…Roller Skate!" Chicago Roller Skate Company 1942 ad. The ad shows the industry support for war bonds, skating for health and post-Hitler wishes. *National Sports Company.*

Additionally, production and raw material shortfalls created hardships for the civilian sector. The government established numerous civilian propaganda campaigns, thoughtfully described as morale-building and participation programs, recruiting nonprofit organizations, recreation centers and local governments to aid in the campaigns to offset these hardships. Several federal agencies were involved and coordinated efforts to build local programs, with support from the Office of Civilian Requirements, the Office of War Information and the Office of Defense, Health and Welfare Services.[354]

Women, as well as minority groups, were called on to fill employment gaps, and they responded in overwhelming numbers. Chicago led the nation in war production, and the war industry was highly dependent on the role women played in its factories. In fact, high school graduation rates were the lowest in recorded history during the war years, as young women chose work over education.

Women worked in traditional clerical roles as well as in war factories. Rosie the Riveter became the face of resilient women who filled the roles once dominated by men.[355] Initially, Rosie was a mural on a building in California where warplanes were built; she was later adopted by the War Production Coordinating Committee as a nationwide campaign theme. No wonder those same tough women thought nothing about roller skating around banked tracks in roller derby competitions with body-to-body contact.

And women had something to prove: they were as good as men, could be as productive and could meet the demands of factory work. To make their point, they grabbed their skates, went to work and displayed an

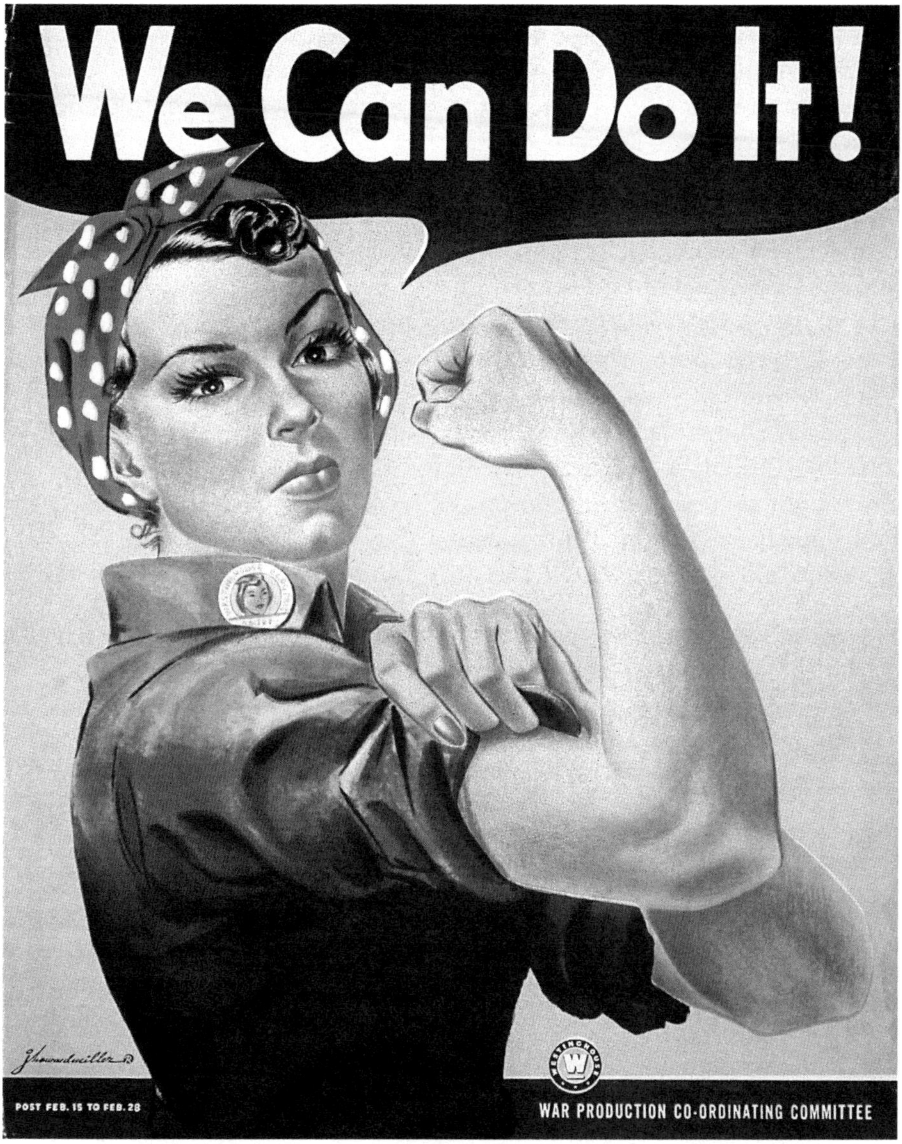

Published in 1943, the iconic "Rosie the Riveter" poster came to depict the liberated, tough woman who symbolized female patriotism and the independent woman working the front lines of the war industry. The poster was commissioned by the Westinghouse Electric & Manufacturing Company and distributed by the War Production Coordinating Committee for only two weeks. *National Museum of American History.*

eagerness to do the work of men in the office or the factory. It became customary that to speed production, workers would use roller skates to move paperwork and coordinate information and interdepartmental messages in huge war plants like Douglas Aircraft in El Segundo, California.[356]

What made skates at work acceptable? Government campaigns directed industries and civilians to save gas, be productive and practice conservation. Skates at work became commonplace in war production facilities, whether in the Midwest building trucks or at M3 Scout Cars (White Motor Company) or in the West Coast Douglas war plants. As a result, women showed up with roller skates. They took street skills and transformed them into essential work skills.

Filling the war production line was not the only expectation of women. They were also expected to meet those traditional roles women have held since the beginning of time: keeping the home fires burning. Women at neighborhood rinks across America worked during the war years by

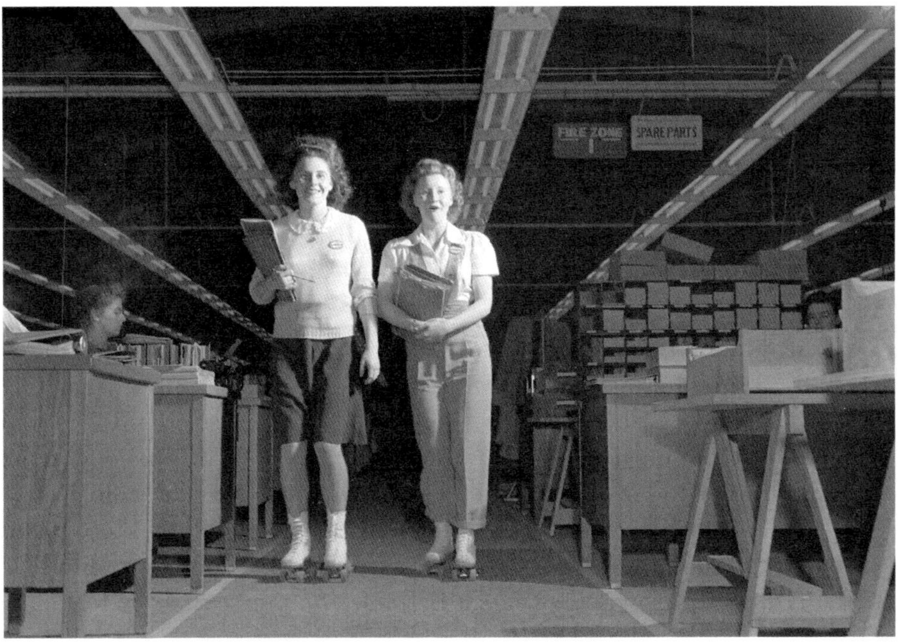

Dolores Richardson and Geneva Carpenter are "expeditors" at Douglas Aircraft in El Segundo, California, where they delivered interdepartmental message on roller skates. Douglas built the A-24 dive bomber for the Army Air Corps and the A-26 for the navy, with a tail hook used for carrier landings. *Library of Congress, Prints & Photographs Division, FSA/ OWI Collection [LC-USW3-029169-D].*

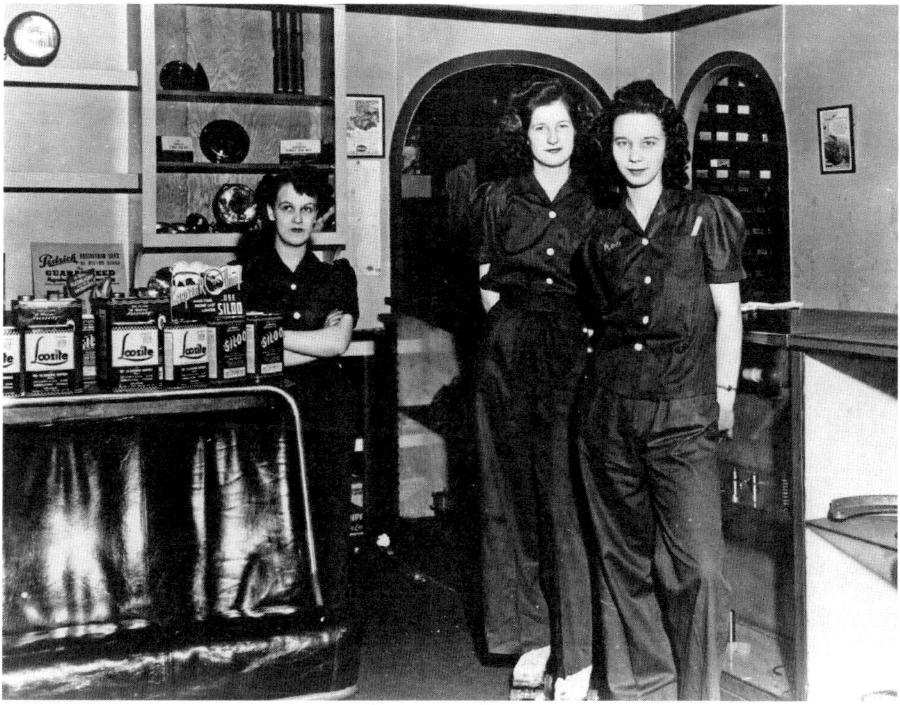

Women in the parts department on roller skates, White Motor Company, Chicago branch, 1942–45. Women are wearing the military-looking outfits with army colors that were trendy in the war years and popular among female defense workers. Note the sign over the oil cans that reads, "Keep 'em ROlling," with a tank that slogs through the capital *O*. According to the original caption, "Roller skates enabled them to give fast service in the delivery of parts from bins to customers or to the repair department. These women have proved to be satisfactory replacement for men who have been called to the armed forces." *National Automotive History Collection, Detroit Public Library.*

fulfilling many diverse roles, from worker to letter writer, homemaker and fitness buff, as well as in the social scene. Slick war ads created by the Office of War Information were quickly adopted by the roller skate industry engaging skaters to support the war effort by buying victory bonds and skating for optimal fitness while working in the war industry. The skate scene continued to grow during those years, while rink operators made adjustments to rink policy that would sustain operations. The instant drain of men from the rink required sudden and dramatic modification to rink policies, such as appropriate dress policies, all-male floor guards and skate couples defined as a male and female.

Rules that had persisted to create an adult scene in roller rinks and that had held fast for years were suddenly changing. For example, partner

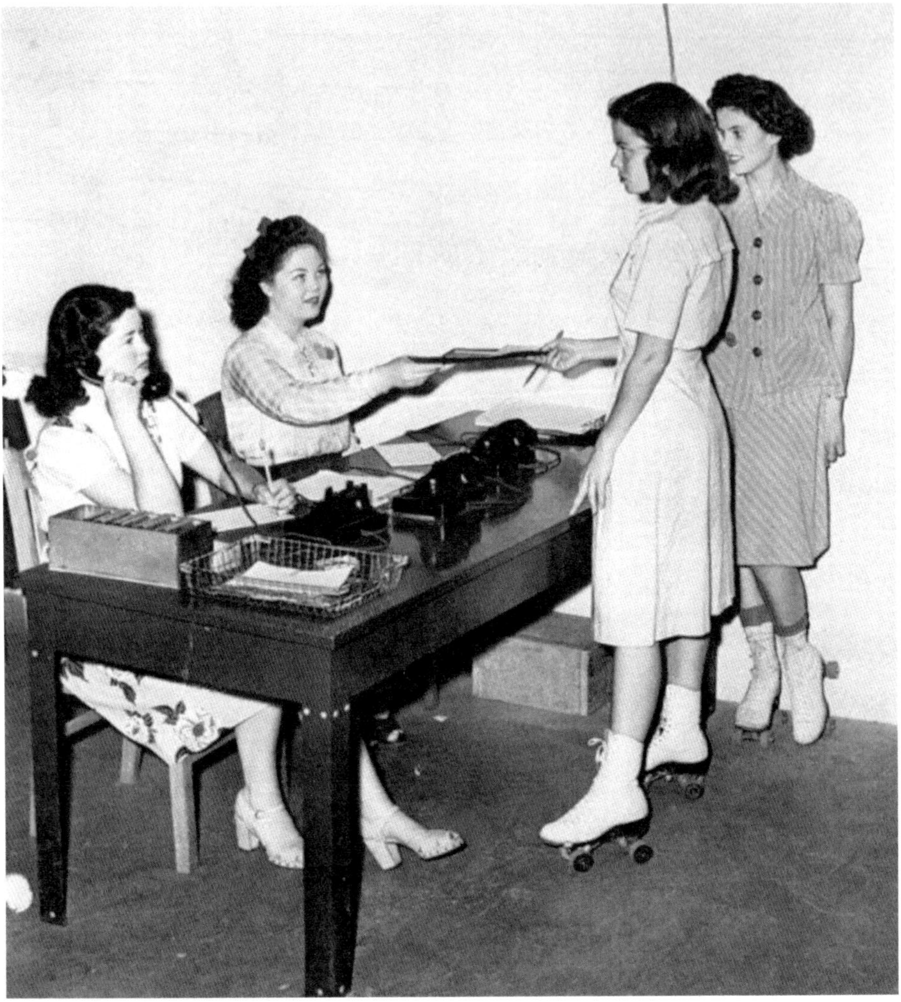

Women with roller skates deliver documents at the Douglas Aircraft Company Santa Monica Plant, May 12, 1943. *Santa Monica Public Library Image Archives, Museum of Flying Collection.*

dancing included a male and a female, but rules were relaxed to keep the skate scene alive. Women were permitted to skate and/or skate dance with each other at rinks around the nation.

Keeping the home fires burning also meant writing letters, lots of them, to many of the boys they knew and stayed connected with overseas. The Office of War Information's poster campaign reminded girls that their duty was to write the boys. The girls at the rinks wrote the boys from their home rinks. They included rink news, how things were going, what the new rink dance was and any new music hits, such as Benny Goodman's "Jersey Bounce." They shared family news, friend news and neighborhood news—anything to deliver a message with the feel that life will be the same when they return. Too often, last letters were returned and the sender informed that her friend was lost in service to his country.

The exchange of correspondence kept family, friends and loved ones in touch during prolonged separations, fostering the emotional ties between senders and recipients. A new technology, V-mail (Victory Mail), adopted by the British and developed by the Eastman Kodak Company, was used to send secured mail. Probably today's generation believe that e-mail was a new phenomenon reserved for millennials. But in 1941, V-mail was a state-of-the-art marvel that bypassed snail mail by sending secured written messages to military personnel. V-mail was scoured or censored and copied to a thumb-sized image in microfilm. Once it arrived at its destination, the microfilm was printed to four- by five-inch paper. It was estimated that thirty-seven mailbags were converted to a single mailbag when V-mail was used.

Another national campaign aimed at wartime industry workers and adopted by RSROA was "Keep 'em Rolling." To sustain maximum production, this particular campaign was developed for numerous industries that built railroads, tanks, artillery, aircraft and anything that rolled. Signs and posters were printed and posted and the message ingrained in the citizenry, including skaters, to support the war effort.[357] The campaign was embraced throughout the country. It was also a perfect fit for the roller industry.

Mobilization also meant conversion of domestic commercial industries to wartime production, such as with roller skate manufacturers. The Richardson Ballbearing Skate Company converted skate ball bearing production to tank, artillery, trucks and aircraft ball bearing requirements. Chicago Roller Skate Company's conversion to war supply production meant it could no longer make skates for civilians, but it did continue to meet military supplies for skates and skate parts. In September 1941, Chicago Roller Skate Company shipped skates to army camps near cities with a roller rink, an action approved by the War Department.

Roller skate manufacturers were considered a critical industry by the War Production Board because of their capability to convert and make war supplies. Thus, these same manufacturers were also included in industrial correspondence and were kept informed of schedules

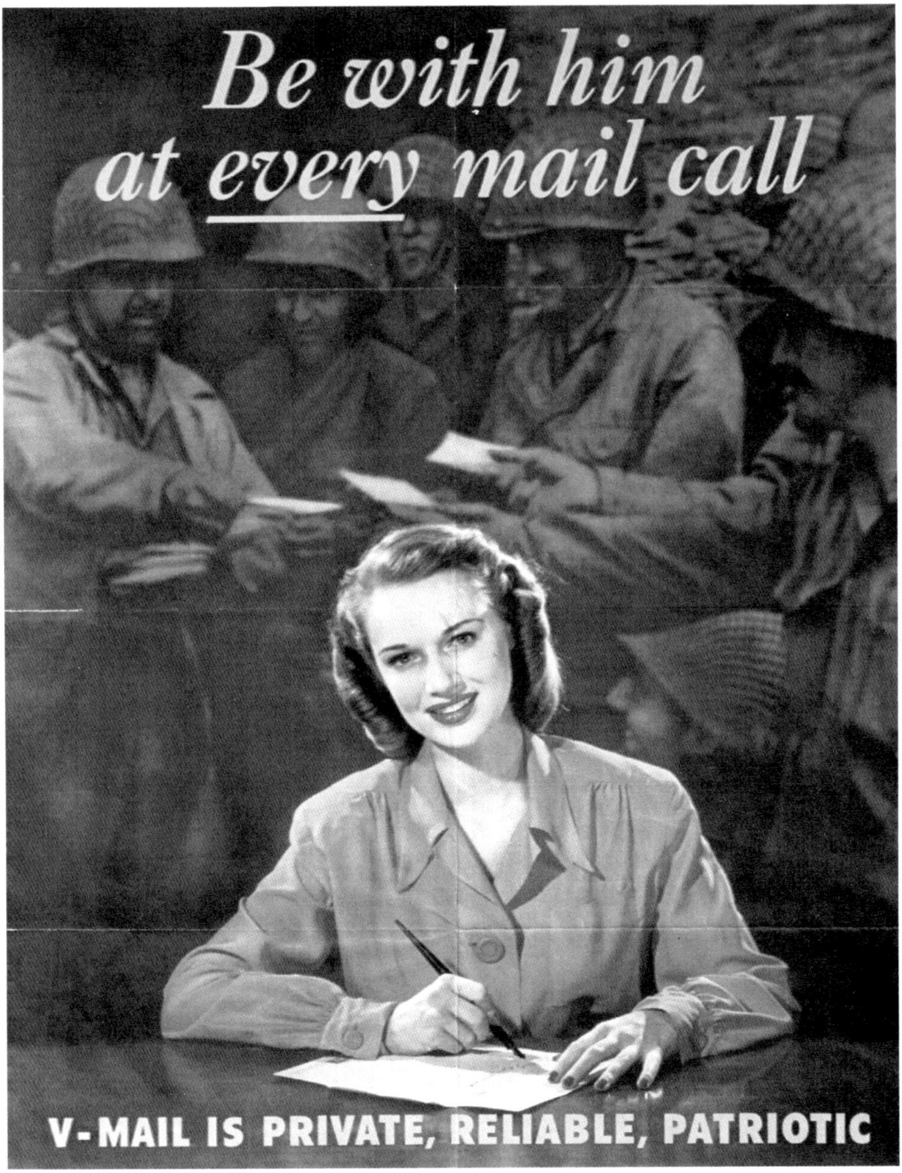

The Office of War Information's V-mail poster shows GI soldiers in the background receiving mail while the young woman writes. The message states, "Be with him at every mail call," and serves as a reminder that V-mail is private, reliable and patriotic. *Northwestern University Library, World War II Poster Collection.*

and shifts in war production requirements. These insights were passed along to roller skate industry leaders, such as RSROA, which could use them to craft messages to support the war while also keeping its members informed of expected changes. RSROA and rink owners used this information to expand their image and ready themselves to emerge from the war years in a position to grow the sport. Throughout the 1940s, the roller skate industry maintained a close association with the war industry, manufacturers and communities. The roller industry understood that roller rinks were considered a critical recreational resource for base personnel at military bases or war industry manufacturer workers. It also meant that rinks expanded their open hours to accommodate the 24/7 shift of war workers.

To illustrate the extent to which roller skating had become enmeshed in the fabric of America's boys in service, active-duty servicemen could find rinks on military bases at home or overseas and skate, relieving the pressures of duty. Both the European and Pacific Theaters hosted rinks where servicemen could skate. Back at home, servicemen skated for free. Today, skating rinks can still be found on domestic and European military bases.[358] American servicemen also showed much ingenuity to keep 'em

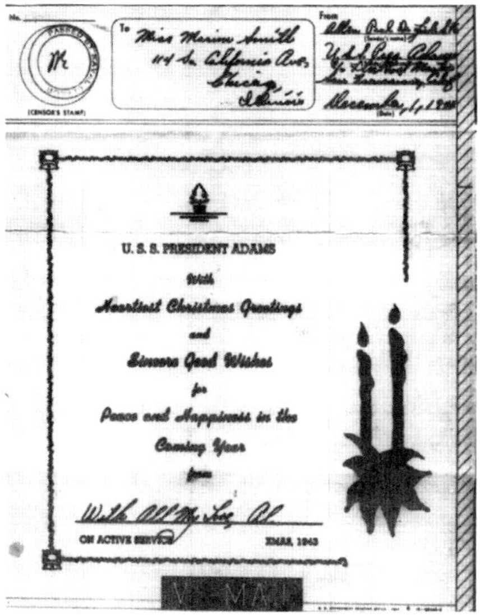

V-mail with holiday greetings from Seaman Second Class Allen DeLisle to Miss Marion Smith, dated December 1, 1943. DeLisle was stationed on the USS *President Adams*. The censor's stamp is in the upper left-hand corner. At bottom center, in the block box, is the "V-MAIL" logo in white letters. *Author's collection.*

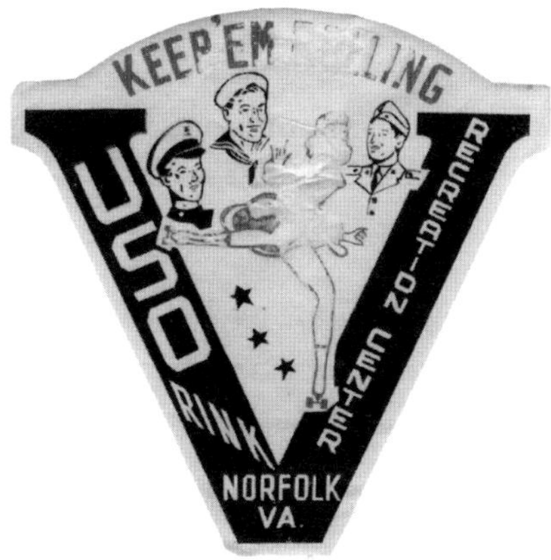

A Norfolk, Virginia military base USO roller skating rink, built for servicemen by the government for recreation, relaxation and morale building. *Author's collection.*

rolling. While stationed in New England and assigned to the U.S. 8th Air Force Bomber Station, servicemen rebuilt skates from B-17 Flying Fortress parts and passed the figure skating tests of the British skating association.[359]

The government worked to meet recreational needs wherever U.S. armed services personnel were sent through both established and new organizational structures. Organizations such as the United Service Organizations (USO), created in 1941, met servicemen's needs for socialization and recreation. Skate clubs made up of marines, soldiers, sailors and civilians were organized stateside or overseas. One such club was started in Hawaii, used a 100- by 200-foot cement rink and played records. The club president appealed to *Skating News* for copies of *The Art of Dance Skating* and *Skating News*, as well as materials to equip the rink and skaters.[360] Skate clubs would host buffet dinners, dances and bunco parties. Chicago's Commission on National Defense and Mayor Edward J. Kelly established the Chicago Service Men's Center in August 1941. This was the servicemen's recreation center and provided conversation, social recreation, refreshments and dances at no cost. Neighborhood rinks supported the center with events that raised funds.

Demobilization

Mobilization for the war was a huge endeavor, but readying communities for returning servicemen was an equally massive undertaking. The war in Europe ended on May 8, 1945, with the Russian capture of Berlin and the unconditional surrender of Germany. Japan's surrender soon followed on August 8, 1945.

The needs of handicapped service personnel required special medical facilities. It was also recognized that a return to normalcy for servicemen required the civilians on the homefront to provide reassurance to returning servicemen that the social scene was essentially unchanged from when they left. The nation's GIs weren't sure what to expect when they returned home. They had been overseas for anywhere from six to eighteen months and did not know what civilian life was like. Pressures on the family structure were immense. Divorce rates reached the highest they had ever been, and the general concern was, "How much can families take?"[361]

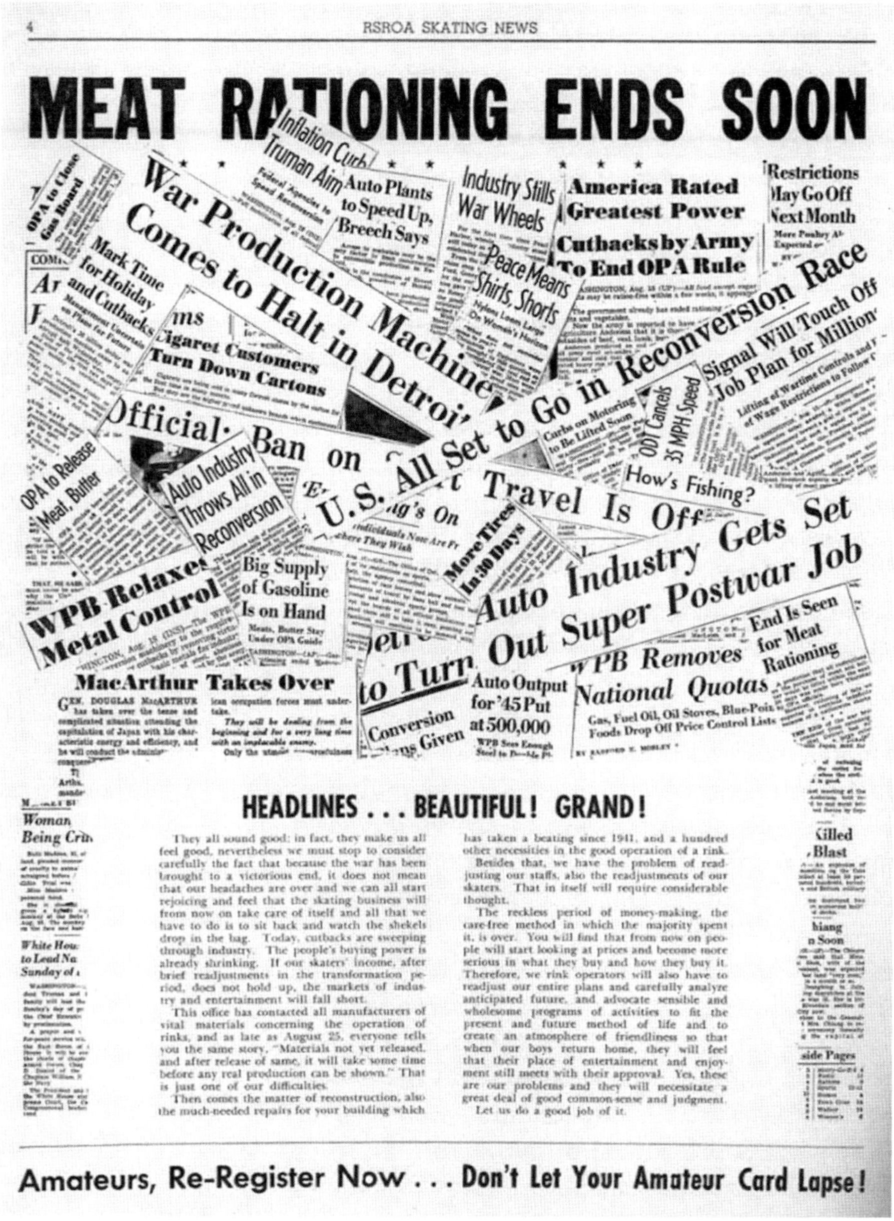

4 RSROA SKATING NEWS

MEAT RATIONING ENDS SOON

Inflation Curb Truman Aim

Auto Plants to Speed Up, Breech Says

Industry Stills War Wheels

America Rated Greatest Power

Restrictions May Go Off Next Month

Cutbacks by Army To End OPA Rule

War Production Machine Comes to Halt in Detroit

Mark Time for Holiday and Cutbacks

Peace Means Shirts, Shorts

Cigaret Customers Turn Down Cartons

U.S. All Set to Go in Reconversion Race

Signal Will Touch Off Job Plan for Millions

ODT Cancels 35 MPH Speed

OPA to Release Meat, Butter

Auto Industry Throws All in Reconversion

How's Fishing?

More Tires In 30 Days

WPB Relaxes Metal Control

Big Supply of Gasoline Is on Hand

Auto Industry Gets Set to Turn Out Super Postwar Job

End Is Seen for Meat Rationing

MacArthur Takes Over

Auto Output for '45 Put at 500,000

WPB Removes National Quotas

HEADLINES . . . BEAUTIFUL! GRAND!

They all sound good: in fact, they make us all feel good, nevertheless we must stop to consider carefully the fact that because the war has been brought to a victorious end, it does not mean that our headaches are over and we can all start rejoicing and feel that the skating business will from now on take care of itself and all that we have to do is to sit back and watch the shekels drop in the bag. Today, cutbacks are sweeping through industry. The people's buying power is already shrinking. If our skaters' income, after brief readjustments in the transformation period, does not hold up, the markets of industry and entertainment will fall short.

This office has contacted all manufacturers of vital materials concerning the operation of rinks, and as late as August 25, everyone tells you the same story, "Materials not yet released, and after release of same, it will take some time before any real production can be shown." That is just one of our difficulties.

Then comes the matter of reconstruction, also the much-needed repairs for your building which has taken a beating since 1941, and a hundred other necessities in the good operation of a rink.

Besides that, we have the problem of readjusting our staffs, also the readjustments of our skaters. That in itself will require considerable thought.

The reckless period of money-making, the care-free method in which the majority spent it, is over. You will find that from now on people will start looking at prices and become more serious in what they buy and how they buy it. Therefore, we rink operators will also have to readjust our entire plans and carefully analyze anticipated future, and advocate sensible and wholesome programs of activities to fit the present and future method of life and to create an atmosphere of friendliness so that when our boys return home, they will feel that their place of entertainment and enjoyment still meets with their approval. Yes, these are our problems and they will necessitate a great deal of good common-sense and judgment.

Let us do a good job of it.

Amateurs, Re-Register Now . . . Don't Let Your Amateur Card Lapse!

A collage of headlines announces that the war is over and demobilization is ahead. *Skating News*, September 1945. *National Museum of Roller Skating.*

D-Day was June 6, 1944, codenamed Operation Overlord, and the entertainment industry was abuzz about postwar plans and anticipated a business boom with the boys coming home. It would be another year before World War II ended with the surrender of Japan. However, in 1944, invasion news affected roller rink activity very little. D-Day was launched with an estimated 156,000 American, British and Canadian forces landing on five beaches along a fifty-mile stretch of a heavily fortified coast off France's Normandy region. Simultaneously, plans were announced for twelve "Super De Luxe Skatoriums," a significant postwar construction plan of enormous magnitude that captured headlines in trade journals. Other expansions called for new rinks in and around New York, including the Bronx, as well as Long Island, Newark and Philadelphia, with other locations to be announced at a later date.[362] Competitor rink operations announced other plans to expand roller skating. For the south side of Pittsburgh, there was planned a fifty-thousand-square-foot facility, with a skating space of thirty thousand square feet, a thirty- by one-hundred-foot beginners' rink, an elaborate lobby, lounges and clubrooms. Another operation also announced plans for a thirty-thousand-square-foot facility and a twenty-thousand-square-foot skating rink.[363]

In the wake of D-Day, the Allies began to release war films in ever greater numbers. Allied governments sought to fight back against the "war is over" sentiment that swept the nation and instead maintain the momentum for war production materials. For example, a two-reel film, *The War Speeds Up*, was distributed by the War Department. General George Marshall requested the film be made by the motion picture industry.[364] The Navy Department also arranged for the production of films to reduce absenteeism and labor turnover. These movies included *Behind Nazi Guns*, *Battle for the Beaches* and *December Seventh*. The Navy Department also authorized two movies be released to war workers captured from the Nazis titled *Return to Guam* and *Invasion—Nazi Version*. *Return to Guam* was a sixteen-minute film of the U.S. marines "hitting the beach" in the return invasion of Guam through a terrific amphibious assault for the first time since Japan overtook the U.S. possession. More than eleven thousand tons of ammunition were used in the bombardment of Guam before the marines "hit the beach."

As the war ended in 1945, the U.S. government expanded all sorts of programs, including specialized rehabilitation programs for wounded veterans. The roller skate industry responded and, in cooperation with the U.S. Army Medical Service (AMS), implemented a nationwide roller skating therapy program. The program assisted returning servicemen who had lost a leg to relearn balance by roller skating. Local rinks recruited skaters who pledged to work with recovering veterans and the Army Medical Service. AMS (today called Army Medical Department, AMEDD) had trained commissioned nurses to assist in this form of physical therapy via exercise.[365]

To show rink operators across the nation that this specialized program worked, twenty-five amputees from the Thomas M. England General Hospital laced up for a demonstration party at New Dreamland Arena, Newark, New Jersey. One soldier with two artificial legs skated alone, backward as well as forward, in the center of the rink.[366] The point was that disabled vets wanted to be treated like anyone else. As a result, vets worked to use artificial limbs and were public about it so that other vets could witness the results. The view was adopted by both veterans and the general public that "disabled veterans are not handicapped unless they think or are made to think so thru constant reminders or exploitation."[367] Their public courage served as a reminder to rink operators and the general public that the collective effort was to return veterans to the physical and mental state they enjoyed before the war.

The end of the war also brought about both the expansion and the disposition of numerous army and naval bases. Along with those conversions came the loss of base-hosted roller rinks. One such rink was the Palace Roller Rink, located on the Pasco Naval Air Station. After the war, the base was sold to the City of Pasco and converted to the civilian Tri-Cities Airport.

The contribution of roller skating to the war effort may have no greater tribute than the roller skating rink located at the U.S. Yokosuka Naval Base in Japan. Yokosuka hosted the Yokosuka Iron Works, which was the Imperial Japanese Navy's largest shipbuilding and repair facility. U.S. forces reopened the facility on April 28, 1947, under the United States flag and converted a warehouse into Fleet Gym and a recreational center that included a roller skating rink.[368]

The Yokosuka roller rink opened during the golden age, when roller skating was the top recreational activity in the nation. Stories are told about roller skating in retrofitted gymnasiums throughout Europe, while Seabees used the lower hangar decks of aircraft carriers to keep up skate speed. Letters to *Skating News* by overseas servicemen asked for copies of the periodical along with skate parts to keep old roller shoes rolling. Robert Ware Jr. of the Chicago Roller Skate Company was interviewed for *Skating News*

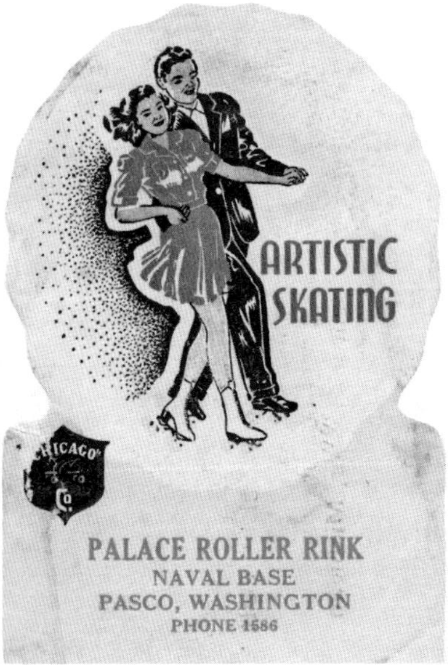

Palace Roller Rink, "Artistic Skating," Pasco Naval Air Station. Built with federal funds, the Palace rink served the Pasco Naval Air Station personnel. *Author's collection.*

in 1985 and shared that the company only made roller skates for the armed forces, and that included skates for sailors' recreational use on aircraft carriers.[369] Jerry Seltzer reported that in later years, a roller derby match was hosted aboard the USS *Ranger*, a Forrestal-class supercarrier.[370]

Not unlike the demise of numerous roller rinks across the nation, the Yokosuka roller rink ultimately closed in May 2006 to make way for a new power plant that would supply power to the USS *George Washington*, a nuclear-powered aircraft carrier launched in 2008.[371] Interviewed for *Stars and Stripes*, base spokesman Bill Doughty wrote in an e-mail, "People aren't disco skating as much as using their laptops." Tools captivated the caveman, and twenty-first-century man continues to be consumed and entertained by gadgets. But the legacy of Yokosuka roller skating lives on with the Yokosuka Sushi Rollers, a women's flat-track roller derby team.

Roller skating emerged from the war years as a mainstream recreation sport represented by national organizations. The sport had contributed significantly to the war effort, grew to populate more than five thousand communities with skate rinks and established national and international competitive prominence. Roller skating became part of pop culture through music, movies and, by the end of the 1940s, television.

Despite setbacks brought about by war, the roller industry pursued a strategic goal to expand roller skating by establishing it as a legitimate sport with competitive skating. It established policies, rules and regulations; defined instructor training programs; and structured local, state and national competitions. Correspondence with rink owners described management techniques to keep operations going. Throughout trade journals and news reports, the industry knew well its status as a recreational sports industry, compared to its competition, and leveraged opportunities to promote itself. It never flaunted its status but also never shied away from sharing that strategic goal. Whether it was raising money for the National Foundation for Infantile Paralysis (March of Dimes) program, collecting scrap metal and tires or conserving the much-needed items for the boys, rink owners and clubs got behind each of these efforts, using their cadre of skaters to support war efforts. The roller industry structured itself to be at the forefront of demobilization once the war ended, positioning itself to become the top recreational sport of the nation.

PART V

THE ORGANIZATIONS OF ROLLER SKATING

It was announced in the fall of 1971 by *Skate*'s editor and RSROA sports administrator George Pickard that roller skating would be whole again after three decades.[372] To rink rats and most other skaters, the reorganization of roller skating's national associations would not affect the joy of everyday roller skating. So why the marriage? It was clearly not Roller Romance. After all, a thirty-year engagement rarely fuses emotions. The most likely explanation is that the Olympic recognition sought by the rival organizations had yet to materialize after many proposals beginning in the 1940s. It was hoped that this new union would bring about roller skating's Olympic ambitions.

The RSROA's U.S. Federation of Amateur Roller Skaters (USFARS) merged with the U.S. Amateur Roller Skating Association (ARSA) on November 1, 1971, forming the newly created governing body called the Artistic Skating Union. By 1973, the new organization would be incorporated as the United States of America Confederation of Amateur Roller Skating (USAC) and today operates as USA Roller Sports.[373] The winners were amateur skaters who would compete under the rules of one organization. Furthermore, the sport would gain credibility and clarify for spectators that there is indeed one set of national champions to represent roller skating.

Prior to the merger, as alluded to in previous chapters, the golden age was not just about skate competitors but about those organizations that competed for control of amateur skate competitions, with a grudgingly common goal to grow the sport of roller skating. While roller skating as a sport can claim a long history, it was the formal, structured, competitive skating that was organized, coordinated and controlled for the masses that had been missing. And this formalized structure was established for emerging new styles of roller skating such as dance, figures, artistic and hockey, in addition to speed skating. As a result, the new organizations emerged to guide and/or control competitions. The inter-sport organizational rivalry contributed to the growth of the sport.

The Formative Years

Setting aside organizational rivalries, other issues clouded roller skating's reputation as an acceptable form of recreation that carried over from the early 1900s, much of which was detailed in earlier chapters. These factors include the rink environment and the role of a rink in local neighborhoods to serve as a community's recreation center, as well as transforming its reputation to one of wholesome, family-centered activity. Owners set out to present roller skating as a professional sport, departing from its view as the playground of roughnecks where "nice people did not roller skate."[374] Its slogan, "Roller Skate to Health," illustrated the recreational intention of the sport to attract young and old alike.

Roller skate rink owners were the first to spike the ball. Seventeen rink owners met in April 1937 in conjunction with the first U.S. Amateur Speed Roller Skate Championship at Arena Gardens of Detroit, and it was then that the Roller Skating Rink Owners Association (RSROA) was formed.[375] Its purpose was to address the lack of standard rules and structure for amateur competitive skating. The view of those present was that "imposters and false records" had claimed legitimacy with no governing body to either sanction the events or counter these claims. Also, those governing bodies in operation had failed to acknowledge the emerging popularity of roller skating and its growth potential as an amateur competitive sport. In its governance role, RSROA set forth to establish rules for speed, dance and figure roller skating. In essence, rink operators and professional skaters had organized to control the sport, dramatically transform its image and provide governance over amateur competitions.

In that same time, it had been brewing that rink owners were critical of the rink environment that would serve those competitors and sought solutions to change the perception. Owners saw the rink organization's constructive

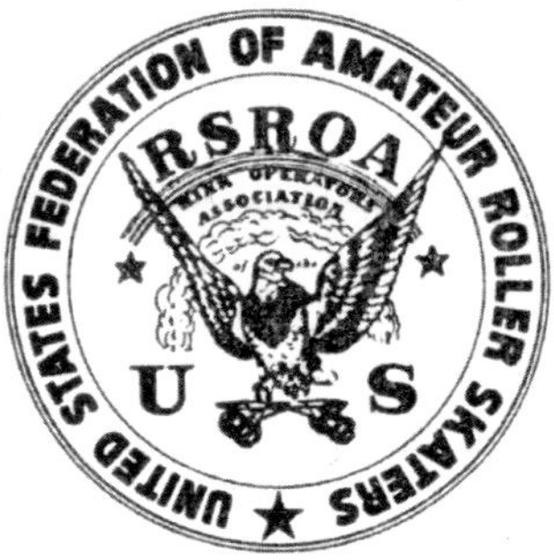

Unites States Federation of Amateur Roller Skating (USFARS). USFARS was RSROA's board of governors, which administered competition guidance for figure, dance and speed skating and provided oversight of amateur status. January 1947. *Author's collection.*

efforts to change those perceptions. Consequently, RSROA supported rink operators by improving management practices, developing standardized training of instructors and skate instruction for enthusiasts, cleaning up the image of rinks and promoting roller skating for the masses. A rival rink group was organized under the name of United Rink Organization (URO) in late 1942 and adopted similar practices to those of RSROA for its member rinks.[376]

In 1940, RSROA held the first U.S. Amateur Rolling Skate Championship.[377] The weeklong contest combined all styles for the first time at the Cleveland Auditorium to include artistic, dance, speed and hockey. The Amateur Skating Union (an ice skate organization) applauded the RSROA leadership for its quick rise to become one of the outstanding governing bodies in United States sports.[378]

The contribution of RSROA was significant and moved roller skating from a special promotion-driven spectator sport during the early 1900s to an individual-participatory competitive sport for the masses. RSROA member rinks and skate clubs organized and managed amateur competitions at state and local events, establishing rules, events and communications with the industry and with its prospective customer base for the adult roller skate enthusiast who sought wholesome, recreational activity. This encouraged the development of new technologies to support rink operations such as rink floors, sound systems and patron amenities. The result was that a clientele base was built while a cadre of amateur competitors was nurtured.[379] Equally important, the work of national organizations in collaboration with rink operators transformed roller rinks to wholesome environments where the public turned for recreation during World War II as a low-cost escape to skate away their cares.

Not to be forgotten, and with much credit, is the competitive positioning that RSROA brought to roller skating. The launch of RSROA challenged the 1930s status quo that resided within amateur sports toward roller skating, brought about the creation of ARSA and formed a competitive rivalry that grew the sport of roller skating to unprecedented heights. The sport experienced tremendous growth, and amateur athletes were the beneficiaries whether their home rink was an RSROA-affiliated rink, an ARSA-affiliated rink or even a rink from the rogue franchise America on Wheels (AOW) network.

Shortly afterward, in an alliance with AOW, the Athletic Amateur Union (AAU), whose domain was governance over amateur sports, saw rink operators/owners and professional oversight of amateur competitions by RSROA as a conflict of interest. At its December 1942 meeting, AAU passed a resolution with a dozen recommendations directing RSROA to disassociate itself with control over amateur competitions.[380] The RSROA counterargument was that AAU had allowed roller skating to lapse into a sport for roughnecks, and rink owners would not permit a return to those days given skating's renewed popularity. As tensions rose between RSROA and William Schmitz, AOW franchise manager, Schmitz claimed that "the sole object of RSROA was the exploitation of the amateur!" RSROA claimed personal injury to its reputation by the Schmitz statement. As a result, RSROA took the alliance of Schmitz, AOW and the AAU to court, asking for $300,000 in damages.[381] The American Skating Union (ASU) would side with the Amateur Athletic Union (AAU), and by 1942, RSROA had resigned from the ASU.[382] The ASU, closely aligned with AAU, was a national organization and promoted itself as an organization that represented all of skating, both ice and roller. The animosity played out in the "Rinks and Skaters" column of *Billboard*, which served as the trade magazine for rink news and organization announcements. A look back at this period of organizational development reveals that the control of amateur roller skating was intense once its popularity and growth potential was realized. Financial investments had been significant, and influential operators were not letting go.

In cooperation with URO, the alliance established the U.S. Amateur Roller Skating Association (ARSA).[383] According to a Mineola newsletter, ARSA was preceded by URO, an outcome of Earl Van Horn's dispute with RSROA leaders. Van Horn's Mineola rink had hosted the first skate dance nationals in 1939. By the early 1940s, three national organizations had emerged, with RSROA pitted against URO and ARSA. The trio controlled amateur roller skate competition and organized rink operators. As a result, a rivalry was set in motion that would eclipse the golden age and persist for three decades. The two roller skate organizations held separate national championships, with both state and regional contests that channeled the best competitors to national prominence. The role of the United Rink

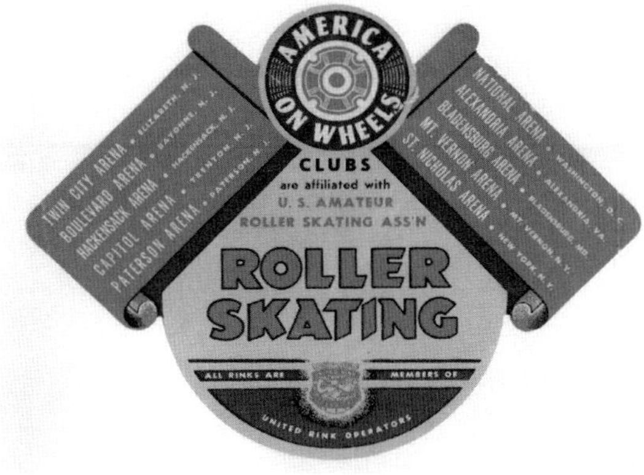

America on Wheels was a chain of East Coast rinks, members of the United Rink Operators Association, that hosted competitions following the rules of the U.S. Amateur Roller Skating Association. This roller skate sticker represents the mid-1940s, when AOW operated ten rinks. *Author's collection.*

Operators—training, rink management and business operations—was not unlike the role and relationship of RSROA to its member rinks.[384]

ARSA stayed true to amateur governance, and its competitive guidance was much more closely aligned with that of ice skating, as was the membership scope of URO.[385] Thus, the rules for both ice and roller skating were quite similar. Those roller skaters who competed under ARSA would comment how similar the skate styles were when contrasting ice to ARSA rollers. In fact, ice skaters cross-trained with roller skating as the seasons changed. Ironically, in its formative years, RSROA used ice skating judges with competition development and competitive judging. In 1956, Arlis Snyder described the ongoing challenges of developing and securing amateur judges for competitions.[386] Skate dance professionals would later intimate that RSROA skaters in their competitions seemed restricted in their routines. By contrast, ARSA skaters had the flexibility to be interpretative during their performances.

The rogue America on Wheels organization was a chain of East Coast rinks, members of the rival national rink association United Rink Operators (URO), that held competition events at member rinks. The AOW rinks adopted the ARSA style of skating and therefore held ARSA memberships. First introduced in 1941, by 1952 AOW had completed its twelfth annual championship.[387] AOW held its first championship with skate dancing but grew to include figures, freestyle, mixed pairs, ladies' pair and speed, with divisions from juvenile to senior, in 1952. At its zenith, AOW operated twenty-two rinks within its fold.[388]

By the early 1970s, America on Wheels had begun to close rinks as real estate values increased and insurance costs skyrocketed. Urban areas became scenes of violence, and the added burden of security added to costs, while declining participation meant lower revenues and an even tighter squeeze on the profit margin. The Levittown Roller Rink is a typical example of the demise of urban rinks. Located in East Meadow, Long Island, New York, Levittown was home to numerous national championships. The rink was sold to a chain drugstore, and in 1986, the building was demolished. Levittown Roller Rink operated for thirty-one years as a site for USARSA-style roller skate dancing.

Merger Overtures

Over the years, association members from both organizations called for a merger of amateur competition roller skating. Numerous attempts were made by leaders who saw the betterment to the whole of roller skating rather than the losses to individual organizations, but the negotiation breakdown was always over the same thing: who would administer amateur roller skating competitions.

Perhaps the first formal meeting was held in October 1944 between representatives of RSROA, ARSA and URO to discuss the merger of roller skate organizations.[389] No agreement was reached. Later, in 1944, *Skating Review* editor Edward Smith, in his report of this meeting among roller skate association heads, held out hope for reconciliation of differences and unification for one national championship.[390] In 1947, Perry Giles, rink owner of the Curvecrest Roller Rink in Muskegon, Michigan, pleaded in a half-page article in *Billboard*'s "Rinks and Skaters" how foolish it was to award rival national champs in each roller style.[391] Using a baseball analogy, Giles pointed out that just as there is a National League and an American League, a single contest, the World Series, crowns one victor. His suggestion was to let the rival organizations run their competitions but wrap up the season with one true national championship competition. But the feud persisted due to what was described as the unwillingness of two prominent rink operators to come together and resolve the differences.[392]

Another overture of a merger among prominent stakeholders was reported in *Billboard* in May 1952 when Victor Brown of New Dreamland Arena, Newark, a staunch RSROA member, was among the celebrities at a Chicago hop contest at the Mineola Rink. Brown donated a thirty-inch gold challenge trophy that was seen by insiders as an overture to settle differences.[393] Earl Van Horn was an early RSROA member but then switched after a dispute with RSROA leaders on dance competition rules. He also had a hand in organizing URO and ARSA. Readers will recall that Van Horn passed in 1962, but it would be another decade before reunification was finalized. According to Turner and Zaidman, once the disputants had all passed, a merger finally moved forward in earnest.[394]

While the national organizations of RSROA and ARSA ran parallel tracks and quibbled over control of amateur competitions, the entire industry received numerous accolades for establishing the Roller Skating Institute of America (RSIA) in 1948.[395] The "Rinks and Skaters" editor called the action a ceasefire, with hopeful enthusiasm that RSIA would end the shots across the bow by the two prominent roller organizations. In a collective public relations campaign to promote the sport, RSIA set a goal to represent all of roller skating.[396] The RSIA was formed to market the sport of roller skating as a whole versus one particular style, amateur organization or rink association. All industry sectors were invited—skate manufacturers, floor purveyors and rink operators, including United Rink Operators. To demonstrate the spirt of cooperation, RSIA swept the nation with the "Roller Skating Song," recorded by Guy Lombardo. LP vinyl records, a new sound technology, were made and sent to disc jockeys across the nation.[397] Lombardo got RSIA's Good Skate Award as the LP reached radio, television, jukeboxes and record stores.

Mergers and music, while good things for roller skating, are not the true legacy of the golden age. A genuine legacy that is evident today are the family-centered values that rinks incorporated into operations and took many forms. Families nurtured eager youth to excel, and it was not uncommon then, and remains today, for professional skaters to coach aspiring athletes from an early age through the series of competition divisions. Perhaps an even greater family-centered characteristic of roller rinks is the way rink ownership became a family affair, with operations and ownership remaining in a family over many decades to ensure that the rink's value system was maintained by the offspring.

Consider, for example, the McCormacks, who owned and operated the Madison Gardens Rink. Harry McCormack started the rink in 1906. His son, Charles, took over when Harry passed in 1919. When Charles passed in 1939, Virginia, his wife, ran the rink until the riots of 1968 scorched an entire neighborhood. Even farther west, on the outskirts of Chicago, was the North Avenue Rollerway, operated for nearly six decades by Steve and Verlin Seipp and then Tom and Carol Seipp. The reader will recall how Carol Seipp closed the doors in 1998, resisting the times and calls for change, crystalizing the memories recalled from childhood. And this trend persists well into the twenty-first century. In continuous operation since 1988, Tom and Loretta Meegan-Curran and their daughter, Kelly Curran, an accomplished skate family, bought the Roller Ranch in Kissimmee. The family remodeled the rink with a tropical décor to fit into the hot and steamy Orlando neighborhood. Skate Reflections is operated as a family-centered and teaching roller rink. Due to its floor size and amenities, Skate Reflections regularly hosts international competitions.

In 1953, the "Rinks and Skaters" column in *Billboard* described the ascent of roller skating as a sport, parallel to the growth of the RSROA.[398] The basis of the sport's first-place ranking was admission figures, but the full story behind this growth is the transformation of its reputation. The roller skate industry's adopted slogan became "Recreation for the Whole Family." Roller skating opponents referred to roller rinks of the 1930s as juvenile delinquency centers, whereas by the 1950s, rinks had become neighborhood recreation centers that hosted Boy Scouts, Girl Scouts and church groups, with alcohol banned. Even ARSA insiders recognized the contribution and marketplace strength of RSROA. A Mineola rink newsletter acknowledged that ARSA took a back seat to the well-structured and efficiently run RSROA network that had prospered over the fifteen years since its founding.

As the golden age came to a close, Stan Musial, chairman of President Johnson's Physical Fitness Committee, applauded RSROA and its work to involve American youth in exercise "helpful to both the individual and the national well-being." Musial reported that 21 million skaters participated at five thousand rinks in the United States.[399] RSROA had skillfully recruited President Johnson's new chairman of the U.S. Physical Fitness Program to endorse roller skating as an integral part of physical fitness. It is this legacy that has made fitness and roller skating one and the same, first introduced by John B. Kelly of the Office of Civilian Defense, Physical Fitness Division in 1942.[400]

Skate So Others Can Walk: A National Project

The theme "Skate so others can walk" was a familiar one to skate enthusiasts during the golden age. Each year, rinks hosted March of Dimes fundraising campaigns across the nation, raising tens of thousands of dollars. It started during the war years, when the polio organization was called National

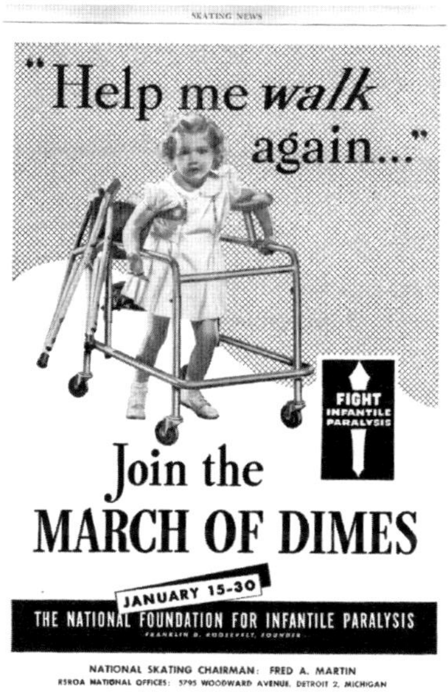

"Help me *walk* again…," RSROA National March of Dimes campaign. Note the reference to the National Foundation for Infantile Paralysis. Published in the January 1947 issue of *Skating News*. *Author's collection.*

Foundation for Infantile Paralysis (NFIP). For years, the NFIP was referred to as the "President's Own Charity."[401]

Local rinks across the country supported the national roller skate campaign and held local benefits for the NFIP under the sanction of RSROA. Benefit shows with top skaters and recently crowned champions from a variety of age groups made up the show, and patrons attended to see the new talent while admiring the pros from recent years. Chicago rinks such as Arcadia Rink, Armory Rink and Swank were among those local rinks that hosted an event for NFIP.[402] More than $13,310 was raised across the nation in 1944 by roller skating rinks.[403] In 1944, the first large-scale roller spectacle was held at Madison Square Garden on President Franklin Delano Roosevelt's birthday by RSROA to supplement its annual March of Dimes campaign. The first year, more than $10,000 was raised, while the second year's haul was more than $20,000. RSROA raised hundreds of thousands of dollars over the decades for NFIP.

Neighborhood rinks supported numerous charitable organizations where they were located, whether it was a local organization, USO or the American Red Cross.[404] Blood donation centers represented an enormous undertaking, and Americans felt a patriotic duty to donate a quart of blood regularly. They also hosted fundraisers for numerous local organizations and those rinks of the golden age. While there was universal support for servicemen, the USO and neighborhood skating rinks also were involved in other charitable efforts.

The notion of roller rinks serving as neighborhood recreation centers, supporting their local community, goes without saying. Rinks felt a duty. They exercised that duty, won local support and formed local emotional ties that lasted for decades. It is no wonder that tears were shed at each golden age rink's closing. What remains is the nostalgia of the best of times now gone.

PART VI
HOW IT ENDS

The caption in the 1904 Decatur newspaper read, "Old Craze Comes Back," adding, "Roller skating promises to be as popular as it was twenty years ago." Reported on October 11, 1904, the statement announced the opening events of a new Decatur roller rink.[405] In 1906, with the opening of another Chicago rink, the *Inter Ocean* newspaper complained that "after twenty years of exemption from the affliction the desire to roll is again taking possession of American adults…the mania has struck Chicago."[406]

Nearly forty years later, Charlie Tyler would write, "This current roller skating 'craze' is nothing new." Tyler wrote for Chicago's *Herald-American* in September 1941 and described the opening of Madison Gardens Rink's thirty-fifth season on the eve of World War II.[407] Tyler was referring to the first roller skate craze[408] at the turn of the twentieth century, when ball bearings revolutionized roller technology and roller skaters staged spectacle events and speed-skating marathons. Clamp-on skates were mass-produced for those with great aspirations. Tyler's reporting attempted to temper the rebirth of enthusiasm for the new roller styles that had become popular, including roller derby and dancing on rollers, suggesting that we had seen this before. Today, the acceptance for roller skating ebbs and flows as the sport persists. Roller skating continues to thrive as a part of pop culture in the form of recreation for leisure, dance and sport. Rollers, past and present, are diehards.

Old-school rollers who contributed to the growth of roller skating as relating to quality of life, the individual, the family and the community during

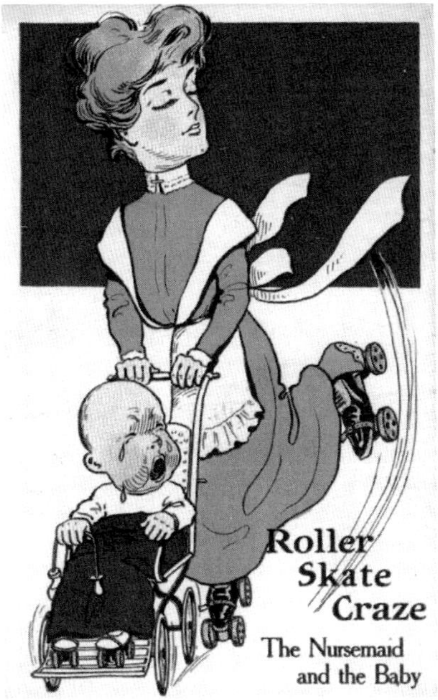

The roller skate craze, captured in a 1909 postcard, "The Nursemaid and the Baby." *Author's collection.*

the golden age remarked on its decline. Their focus was the waning status of traditional styles of roller skating such as those "graceful skating" contests hosted at Madison Gardens in the 1940s. For example, Rob's Roller World offered a description of the demise of roller skating from the perspective of one who witnessed over several decades the dwindling of traditional roller skate styles that once prospered during the golden age.[409] But the debate among roller skate association insiders persists on the pages of Facebook whether artistic and dance competitive skating can survive and what can be done to save it. Some stay true to the nostalgia of pre-1971 organizations, when roller skating was in its heyday.

However, the revival of roller derby in 2004[410] through the Women's Flat Track Derby Association (WFTDA)[411] suggests that the nine lives of roller skating have yet to end, while skate dancing has emerged in quite a different form. Writers from each generation called roller skating a fad, but given that it has entered its third century, the craze persists. Young people discover that it is fun and one of the best all-around fitness activities and adapt it to all styles of dance; it offers the cardio fitness benefits of running without the impact on joints, ligaments and tendons.

Today, as in the past, the fitness benefits of roller skating are touted for why children, families and adults should continue with the skating that dominated their youth. Golden age coaches recognized the benefits of cross-training for those roller competitors they coached, suggesting bicycling and running and the avoidance of tobacco, alcohol and late nights as improving an athlete's competitive edge. Those coaches understood that roller skating worked the major muscle groups such as the quadriceps (thigh), glutes or gluteal muscles, calf muscles, abdominals and arms and that other exercises that worked the same muscle groups would improve overall performance. Coaches understood that top performers required a balanced regimen of cardiovascular workout, endurance training and strength training for top performance. Roller skating as an activity also provides elements of both balance and coordination.

The American Heart Association claims that roller skating rivals running and bicycling as an effective form of aerobic exercise. Ironically, the calorie burn was known as far back as 1979, when a runner wrote to Dr. Bachman stating that he wanted to get into the "roller skating craze" and asking if it was okay to intersperse roller skating with running. Dr. Bachman wrote that "roller skating burns 600 calories an hour the equivalent of running a ten-minute mile."[412] The Roller Skating Association lists several scientific studies that support its health and fitness benefits. As an alternative to running, one hour (six miles per hour) of moderate roller skating burns 330 calories for a 143-pound person. If that individual skates at ten miles per hour, he or she will burn 600 calories an hour—pretty impactful. Studies also reveal that roller skating, compared to running, results in 50 percent less impact shock to joints.[413] Skate for twenty-five minutes three times a week and a skater burns 750 additional calories per week.[414] Rinks report an upswing in attendance for "skate" fitness classes, which have become quite popular with seniors who seek low-impact exercise alternatives.

Roller Skating and Pop Culture

Hollywood movies depict snapshots of American life, and roller skate movies deliver intriguing insights into an era's view of the sport while documenting its evolution. Mel Seltzer's live extravaganzas of Skating Vanities from 1942 to 1953 offered audiences roller events, while movies that feature roller derby and disco skate dancing depict the evolution of roller skating styles of dance that departed dramatically from mainstream 1940s skate dancing. Even YouTube, as a mass medium, offers viewers a chance to pick up the latest styles, whether it is a neighborhood rink or the urban centers of America.

Movie stars from as far back as the silent movies to the talkies and today's high-definition features have donned roller skates to make their mark. The great dancer Gene Kelly used roller skates in a dance routine with none other than Marilyn Monroe. Of course there was Mickey Rooney in *The Fireball*, also skating with Marilyn Monroe. But it was the silent movie *An Awful Skate* that brought roller skating to the masses when hobo Ben Turpin careened down the streets of Chicago's Old Town in 1907. Later, Charlie

Chaplin as a clumsy waiter used *The Rink* (1916) to show the grace of roller skating to win a young girl over.[415] In 1944, *Pin Up Girl* with Betty Grable, a model for soldiers, also featured the blond roller skate sensation Gloria Nord, who became the boys' newest idol with a scene that depicted the Skating Vanities and the spectacle that roller skating had become. High energy and choreographed skating events with glitz and thrill glamorized rollers in the 1944 movie.

By 1950, the mass production of televisions had created tremendous exposure to sporting events. The theatrics of roller derby were an immediate sensation. Roller derby movies followed, with Mickey Rooney in 1950 with *The Fireball* and 1972's *Kansas City Bomber* with Raquel Welch. The 2009 release of *Whip It* introduced the twenty-first century to the rollergirls' flat-rink style of derby, departing from the traditional banked track.

Ballroom-style dance routines that golden age skaters danced to in the 1940s changed to become the roller disco skating craze in the 1970s. Disco skating had faded by the turn of the twenty-first century, but *Roller Boogie* with Linda Blair and *Skatetown, U.S.A.* with Patrick "Ace" Swayze, both in 1979, captured the essence of roller boogie and disco music, following the forever popular movie *Saturday Night Fever* in 1977. In 2005, *Roll Bounce* reminded us of the roller disco era and depicted a skate dance style that gave way to jam skating. Ironically, rink managers made great efforts in the 1940s to reduce the fog of rinks attributed to the use of floor rosin. However, the disco era brought back the fog machines, which offered skaters steamy but exhilarating experiences, with traffic lights and rotating mirrored balls that contributed to a vibrant urban subculture of roller dancing, while mainstream roller skating continued its long, steady decline.[416]

To read the works of twenty-first-century writers, one would get the impression that roller skating achieved mainstream status and became a facet of pop culture with roller disco in the late 1970s.[417] However, the history of the golden age reveals that roller skating became mainstream in the early 1940s, prior to the idea of "pop culture" even arising. Consider, for example, the extent to which the government incorporated roller skate images during World War II and called on roller skating in its recreational and "save gas" campaigns. U.S. government posters featured roller skate images in many different forms: "Jenny on the Job," the 1941 marching soldiers cartoon or the government's advocacy for roller skating on the job. The fact that roller skating impregnated the fortress of the war industry as a war resource remains a testament to the impact roller skating had as a mainstream sport long before the arrival of pop culture.

Hollywood's Twentieth Century Fox sent out 2 million copies of Grable's pin-up posters to servicemen around the world, making her the number one pin-up girl of World War II GIs.[418] The studio's objective was to highlight Grable's new 1942 movie, *Pin Up Girl*, which had not only incorporated a new technology, Technicolor, but also embedded subtle but scripted war messages outlined by OWI. The movie was flush with scenes that were overtures to the war and its appeal to servicemen, but it was equally effective in giving a promotional overture to the acceptability of roller skating, with Gloria Nord as a star, incorporating a Skating Vanities scene.

Rink promoters of the golden age exploited all sorts of media opportunities to generate publicity for roller skating, including those the U.S. government offered during the war years. Music was described as fundamental to roller skating's popularity, whether the nostalgic Wurlitzers or the new technologies of LP recordings. All of these were accompanied by emerging multimedia formats that included talkies (movies), television, glitzy spectator events and even traditional print formats such as newspapers and magazines. The extent to which government promotional efforts, colored by propaganda campaigns, to foster recreation, especially roller skating, vaulted it to the forefront of participatory sports is a topic worthy of further study. The government's impact was significant, as it endorsed roller skating, earmarked funds, built rinks, linked the sport to the physical fitness movement and wrote federal policy that named it a war resource. Roller skating as pop culture lives with us today, but it was established in the golden age.

Roller Rhythms

There persists an irony within this brief snapshot of roller skate history, coupled to dance ballrooms when dance halls openly solicited African American jazz bands to entertain white audiences because patrons sought out unique dance styles. Those routines were typically not on display at all-white ballrooms. Dance sequences became roller dance routines, and the jitterbug is one example that became a hit roller dance at most rinks in the 1940s. This mix of subcultures with sport, recreation and dance is central to roller skating today.

Nowadays, rink visitors will note a diversification of skate dancing in major urban areas that represents unique rhythm-style skate cultures.[419] There is shuffle skating, bounce skating, jamming, R&B skating, funk skating, freestyle and rock. In Chicago, a new corps of skaters described themselves as "JB skaters," followers of James Brown's songs and a style reminiscent of rhythm-and-blues. This style emerged during the 1970s, what some have described as the height of the roller revolution, as well as when Chicago became known as a roller skating city.[420] The JB style of roller skating, which originated in Chicago, consisted of grooves and bounces, fancy footwork and standing dance routines borrowed from the Godfather of Soul himself and dating back to the 1970s.[421] That bounce is a throwback to a style that differentiated Madison Gardens skaters from those of Chicago rinks. Where did Madison Gardens pick up on these distinctive steps? Skate dance historians have yet to trace the origins of such styles. Chicagoland skaters created this unique style of skate dancing, and various elements have since been incorporated into R&B, hip hop, gymnastics and break dancing.

Another style is called roller dance, a dance style that is like line dancing on wheels and which emerged from the West Coast. Groups of skaters roll dance to a set sequence of steps in a series of choreographed movements not unlike what has become popular with line dances. Skaters who know the moves jump up, roll in and skate dance until their legs give out. In roller dance, the skaters remain in about a three-square-foot circle, but if you are looking for floor movement, trains have become another technique—a group rhythm movement but with groups of three to a dozen or more. Trains are composed of individual skaters who hook up on the rink floor and use the entire floor real estate to move the train around the rink perimeter.

Rhythm skating is believed to have begun as early as World War II, with its origins in the Detroit area. Arcadia and Arena Gardens of Detroit were hubs for competitive skating that included artistic, dance and speed. But with no outlet for black skaters, the Forest Club in Paradise Valley[422] became the nucleus for the black expression of dance on skates.[423] A subculture of skating emerged that had become the basis for "bebop" skating by the late 1950s and 1960s. A unique "soul skate" style emerged along the same timeline as the sounds of Motown and southeastern Michigan's "Soul Nights" became weekly events. Detroit is the home of the Motown sound, and the skate dance style that emerged is unique to Detroit, not unlike the JB style that grew up in Chicago. In summarizing the decline in organ-driven rink skating furthered by the rock-and-roll genre, Romy Poletti suggested that it was those black rinks where the next generation's musical preferences were incubating and surged for roller disco:[424]

African American roller skating rinks retrieved roller skating from complete culture obsolescence because the music that was found at these rinks "worked" with the roller rink music paradigm. With R&B, and then eventually disco, roller skating and its rinks would see another revival in mainstream culture in the late 1970s.

The persistence of a black subculture in roller skating, associated with the likes of Paradise Valley and the Savoy's Jimmy Davis, thrives in the twenty-first century, arguably serving as a legacy of the golden age despite the segregated actions of its whites-only rinks. Compare *Roller Boogie* in 1979 at the height of roller disco to *Roll Bounce* in 2005. It's roller disco, with a music genre that is quite similar. The only difference is white rollers in 1979 versus black rollers in 2005. Perhaps in 1979, Hollywood and its audiences were not quite ready for all-black roller skaters. Today, it's all about roller skating. How many modern-day roller rinks host JB and rhythm skate clubs with skaters of all races? The best are those who have skated since their youth. The Port City Rollerz of Wilmington is one example, where both Scooter's and Jelly Beans host the R&B mix of skaters who do it for the joy of recreational skate dancing. And when they perform, the young hang around, eager to pick up that old style that harkens back to not only the disco era but the golden age as well.

In 1946, the pleasure of roller skating was described by a "Rinks and Skaters" writer in *Billboard*: "Everything violent, angular or stiff is to be avoided. There should be no strong effort and the impression should be given that the figures are executed with ease and poise."[425] The technical aspects of skating that were debated in the 1940s pitted skate edges versus flats and the flexible skate versus stiff, as well as wobble versus true balance.[426] Pros and serious skaters preferred flexible skates, while beginners performed better on nonflexible skates. By the late 1940s, rink promoters could see that skate technology was ready to launch the sport to the masses, especially with the advent of television.

That guidance persists today. Most jam skaters keep the boots laced lightly to increase flexibility beyond the envelope pushed in the 1940s. That adds another technical option given the improvement in skate technology. Robert Ware of Chicago Skates reported that adults avoided skating due to three factors: physical stamina, lack of idle time and the capacity for play that belonged to teenagers. Today's adults skate for play. They recognize that health and fitness are wasted on youth and that stamina and play are for those who pursue it.

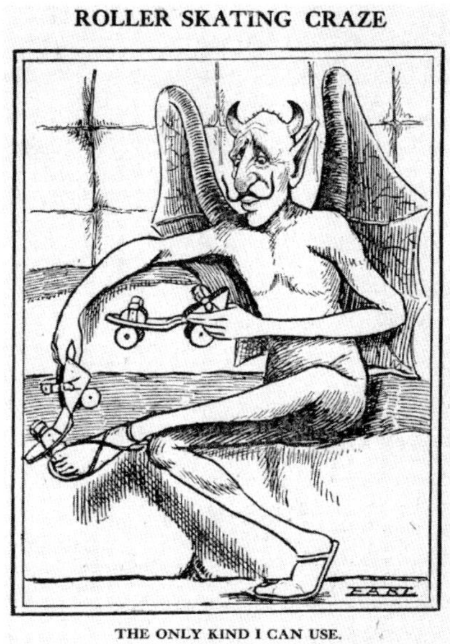

The roller skate craze, captured in a 1909 postcard, "Devil with Clamp-on Skates." *Author's collection.*

Not all skate styles are equal, and individuals whose passion drives them to excel in a particular skate style learn this as they advance from local to state and into national competitions. Perhaps this is driven by spectator preferences and the general public at large. Gloria Nord thought that roller derby would ruin the sport and was insistent that the name Roller Follies not be used to describe what would become Skating Vanities. Her strong view was that Skating Vanities should not be confused with roller derby and its programmed antics. Choreography of artistic movements was much more palatable to her.

Speed skating has history on its side, and much has been written about this particular roller style, even though it did not gain the stature of artistic and figure skating established in the national competitions.[427] One such *Skate* article as late as 1966 continued to argue the merits of speed skating, contrasting it to artistic skating: "'Victory in artistic skating is something the judges sometimes give you but in speed skating you win yourself!' That's the code of the speed skater—speed skating is the most demanding of all roller skating competition because it is a constant battle for survival."[428]

Over the decades, controversy persistently simmered whether the new ironmen of speed skating could beat the fifty-year-old marathon record of Fred Martin set in the early 1900s.[429] One old-timer speed skater, Al Kish, expressed doubt that the men of the 1960s could do it.[430]

The match was set for a marathon showdown at the 1965 New York World's Fair. The modern ironmen accepted the challenge to beat the record of one hour, eighteen minutes and forty-five seconds for a 26-mile, 385-yard marathon set by Fred A. Martin in 1915. The speed event of the century was canceled, and to date, evidence does not exist it took place. Today, speed skating continues to be a sanctioned discipline of the Roller Skating Association along with figure (artistic), including dance. Ironically, speed skating (inline) remains the sole roller skate style to become a demonstration

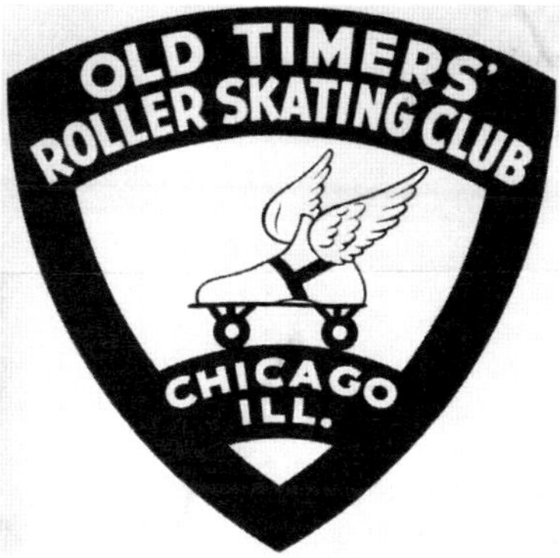

Old Timers' Roller Skating Club of Chicago. *Author's collection.*

sport at the Olympics. But the crowds of today, along with competitors at national events, reflect the diminished participation in roller skate competition.

How does roller skating end? Roller skating has remained resilient over three centuries, fueled by evolving new technologies and adaptations to the musical whims of succeeding generations, among other cultural shifts that create nostalgia for each generation. The physical biomechanics of roller skating connect with the human center in a way quite unlike any other sport. It is perfected by the professional, enjoyed by the masses and modified by eccentrics to become one of among the dozens of extreme sports humans engage in on a daily basis.

Whether the roller craze is back is anyone's guess. Rink operators report that interest has fallen off, and rollers continue to compete with alternative forms of recreation and technologies that keep youngsters tapped into the immediate gratification of their social media scenes. But roller skating demonstrates an ability to survive generational adaption to a recreational activity that delivered (and still delivers) elation to skaters of all ages. Roller skating as a sport adapted to generational changes to reinvent itself and acquire a following among the young. The exhilaration of roller skating never left those old-time roller skaters, whose passion compels them to seek out one more adrenaline rush around an old wooden hardwood maple floor, regardless of skate style. Just add fog.

CONCLUSION

The origins of the golden age were rooted in a vision that roller skate rinks should host wholesome social recreation for the adult classic skater yet be trendy enough for youthful jitterbug skaters. Skate sessions were defined as being for adults only, with children not permitted after certain hours on certain evenings. Turner wrote sixty years later that "roller skating has changed from traditional adult entertainment to one exclusively as children's recreation."[431]

Two decades have passed since that was written. Unsurprisingly, a tour of rinks around the country reveals a business model shift for roller rinks whereby they have become a depot intended for children's play, with a skate floor captured among a collage of games, laser tag and arcade fantasies. Promoted as amusement, recreation and nostalgia, rinks of this model showcase a playground but remain profitable for rink owners. The rink as an adult recreation venue has been sidelined, with limited, if any, formalized programs to incentivize adult patrons to improve skate ability or use the rink as a main recreational source.

But there also persists pockets of old-school roller rinks, whether Charlotte, Portland, Orlando, the fringes of Chicago or along the eastern seacoast. Most of them are teaching rinks, meaning they coach the artistic forms of roller skating and ready young people for a campaign of amateur competition. Call them legacy rinks if you wish, but these rinks subscribe to the legacies established in the golden age of family appropriateness, instruction in the classic styles of roller skating and hosting competitions. You may very well find an old Hammond organ playing to adult-only skate sessions with quad-skate shuffle skating. Those same rinks probably host R&Bs sessions as well.

While roller skating is not the mainstream recreational pursuit it was during the golden age, the passion for this form of social recreation remains mainstream among those who continue their weekly pilgrimage to the neighborhood rink. Interestingly enough, rink managers report that senior fitness classes have become popular, as those who roller skated in their youth realize its value as a low-impact form of exercise.[432] Since the merger years of ARSA and RSROA, the number of competition classes has increased, and the age range among those who compete has stretched well into their sixties! Specific competition classes have been added for adult competitors, such as master and esquire. Back in the day, the senior class/division was eighteen years and older. Usually by the age of thirty, roller athletes retired from competition. Not true today! The longevity of boomers has exceeded both their parents and their grandparents, and many remain active well into those senior years.

Contemporary writers report that roller disco was a boom period for roller skating, as they contrast skating today with the good times of three decades ago. The reality is that the disco era was no more than a blip on roller skating's bear market, begun in the vestiges of the golden age. Roller skating continues in a bear market to this day. Yet there perseveres pockets of optimism around the country for adult-related, recreational roller skating. Adult skate sessions target jam skaters and JB skaters, as well as those who prefer a graceful skating style along with a Jersey Bounce shuffle skate. The remnant of roller disco, it could be argued, is its music genre that continues to find space on a rink's playlist. But the Chicago rink rat story described the origins of roller disco back to black roller skate rinks, where jazz bands played to R&B skate dancers.

The first roller skating boom is marked by the 1880–1910 years, with achievements that reign to this day. Skate technology improved dramatically with Plimpton's four-wheel steerable truck assembly, Richardson's introduction of ball bearings and skates that allowed the likes of vaudeville trick skaters to use skate edges for spills and thrills. World War I took the wind out of roller skating's popularity, as it competed with automobiles, the dance craze and movies. The talkies had yet to arrive, but today's skaters still use those edges for trick moves at rink center.

Not unlike rinks in the 1900s that battled for the attention of adults and youth, today's roller skating rinks have their competition. Rinks today compete with extreme sports, of which there at least fifty; cellphone technologies that power all sorts of social media models; and helicopter parents who fly their kids to sports camps and game fields to fulfill their recreational needs. But the rinks of the golden age had their opposition as well—not only within the industry among ARSA, RSROA and URO but also in the dust-up that became World War II and its related war industries, all of which drained the skate industry of manpower, raw materials and infrastructure supplies needed for a growth industry. It overcame these challenges with organization, leadership and a promotional instinct that leveraged opportunities as they came along.

A Reuters article as recent as 2015 announced that roller skating had become a threatened species, with rinks closing throughout the nation.[433] Its author made the point that roller skating had also seen a skating renaissance of urban-style skate dancing over the past fifteen years, brought about by social media as like-minded rinks connect online. But is this really new? Rinks networked during the golden age and staged spectacular competitions using telephone landlines. Think of what they would have accomplished today with social media and online media forums.

The question remains: Is roller skating in a boom period that rivals that of the golden age as it closes the second decade of the twenty-first century? History suggests that the next boom period in roller skating will not be realized until the roller skate industry and its rinks establish formalized adult-related programs that attract adults back to the rinks as their main recreational resource,[434] whether as fitness classes, amateur-related coaching, JB/jam skates or those graceful skating sessions. The recreation-minded adult of today is not unlike those of a century earlier. Adults seek what adults did in the 1930s: a rink environment that hosts wholesome roller skate recreation.

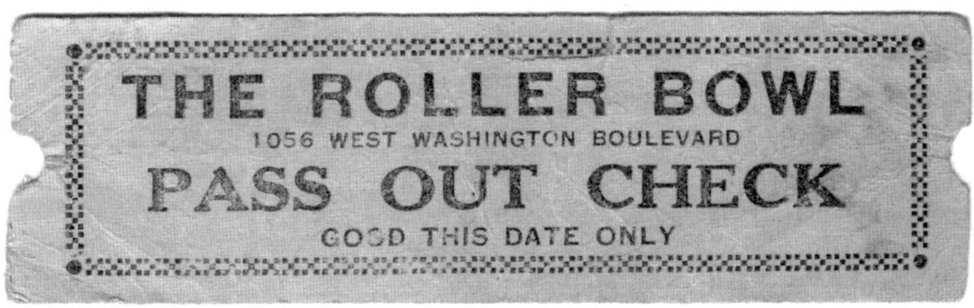

Roller Bowl admission ticket, circa 1940s. *Author's collection.*

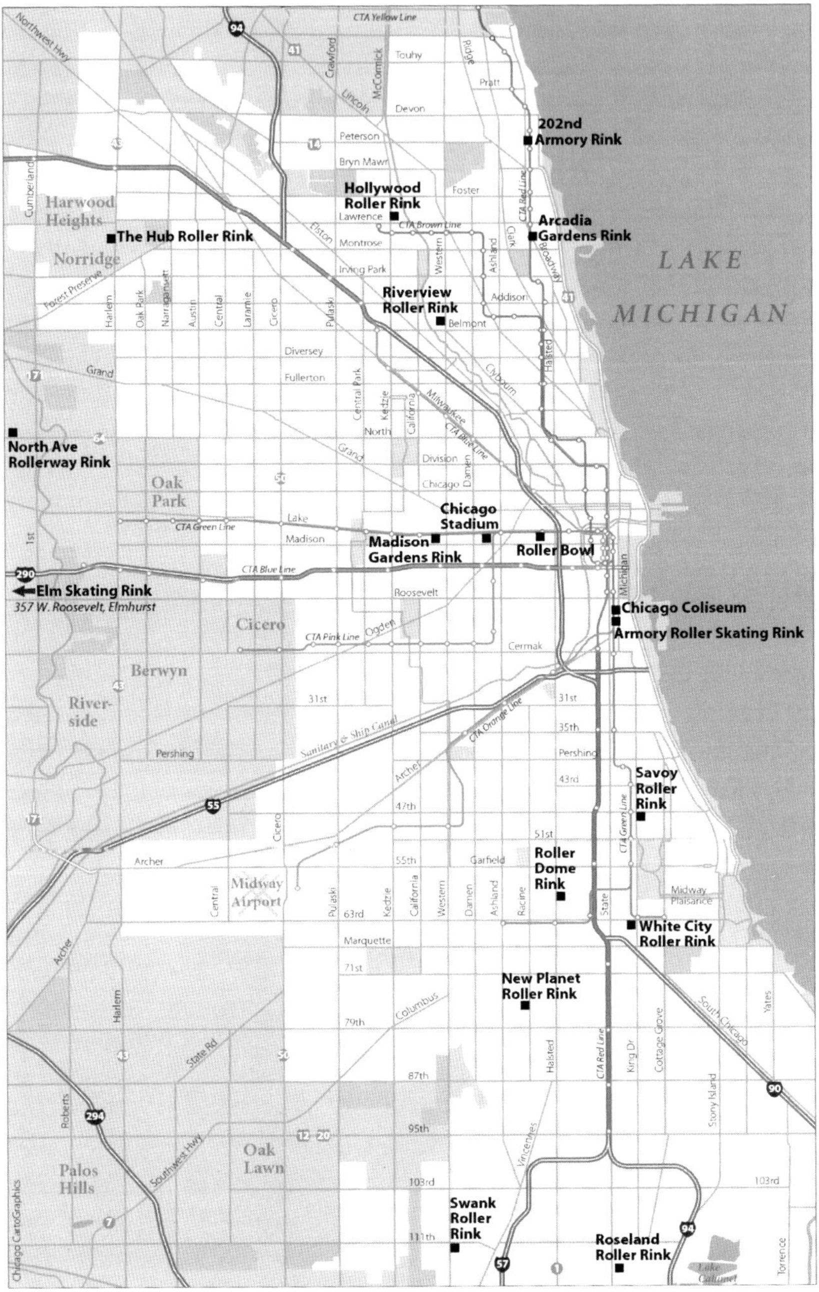

LAKE MICHIGAN
202nd Armory Rink
Hollywood Roller Rink
Arcadia Gardens Rink
The Hub Roller Rink
Riverview Roller Rink
North Ave Rollerway Rink
Chicago Stadium
Madison Gardens Rink
Roller Bowl
Elm Skating Rink
357 W. Roosevelt, Elmhurst
Chicago Coliseum
Armory Roller Skating Rink
Savoy Roller Rink
Roller Dome Rink
White City Roller Rink
New Planet Roller Rink
Swank Roller Rink
Roseland Roller Rink
Harwood Heights
Norridge
Oak Park
Cicero
Berwyn
River-side
Midway Airport
Oak Lawn
Palos Hills
Lake Calumet
CTA Yellow Line
CTA Red Line
CTA Brown Line
CTA Blue Line
CTA Green Line
CTA Pink Line
CTA Orange Line
Sanitary & Ship Canal
Northwest Hwy
Touhy
Pratt
Devon
Peterson
Bryn Mawr
Foster
Lawrence
Montrose
Irving Park
Addison
Belmont
Diversey
Fullerton
North
Division
Chicago
Lake
Madison
Roosevelt
Cermak
31st
35th
Pershing
43rd
47th
51st
55th
Garfield
63rd
Marquette
71st
79th
87th
95th
103rd
111th
Chicago CartoGraphics

APPENDIX A

MAP OF CHICAGO ROLLER RINKS, 1937–1959

This map locates Chicago rinks in operation from 1937 to 1959 and their relationship to both interstates and Chicago Transit Authority (CTA) rail lines in operation. Construction for Chicago-area interstates would not have begun until after 1953, and so those depicted illustrate the position of roller rinks of the period in relation to interstates as they exist today. Currently, the CTA operates the nation's second-largest public transportation system and includes the city of Chicago and the thirty-five surrounding suburbs.

The CTA rail lines are labeled on the map and approximate those rail lines in operation during the golden age. The map displays the accessibility of rinks to public transportation, both trains and buses. CTA bus routes provided the final link to rink destinations as rink rats traversed the city.

Chicago Transit Authority Rail "L" System (the color reference coincides with CTA's published color coding and map depiction):

CTA Blue Line: *Between O'Hare Airport, Downtown and Forest Park*
CTA Brown Line: *Between Kimball and Downtown*
CTA Green Line: *Between Harlem/Lake, Downtown and 63rd Street Terminals*
CTA Orange Line: *Between Midway Airport and Downtown*
CTA Pink Line: *Between 54th/Cermak and Downtown*
CTA Red Line: *Between Howard, Downtown and 95th/Dan Ryan*
CTA Yellow Line: *Between Dempster-Skokie and Howard*

APPENDIX B

CHICAGO ROLLER RINKS

SKATE FLOOR DIMENSIONS

Roller Rink	Location	Rink Floor Size (square feet)	Chicago Sides
Arcadia Gardens Rink	4444 North Broadway	15,000 est.	North Side
Armory Roller Skating Rink	1566 South Michigan	34,500	Near South Side
Chicago Stadium	1800 West Madison Street	?	West Side
Coliseum Roller Rink	1513 South Wabash Avenue	?	Near South Side
Elm Skating Rink	357 West Roosevelt	20,000	Far West Side
Hollywood Rink	4825 North Kedzie Avenue	8,000 est.	Far North Side
The Hub Roller Rink	4510 North Harlem	26,125	Far Northwest
Madison Gardens Rink	2560 West Madison Street	11,400	West Side
New Planet Roller Rink	7534 South Racine Avenue	21,000	South Side
North Avenue Rollerway	8490 West North Avenue	24,000	Far West Side

Appendix B

Roller Rink	Location	Rink Floor Size (square feet)	Chicago Sides
Riverview Roller Rink	Belmont and Western Avenue	30,000 est.	North Side
Roller Bowl	1058 West Washington Street	24,000	Near West Side
Roller Dome Rink	5955 South Halsted	10,000	South Side
Roseland Roller Rink	23 East 115th Street	8,000 est.	Far South Side
Savoy Roller Rink	4733 South Parkway	12,500	South Side
Swank Roller Skating Rink	2345 West 111th Street	8,100	Far South Side
202nd Armory Rink	5917 North Broadway	34,500	Far North Side
White City Roller Rink	63rd Street and South Parkway	33,000 est.	South Side

APPENDIX C

A ROLLER RINK POEM

The roller skate poem "The Roller Rink" was written by Laverne Larson and published in a 1953 South Side newspaper.[435]

Fairyland of lights and music
A sport for young and old,
You'll find your feet have tiny wings
As pleasant hours unfold.

Waltzes, fox-trot, conga
Learn to do each one,
Dancing on your roller skates
Can really be good fun.

Smiling Friendly faces
Greet you every night,
Laughter chimes like silver bells
And hearts know pure delight.

The roller rink is wonderful
And you will find it's true,
Golden carefree hours
Are waiting there for you.

So join the happy crowd
At the roller rink real soon,
For an evening packed with fun
Played to a jolly tune.

NOTES

Part I

1. *Billboard*, "Freeman Hits at Differences," May 22, 1943, 37, 47. At the May 15, 1943 national convention of RSROA, President Freeman reported 4,000 rinks with an average of 5 million skaters participating per week. In 2014, estimates put the number of rinks at 1,200, down from a high of between 1,600 and 2,000 in the 1980s. See *Wall Street Journal*, "New Rinks Putting a Different Spin on Roller Skating in New York City," July 11, 2014, http://www.wsj.com/articles/new-rinks-putting-a-different-spin-on-roller-skating-in-new-york-city-1405126437.
2. *Billboard*, "Middlewest Ops Probe Problems," April 7, 1951, 47. By the early 1950s, the rink operator of Hoosierland Roller Rink, Roy H. Seibert, stated that there were nearly five thousand rinks in the United States.
3. Earl Van Horn, "Personal Contact in Rink Management," *Billboard*, August 30, 1941, 67, http://www.americanradiohistory.com/Archive-Billboard/40s/1941/BB-1941-08-30.pdf. Earl Van Horn described how the lessons learned from his Mineola experience changed from past perceptions (1934) to what roller skating had become as an acceptable form of social recreation by 1941.
4. *Billboard*, "Wartime Competish Defended by URO and ARSA Officials," September 30, 1944, 40.
5. *Skating News*, "Grantland Rice Dies," Championship Issue, 1954, 10. Grantland Rice, sports columnist and "Dean of Sportswriters," is credited by RSROA as the first columnist to have recognized roller skating as

the top participation sport in America. His column "The Sportlight" appeared in more than one hundred newspapers.

6. Brooks, *Skate Crazy*, 18–20. Brooks credits RSROA's formation in 1937 as the onset of the golden age. The organization's emphasis on elegance and etiquette at rinks initiated the return of wholesome, classic skaters back to roller skating's fold.
7. *Billboard*, "Rinks and Skaters," October 24, 1942, 46. The "Rinks and Skaters" column named Gloria Nord as a Chicago girl.
8. Ibid., "Gloria Nord Is Acclaimed by Roller Fans in Chicago," October 2, 1943, 39. Gloria Nordskog, discovered by Sid Grauman in 1937 at the Hollywood Roller Bowl, California, was offered a job and went pro at the age of fifteen. Soon afterward, Nordskog appeared as Gloria Nord, her show business name.
9. Cairo-Purling Roller Rink, "And Then What Happened?," http://www.cairopurlingrollerrink.com/now.html. This New York rink, in operation since 1933, offers perspective of the rink's experience during the golden age.
10. *Billboard*, "Mass-Produce Meal Tickets to Skate Thru a Depression," August 9, 1947, 88.
11. Ibid., "Johnny-Come-Lately to Blades Compares Icers vs. Rolleries," February 1, 1947, 37.
12. *Chicago Daily Tribune*, "Roller Skating Vanities to Open in Arena Tonight," September 9, 1942, 27.
13. Edward Prell, "Gloria Takes Tumble; Roller Vanities' Success Is Assured," *Chicago Daily Tribune*, September 15, 1943, 25.
14. *Billboard*, "Roller Skate Review, Skating Vanities," September 25, 1943, 4.
15. Harry Grayson, "Gloria Nord, Star on Wheels Puts Roller-Skating in Movies," *Blytheville Courier News*, June 16, 1943, 8.
16. *Billboard*, "Henie After Record in Chicago Icery," January 8, 1944, 4.
17. Ibid., "'Skating Vanities' Gets Cincy Raves; Off Slowly but Ups," January 8, 1944, 4.
18. Ibid., "'Ice Follies' Hits Record 400G in Hub," March 4, 1944, 4.
19. Ibid., "Sonja Henie Skates Ice to Gold Again as Hollywood Revue Hits New Grosses," January 29, 1944, 4.
20. Ibid., "Skating Program Set by OCD Seen as Business Hypo," February 28, 1942, 44.
21. Ibid., "Ads Cite Morale Value of Rollers," March 20, 1943, 44.
22. Ibid., "Higher Levels Due for Sport," December 2, 1944, 55.

23. Ibid., "Clevelanders Rush to Rinks' Defense vs. Pick-up Charges," September 19, 1942, 45.
24. *Skating News*, "The Bride Wore Skates," June 1952, 21.
25. *Billboard*, "RSIA Sets Up Shop in Chicago: Plans Formed, Execs Named," October 16, 1948, 79.
26. Ibid., "530 Kids Ready for RSROA American Championships in D.C.," July 9, 1949, 112.
27. Ibid., "Washington Paper Plugs Roller Art as No. 1 Pastime," May 15, 1948, 84.
28. *Skating News*, "Roller Derby Clicks B'way," January 1949, 4.
29 Bill Mauldin, first published in the *Oklahoma City Times*, July 14, 1941.
30. The War Production Board was an emergency committee set up to identify and secure sources of raw materials to support the war effort. Volunteers staffed the WPB and were called "dollar-a-year men."
31. *Billboard*, "Prexy Brown Nixes RSROA Conclave," February 17, 1945, 46.
32. Ibid., "Biz Off a Third in Birmingham," April 7, 1945, 46.
33. Ibid., "Robert Ware, Sr.," May 5, 1945, 48.
34. Ibid., "Truman, Congress Tax Experts Mull End-of-Emergency Date," September 29, 1945, 3.
35. Ibid., "Wheels' Wartime Value Is Officially Okayed in Norfolk," January 6, 1945, 45.
36. Ibid., "Rebuild Burned Rollerdrome," January 6, 1945, 45.
37. *Skate*, "Roller Skating Will Prosper without Olympic Participation," November 1959, 8.
38. Poletti, "Residual Culture of Roller Rinks," 39.
39. Mary K. Miller, "It's a Wurlitzer: The Giant of the Musical Instrument Collection Makes Tunes Rootin' Tootin' or Romantic," *Smithsonian Magazine*, April 2002.
40. Wolcott, *Race, Riots and Roller Coasters*, 56.
41. Smith, "Congress of Racial Equality (CORE)."
42. Jimenez, "To the Core," 4.
43. Juanita Williams, "My First Month with the Freeman Plan," 10. Williams of Arcadia describes learning advanced skate techniques following the Freeman Plan, taking a course hosted at the Roller Bowl. She was one of thirty-two who graduated the four weeks of lessons; one hundred started the class.
44. Grisham, "Silent Movie Capital."
45. Charles Bartlett, "Roller Derby Returns—It's the Thriving Babe of Sport," *Chicago Daily Tribune*, November 3, 1937, 23, http://archives.

chicagotribune.com/1937/11/03/page/23/article/all-stars-win-morenz-hocky-game-6-to-5.

46. Cecilia Rasmussen, "The Man Who Got Roller Derby Rolling Along," *Los Angeles Times*, February 21, 1999, http://articles.latimes.com/1999/feb/21/local/me-10190.
47. Fred A. Martin, "The Birth of an Idea," *Skating News*, March 1950, 10.
48. National Roller Derby League, "First Annual Roller Derby Year Book—1951," 37–39. This shows members of the 1951 Chicago Westerners roller derby team. Also, Seltzer presents a history of roller derby since its 1935 inception.
49. Pickard, *Titans and Heroes*, 91–93.
50. *Skating News*, "Who Said 'No Speed Skating'?," June/July/August 1946, 10.
51. *Billboard*, "Future of Speed Skating," July 31, 1943, 60.
52. Edward Smith, *Skating Review*, July 1941, 3. Nord's last name was shortened by either her promotion team or others with vested interest.
53. *Skating Review*, "Gloria Nordskog Rehearses at Arcadia Gardens, Chicago," June 1941, 6.
54. According to Team USA (U.S. Olympic Foundation), race records are frozen from 1976, the last year race distances were measured in miles and yards. Initial speed events were measured in yards with twelve to fourteen laps per mile. In 1977, roller skating adopted the metric kilometer by United States roller skate associations.
55. *Inter Ocean*, "Roller Skating Race League," March 21, 1904, 4, https://www.newspapers.com/image/34583014/?terms=Armory%2BRoller%2BSkating%2BRink%2Bin%2Bchicago.
56. *Skating News*, "What, No Speed Skating? Why?," May 1946, 7.
57. *Skating Review*, "Better Skating in Vanities," September/October 1942, 6.
58. Kermit Holt, "Birds on Wing; Kids on Wheels; Sure, It's Spring," *Chicago Daily Tribune*, April 10, 1952, part 4, 6, http://archives.chicagotribune.com/1952/04/10/page/66/article/birds-on-wing-kids-on-wheels-sure-its-spring.
59. The original Chicago Roller Skate Company was located at Madison and Chicago River.
60. F.B. Bell, "50 Golden Years in Roller Skating: Chicago Skate Co. Reaches Half-Century Mark," *Skating News*, March 1955, 6.
61. *Daily Herald*, "Roller Skate Tourney Aug. 3 at New Stadium," June 28, 1929, 6.
62. *Billboard*, "Four-Legged Skater Puts on Show," July 12, 1952, 45.
63. Ibid., "New Competish for National Skating Meets," May 31, 1952, 46.

Part II

64. Ibid., "Bacon Spending 85G on Jackson Rink, Penthouse," September 22, 1945, 69.
65. *Skating News*, "The Rink that 'Laury' Built," June 1952, 11.
66. *Skate*, "Current Amateur Registration Leaders," January 1963, 8.
67. Aspheldium mastic was a building material used for paving, roofing and flooring. Today, mastic asphalt is the preferred material due to its waterproofing characteristics.
68. *Billboard*, "How to Eliminate that Floor Noise," June 22, 1945, 86.
69. Ibid., "More About Plastic Flooring; Perry Giles Praises It Highly," July 20, 1946, 85.
70. Ibid., "180 Skaters View for Top Slots in RSROA Northeastern Regional Meet," May 24, 1947, 78.
71. Ibid., "A Straight Line and a Curve or Scooting Versus Skating," September 9, 1944, 44.
72. Ibid., "Man of Many Talents Needed to Fill Role of Good Manager," December 21, 1946, 68.
73. *Skating News*, "What About Rink Music," June 1950, 12.
74. *Billboard*, "Feet-on-Desk Passe, Says Cap Sefferino," October 25, 1947, 74.
75. Ibid., "America on Wheels Notes," June 20, 1942, 43.
76. Ibid., "'Skating Vanities' Fair in Garden Bow; New York's First Roller Show," June 13, 1942, 4.
77. Ibid., "'Roller Vanities' to Play Chi Arena," August 8, 1942, 4.
78. Ibid., "Garden Gets 2nd 'Vanities' Roller Show," June 10, 1944, 3.
79. Sengstock, *That Toddlin' Town*, 77.
80. Ibid., 68. The Merry Gardens Ballroom (3136 North Sheffield Avenue) on the North Side was considered intimate with its mid-sized 14,535 square feet.
81. Trianon was pronounced "*tree*-a-non."
82. *Chicago Daily Tribune*, "What Chicago Thinks of Trianon," December 12, 1922, 17.
83. Melanie Zeck, "Dancing in Chicago: The Trianon," *CBMR Digest* (Spring 2014), http://www.colum.edu/cbmr/digest/2014/spring/trianon.php#fn1.
84. Sengstock, *That Toddlin' Town*, 68.
85. Ibid., 56.
86. Ibid., 79.

87. Sengstock estimates the floor size of Arcadia at 15,000 square feet (See Appendix B). Rink floors were constructed with some standardization of dimensions and size—for example, either a 185- by 80-foot surface (14,800 square feet), 180- by 85-foot (15,300 square feet) or 185- by 85-foot surface (15,725 square feet). Still today, measurements of rink floors are standardized as they were in the early 1900s. Appendix B compares floor size for rinks of the 1940s and 1950s.
88. *Skating News*, "What Is a Small Rink?," January 1949, 8.
89. Fran Zell, "As the Wheels Turn in Family Roller Skating," *Chicago Tribune*, February 18, 1973, 16.
90. Jody Homer, "Skaters Do Wheel Things at Area Rinks," *Chicago Tribune*, January 3, 1983.
91. Jazz Age Chicago, "Arcadia Ballroom," January 12, 1997, http://web.archive.org/web/20110927070743/http://chicago.urban-history.org/ven/dhs/arcadia.shtml.
92. Charlie Tyler, "Rollin' Round Roller Rinks," *Chicago Herald-American*, October 23, 1941.
93. Kenan Heise, "Leon C. Berry, 82, Roller Rink Organist," *Chicago Tribune*, August 27, 1996, http://articles.chicagotribune.com/1996-08-27/news/9608270120_1_rink-owners-mr-berry-lawrence-welk.
94. *Billboard*, "Fire Damage at Chi Arcadia Rink Estimated at $100,000," August 31, 1946, 84.
95. Ibid., "Seltzer, Morelli Get Chi's Arcadia Gardens," 1946.
96. Ibid., "Chi's Arcadia Bow to Record Throng," August 31, 1947, 77.
97. Ibid., "Arcadia Big Winner in ILL. Championship," April 13, 1946, 81.
98. Ibid., "Heavy Response for RSROA Ill State Contests," April 19, 1947, 85.
99. William Matteson, "Roller Skating at the Arcadia Roller Rink," Uptown Chicago History, January 12, 2012, http://uptownhistory.compassrose.org/2012/01/roller-skating-at-arcadia-roller-rink.html. Matteson reminisces about skating at Arcadia in the 1950s.
100. *Chicago Daily Tribune*, "Arson Probe Ordered in Fire in Roller Rink," January 5, 1959, 16.
101. Rogers Park/West Ridge Historical Society, "Broadway Armory," http://rpwrhs.org/w/index.php?title=Broadway_Armory.
102. *Chicago Daily Tribune*, "Coast Artillery Mat Set for January 10," December 26, 1926, 2.
103. Michigan Skating Association, "United States Amateur Speed Roller Skating Championship Races," April 1937.

104. Chicago Park District, "History of Broadway Armory Park," 2017, http://www.chicagoparkdistrict.com/parks/Broadway-Armory-Park.
105. *Billboard*, "New Armory Opened in Chicago," June 26, 1943, 45.
106. Suzanne Avery, "75-Year-Old Armory Not Ready for Sounding of Final 'Taps,'" *Chicago Tribune*, South Neighborhood News, September 19, 1965, 2.
107. *Chicago Daily Tribune*, "Football? Hockey? No, Sir, It's Roller Derby Back Again," October 22, 1942, 29.
108. *Billboard*, "Chi Braillers Visit Arena," September 16, 1950, 81.
109. *Chicago Daily Tribune*, "Coliseum Roller Skating Rink—Grand Opening," December 29, 1902, 5.
110. *Billboard*, "Deal Sets Revival for Chicago Coliseum," January 22, 1944, 3.
111. Chicago Area Theatre Organ Enthusiasts, "Remembering the 'Big Barn on W. Madison' and Its Big Barton Pipe Organ," February 13, 2013, http://www.catoe.org/barton.html.
112. David Condon, "The Stadium: One Man's Memories of the Great Gray Lady on Madison Street," *Chicago Tribune*, April 1, 1984, 11, 13.
113. Vikki Ortiz, "Elmhurst Skating Rink Was Where the Well-Wheeled Hung Out," *Chicago Tribune*, February 13, 2009, http://articles.chicagotribune.com/2009-02-13/news/0902110635_1_roller-rink-skate-cool-kids.
114. The Free Library, "Letting the Good Times Roll," April 1, 1988, http://www.thefreelibrary.com/Letting+the+good+times+roll.-a06525655.
115 *YouTube*, "Tony Tahlman at the Elm Rink," August 23, 2012. Tony Tahlman plays "Honky Tonk," composed by Billy Butler, on the 4/24 organ at the Elm Rink and captured on YouTube.
116. *Skate*, "Elm Skating Club Tops Amateur Registrations," January 1964, 12.
117. Ibid., "Elm Rink Sets Pace," January 1965, 5.
118. Bruce R. Dold, "Obstacles to Liability Insurance Have Rinks Skating on Thin Ice," *Chicago Tribune*, November 24, 1985, Section 2, 1.
119. *Elmhurst Press*, "What Is the History of the Elm Roller Skating Rink?," My Suburban Life, 2011, http://www.mysuburbanlife.com/2011/06/08/what-is-the-history-of-the-elm-roller-skating-rink/z7wkj2w.
120. Edward Mazur, "Looking Back at Albany Park When It Was Jewish," Chicago Jewish History, Fall 1990, http://chicagojewishhistory.org/media/931/Fall_1990.pdf.
121. *Billboard*, "Season Starts Big for Chi Locations," October 2, 1943, 39.
122. The four blondes featured in the 1941 skate label would have preceded Marilyn Monroe, though they were well-known Hollywood blondes

popular in the early 1940s. See 1950s Classic Hollywood Blonde Bombshells, www.hubpages.com/entertainment/Blonde_Bombshells.

123. William Howard Taft High School Reunion, "The Hub Roller Rink," 1959, http://www.taftreunion1959.com/Hub_Roller_Rink_Story_082310.pdf. An interesting collage of Hub memorabilia.

124. *Greenville News*, "Disco Fever Rolls into Skating Rinks," September 19, 1978.

125. Digital Research Library of Illinois History Journal, "Hub Roller Skating Rink," Living History of Illinois, December 31, 2016, http://livinghistoryofillinois.com. A collage of images and stories related to the Hub rink.

126. *Billboard*, "Chicago's Hub Kicked Off by Bendler, Benson," March 3, 1951, 40.

127. Ibid., "Passing of John C. McCormack," September 16, 1939, 39.

128. Ibid., "Chi Madison Gardens Opens," October 4, 1947, 67.

129. Ibid., "Madison Gardens," September 26, 1942, 42.

130. *Inter Ocean*, "Roller Skaters Will Race," February 22, 1914, 20.

131. *Billboard*, "Park Rinks—Chicago," May 26, 1917, 51.

132. Chicagology, "West Chicago Street Railroad Company," https://chicagology.com/transportation/westchicagostreetrailroad.

133. *West Chicago St. R.R. Co's. Cable Power House*, Sanborn Insurance Map, 1896, and *Madison Gardens Roller Rink*, Sanborn Insurance Map, 1922. Sanborn Insurance Maps trace the redevelopment and transfer of ownership for the Rockwell Powerhouse through a series of maps dated 1896, 1922 and 1950. The 1896 map shows the car barn before its 1906 closure. Personal correspondence with William Vandervoort, February 6, 2016.

134. Borzo, *Chicago Cable Cars*, 9.

135. Greg Borzo, "Cable Car Remnants," Forgotten Chicago, http://forgottenchicago.com/features/cable-car-remnants.

136. *Madison Gardens Roller Rink*, Sanborn Insurance Map, 1950. The 1896 map shows the car barn before its 1906 closure. The 1922 and 1950 map show the location as Madison Gardens Rink. Personal correspondence with William Vandervoort, February 6, 2016.

137. Bryce Engle, "Looters Have a Grim Carnival on West Side," *Chicago Tribune*, April 6, 1968, 5.

138. *Chicago Tribune Magazine*, "The Riot: A Story in April that Rocked the City," July 28, 1968, 35–47, http://archives.chicagotribune.com/1968/07/28/page/214/article/the-riot.

139. Michael Smith, "West Side Riot Area Rubble Is Gone but Not the Scars," *Chicago Tribune*, March 30, 1969, 3.
140. Tyler, "Rollin' Round Roller Rinks," November 6, 1941.
141. Ibid., October 23, 1941.
142. *Suburbanite Economist*, "Industry and Food Exhibit to Be Held," March 27, 1955, 1.
143. Ibid., "17th Economic Home Show Opens Thursday," October 3, 1971, https://www.newspapers.com/image/54269214/?terms=New%2BPlanet%2BRoller%2BRink%2BChicago.
144. Ibid., "Skaters Reunion," March 11, 1962, 10.
145. *Billboard*, "ARSA Shifts '56 Contests to Chicago," February 25, 1956, 77.
146. *Daily Herald*, "Skating Finals Slated," May 28, 1964, 64.
147. *Billboard*, "11 Groups Swell QARSA Roster of Clubs to 186," February 2, 1952, 51.
148. Bill Boyce, "Melrose Park Rink Rolls Against the High-Tech Flow," *Chicago Tribune*, November 18, 1984, section 4, 3.
149. Mo Ryan and Jimmy Greenfield, "The Good Times to Roll No More," *Chicago Tribune*, March 26, 1998.
150. Boyce, "Melrose Park," 3.
151. *Daily Herald*, "Roller Skate Tourney Aug. 3," 6.
152. Ralph Waldo, "Coney Island Suffers in Comparison with Chicago's Riverview Park," *Inter Ocean*, June 30, 1907, 34.
153. James Coates, "Fire Claims Roller Rink," *Chicago Tribune*, June 17, 1971, 1A, 14.
154. *Billboard*, "Chi Riverview to Aid Service Center," October 3, 1942, 45.
155. Troy Taylor, "The Eastland Disaster," American Hauntings, January 24, 2016, http://troytaylorbooks.blogspot.com/2016/01/the-eastland-disaster.html.
156. Chicago Architecture Info, "Harpo Studios," http://www.chicagoarchitecture.info/Building/1342756910/Harpo-Studios.php.
157. Taylor, "Eastland Disaster." Employees of Western Electric Company and their families boarded five steamers to cruise from Lake Michigan to Michigan City, Indiana, for a picnic. The steamer was overloaded and capsized; 880 people drowned. The *Eastland* is the greatest inland waterway disaster in American peacetime and the worst in Chicago history.
158. Hannah, *Manhood, Citizenship, and the Formation of the National Guards*, 11, 39. The 2nd Regiment was formed in Chicago shortly after 1875 with those men who did not qualify for the socially prestigious 1st Regiment.

Available at https://kb.osu.edu/dspace/bitstream/handle/1811/24316/1/Hannah_T-S_Final.pdf.

159. *Billboard*, "New Chi Bowl Gets Good Bow," July 18, 1942, 45.

160. The Hammond Novachord is an all-electronic polyphonic synthesizer that was produced by the Hammond Company between 1938 and 1942 and was intended not to sound like a pipe organ. Lack of parts during the war ended production. Today, fewer than two hundred are known to exist, with even fewer in operation.

161. *Skating Review*, "New Rink Opens in Chicago," August 1942, 7.

162. *Billboard*, "Roller Bowl in Chi $80,000 Investment," November 8, 1941, 45.

163. Ibid., "Chi Bowl Fosters Class Instruction," November 7, 1942, 41.

164. Ibid., "Bob Ryan," December 19, 1942, 46.

165. Ibid., "Starts Big for Chi Locations," October 2, 1943, 39.

166. Ibid., "Arcadia, Roller Bowl Open Door for Chi Braille Center Skaters," February 26, 1950, 79.

167. U.S. Amateur Roller Skating Association, "1942–1949 Championships," http://www.usarsarollerskaters.org/1942-1949USARSANationalChampionships.html.

168. *Billboard*, "ARSA Champs Are Set for Chicago," February 12, 1944, 46.

169. Ibid., "ARSA Meet in Chicago Attracts 300 Entrants," May 13, 1944, 45.

170. *Southern Economist*, "Skateland's Opening Attended by Many Roller Fans," December 1, 1943, 12.

171. *Billboard*, "Wolak Shutters in Chi; Pushes Tape-Sound Co.," May 12, 1951, 40.

172. Vic Short, "Planet Roller Rink," *Southern Economist*, December 8, 1943, 14.

173. *Chicago Daily Tribune*, "Tower Ticker by Savage," January 4, 1950, 26.

174. Encyclopedia of Chicago, "Roseland," http://www.encyclopedia.chicagohistory.org/pages/1094.html.

175. *Chicago Daily Tribune*, "Roseland Postal Station Is Made into Roller Rink," October 22, 1939, part 1, 23.

176. Russell Lee, "Roller Skating at the Savoy Ballroom, 1941," Calumet 412, http://calumet412.com/post/42275471766/roller-skating-at-the-savoy-ballroom-1941.

177. Erica Gunderson, "The Story Behind an Iconic 1940s Bronzeville Photo," WTTW Chicago Tonight, November 25, 2015, http://chicagotonight.wttw.com/2015/11/25/ask-geoffrey-story-behind-

iconic-1940s-bronzeville-photo. Russell Lee was a white photographer hired by FSA to document the migration of the rural poor. To understand where they migrated to, Lee traced their journey to Chicago from the rural South. This story is told by Chicago's WTTW station.

178. Jazz Age Chicago, "Savoy Ballroom," http://web.archive.org/web/20110613034948/http://chicago.urban-history.org/ven/dhs/savoy.shtml.

179. Sengstock, *That Toddlin' Town*, Appendix D.

180. A Chicago Thing, "The Savoy Ballroom Chicago," July 8, 2011, http://www.achicagothing.com/the-savory-ballroom-chicago.

181. D. O'Hara, "Skating through the Color Barrier: Jimmy Davis's Persistence Led to the First Roller Rink Open to Black Enthusiasts," *Chicago Sun-Times*, April 29, 1987.

182. A collection of images of black skaters at the Savoy is archived at the Farm Security Administration/Office of War Information (FSA/OWI), http://www.loc.gov/pictures/collection/fsa. Also see Library of Congress, Prints & Photographs Division, http://hdl.loc.gov/loc.pnp/pp.print.

183. Poletti, "Residual Culture of Roller Rinks," 45.

184. Andrew Martin, "At Long Last, Lou Rawls Center Gets Off Ground," *Chicago Tribune*, May 14, 1998, http://articles.chicagotribune.com/1998-05-14/news/9805140181_1_ground-breaking-800-seat-theater-cultural-center.

185. Ibid.

186. Powers, *Last Catholic in America*, 275–92.

187. *Billboard*, "Chi Swank Club Slates 4th Invitational Meet," December 4, 1954, 66.

188. Ibid., "Illinois ARSA Events to Swank Skatery," June 2, 1956, 49.

189. U.S. Amateur Roller Skating Association, "Jack Countryman, National Speed Champion," http://www.usarsarollerskaters.org/SheratonHotel.html.

190. The *Blue Island Sun Standard* and the *Suburbanite Economist* were two local newspapers that reported the weekly events at the Swank Rink.

191. George Estep, "The Roller Coaster Life of Towering and Tawdry White City," *Chicago Tribune*, April 6, 1986, http://articles.chicagotribune.com/1986-04-06/features/8601250232_1_south-park-tower-fires.

192. Wolcott, *Race, Riots, and Roller Coasters*, 66–67.

193. Chicago Time Machine, WTTW, "White City Amusement Park," http://interactive.wttw.com/timemachine/white-city-amusement-park.

194. *Chicago Sunday Tribune*, "Fire Destroys White City Roller Rink," November 29, 1959, part 1, 12.
195. *Billboard*, "Washington Paper Plugs Roller Art," 84.
196. Historic Detroit, "Arcadia Ballroom," http://historicdetroit.org/building/arcadia-ballroom.
197. *Billboard*, "RSROA Nationals, Meeting to Cleveland," December 27, 1947, 66.
198. USA Roller Sports, "George Pickard, 1930–2016," http://www.teamusa.org/USA-Roller-Sports/Features/2016/March/21/George-Pickard.
199. National Museum of Roller Skating, newsletter, June 1, 2012, http://www.rollerskatingmuseum.com/members/magazine/Jun%202012.pdf.
200. *Billboard*, "Martin Preps Final Curtain for Arena," April 25, 1953, 75.
201. Encyclopedia of Cleveland History, "Rollercade," June 20, 1997, http://ech.case.edu/ech-cgi/article.pl?id=R5.
202. A YouTube video is accompanied by the Cleveland Rollercade's Wurlitzer played by Bill Zopfi, Rollercade organist, https://www.youtube.com/watch?v=IUg48wsoZts.
203. *Billboard*, "RSROA Records New Highs as Second Decade Opens," August 7, 1948, 83.
204. Ibid., "Rollercade of Akron Awarded ARSA National," January 31, 1953, 45.
205. Poletti, "Residual Culture of Roller Rinks," 45–47.
206. *Skating Review*, "Empire Rollerdrome," March 1941, 4.
207. *Brooklyn Daily Eagle*, "John T. Swanson," October 3, 1949, retrieved from http://www.forgottenrollerrinksofthenortheast.com/empire%20In%20Memoriam.html.
208. Suzanne Spellen, "A Look at Brooklyn, Then and Now," Brownstoner, May 16, 2014, http://www.brownstoner.com/history/past-and-present-the-empire-rollerdrome.
209. *Brooklyn Dailey Eagle*, "Roller Skate," October 22, 1948, 19.
210. Ibid., "Roller Skate," April 1, 1949, 25.
211. Jennifer Bleyer, "The Last Last-Up," *New York Times*, April 22, 2007, http://www.nytimes.com/2007/04/22/nyregion/thecity/22empi.html?_r=0.
212. *Billboard*, "Gay Blades Rollerdrome," August 25, 1945, 54. This column in "Rinks and Skaters" in 1945 lists Gay Blades as the Gay Blades Rollerdrome.
213. *Billboard*, "First Eastern School for Pros Set by RSROA," November 20, 1943, 37.

214. *Brooklyn Daily Eagle*, "Convert Ice Rink," April 22, 1939, 11.
215. *Billboard*, "Record Turnout for Convention," July 6, 1946, 78.
216. Ibid., "Gay Blades Is Doomed; Last Manhattan Rollery," August 18, 1956, 79.
217. *Brooklyn Daily Eagle*, "Roller Skating," April 18, 1948, 14.
218. Jerry's Brokendown Palaces, "Roseland Ballroom," June 15, 2012, http://jerrygarciasbrokendownpalaces.blogspot.com/2012/06/roseland-ballroom-239-west-52nd-street.html.
219. *Billboard*, "N.Y. Gay Blades Switching to Dance," July 31, 1948, 118.
220. Ibid., "Lou Brecker Denies Gay Blades Closing," August 7, 1948, 83.
221. Ibid., "AOW Near Completion on Levittown Arena," February 26, 1955, 65.
222. Rob's Roller World website, http://robsrollerworld.homestead.com.
223. Michal Winerip, "Demise of Roller Rinks Cause for Tears," *New York Times*, *Ocala Star-Banner*, September 30, 1986.
224. Ibid., "Our Towns; Sun Sets on a Rink with a Heart," *New York Times*, September 23, 1986, http://www.nytimes.com/1986/09/23/nyregion/our-towns-sun-sets-on-a-rink-with-a-heart.html.
225. Marcelle S. Fischler, "With Each Rotation, 81-Year-Old Skater Keeps Order at the Rink," *New York Times*, October 28, 2007, http://www.nytimes.com/2007/10/28/nyregion/nyregionspecial2/28skateli.html.
226. Scott Garner, "From Ballrooms to Discos, Tracking 150 Years of Roller Rinks," Curbed, October 23, 2014, http://www.curbed.com/2014/10/23/10034408/history-of-the-roller-rink.
227. For a brief summary of Mammoth, along with photos, see RSORA National Championship Program Book, July 1950, http://www.rollerskatingmuseum.com/members/magazine/1950%20Nationals.pdf.
228. Fillmore Auditorium information, http://www.fillmoreauditorium.org/fillmore-auditorium-info.
229. Neil Young, Village Historian, "Looking Back," *Mineola American*, Mineola Skating Rink, April 2, 1999.
230. Van Horn, "Personal Contact in Rink Management," 67.
231. Ferd Browing, "Roller Dances, Fancy Figures and Races Sweep Modern Rinks in Skating Revival," *Evening Review*, April 16, 1940, 11.
232. National Roller Skate Museum, "First Official U.S. Roller Skating Dance Championship Program, 1939," RSROA.
233. *Skating News*, "Van Horn Organization Affiliates with RSROA," December 1957.

234. *Ogdensburg Journal*, "Skating Star Said Killed by His Wife," October 20, 1959, 1.
235. Robert Bollinger, The Oaks Rink, http://www.rbollinger.com/shtml/oaks_sk8sho1940.shtml (site no longer extant).
236. Robert Bollinger, "Fifty Years Beneath the Oaks," *Northwest Roto Magazine*, August 14, 1955.
237. *Billboard*, "Oaks Amusement Park Rink," August 8, 1942, 45.
238. The Bank Organ was upgraded to a four-manual console with thirteen sets of pipes and replaced in 1955 by a four-manual Wurlitzer pipe organ.
239. Oaks Park Skating Club, "Welcome," http://oaksparkskatingclub.com.
240. Puget Sound Theatre Organ Society, "Puget Sound Pipeline: Oaks Park Rink," http://www.pstos.org/instruments/or/portland/oakspark.htm.
241. *Skating News*, "Cincinnati Rollerdrome Closes Its Doors," January 1957, 10.
242. C.F. (Cap) Sefferino, "Speed Skating," *Billboard*, July 13, 1940, 48, http://www.americanradiohistory.com/Archive-Billboard/40s/1940/Billboard-1940-07-13.pdf.
243. Edward W. Smith, "Stop Skating Please, to Meet Bill Sefferino," *Skate Review*, January 1941.
244. Cleveland Memory Project, "March 17, 18, 19 at Sefferino's Rollerdrome," *Skateland Newsletter*, Cleveland Roller Club, March 1941, http://images.ulib.csuohio.edu/cdm/singleitem/collection/general/id/6399/rec/20.
245. *Rolling through Time*, National Museum of Roller Skating, July 1, 2014.
246. *Billboard*, "Sefferino's 12,000 Members," November 2, 1946, 68.
247. Ibid., "2nd Best Year for Sefferino," April 12, 1947, 81.
248. Wolcott, *Race, Riots, and Roller Coasters*, 67.
249. Ibid., 193.
250. Ibid., 70.

Part III

251. DeFiore, *My Journey through Time*, 116, 125, 129. Madison Gardens' layout is described by DeFiore, who grew up in Chicago and skated at the rink in the 1940s.
252. Grumpa Joe posted his first experience at the Swank Rink, titled "Dancing on Wheels," which was adapted to describe how one new skater viewed the action for the first time. Retrieved from http://grumpajoesplace.com/tag/swank-roller-skating-rink.

253. *Billboard*, "Warning! Termites at Work on Box-Office Foundations," August 14, 1948, 6.
254. *Skating News*, "What, No Speed Skating? Why?," 7.
255. *Skating Review*, "Leroy Junge, Illinois State 1940 Speed Skating Champion," April 1941.
256. Ibid., "The Fastest Amateur on Wheels," May 1941.
257. Pickard, *Titans and Heroes*, 89, 91.
258. Emma Brow, "Nord, 87, Skating Star of 1940s and 1050s," *Washington Post*, January 8, 2010, http://www.washingtonpost.com/wp-dyn/content/article/2010/01/07/AR2010010703826.html?nav=E8.
259. *Skating Review*, "Rollers First Big Pro Show Seems a Success," February 1942, 2. The magazine *Skating Review* included a series by Gloria Nord to incorporate ballerina fundamentals into dance skating. *Skating Review* was not adopted as the official magazine of RSROA until October 28, 1942.
260. Elaine Woo, "Gloria Nord Dies at 87: Skating Star of the 1940s and '50s," *Los Angeles Times*, January 7, 1010, http://www.latimes.com/local/obituaries/la-me-gloria-nord7-2010jan07-story.html.
261. *Billboard*, "Skating Vanities of 1947," October 12, 1946, 4.
262. Ibid., "Racing Put Under Microscope: The Box Office Says 'Use It!'" June 7, 1947, 80.
263. Ibid., "USARSA Speedsters Draw Throng at Philly Events: Greeted with Enthusiasm," June 28, 1947, 82.
264. Bill Hay, awarded the Rodney R. Peters Senior Men's Speed Skating Trophy as the 1941 national champion, trained at Madison Gardens Rink and wore the insignia of Chicago Roller Skating Club, originally from Hollywood Rink.
265. *Skating Review*, "Interviews Show National Spread of International Style Dances," November 1941, 6.
266. Chicagology, "Chicago Newspapers," https://chicagology.com/newspapers. The *Chicago Herald-American* (1939–53) was one of many Chicago newspapers before television began to erode the subscriber newspaper base. The *Herald-American* was bought by the *Chicago Tribune*, renamed *Chicago American* and eventually merged with the *Tribune*.
267. This Day in History, "FDR Reacts to Pearl Harbor Bombing," http://www.history.com/this-day-in-history/fdr-reacts-to-news-of-pearl-harbor-bombing.
268. Miller Nichols Library, Radio Newscasts, "The Day of Infamy, December 7, 1941," University of Missouri, http://library.umkc.edu/spec-col/ww2/pearlharbor/ph-txt.htm.

269. Baruch, *Public Years*, 293.
270. Learn NC, "World War II on the Home Front: Rationing," UNC–Chapel Hill School of Education, http://www.learnnc.org/lp/editions/ww2-rationing/contents.
271. *Billboard*, "Speed Skating 'Rough Stuff,'" October 23, 1943, 44.
272. Ibid., "Barred," June 17, 1944, 43.
273. Tyler, "Rollin' Round Roller Rinks," January 2, 1942.
274. *Skating News*, "RSROA—USFARS Clubs," May 1946, 5.
275. *Billboard*, "Madison Gardens," May 30, 1942, 57.
276. George Pickard, "Series of Instruction for the New Skater: The Flow of the Dance," *Skate*, November 1959, 16.
277. Forgotten Chicago, "Forum Recollections of Mariann Pepitone," September 3, 2014, http://www.forgottenchicago.com/forum/5/2734/roller_rinks.
278. Barbara Iehl, "Skating Takes Seniors Back to Youth," *Chicago Tribune*, November 15, 1999, http://articles.chicagotribune.com/1999-11-15/news/9911150107_1_skating-rinks-older-adults.
279. Tyler, "Rollin' Round Roller Rinks," May 21, 1942.
280. *Skating Review*, "Skate Dancing Growing in Popularity," Arena Gardens Issue, 1943, 9.
281. *Billboard*, "Hayes to Open New Chi Spot in Armory," June 19, 1943, 44.
282. Perry Rawson, "Skate Dancing," *Skating Review*, May 1942.
283. U.S. Amateur Roller Skating Association, "It Happened on Long Island," http://www.usarsarollerskaters.org/bayshore.html.
284. *Skating Review*, "Plain Skating," May 1942.
285. *Billboard*, "Business Holds Up Well in Chicago," January 23, 1943, 41.
286. Ibid., "Contests in Philly Hit by Driving Ban," February 27, 1943, 44.
287. Ibid., "Fritz Huber," May 16, 1942, 51.
288. Ibid., "No Short Cut to Dance Skating," April 10, 1943, 55.
289. Treadwell, "United States Army in World War II," 460.
290. *Billboard*, "Illinois Speedsters Meet in Arcadia," March 13, 1943, 44.
291. Ibid., "Results of the Illinois State Roller Skate Championship," March 20, 1943, 44.
292. Ibid., "Illinois Winners Qualify for Detroit," March 27, 1943, 44.
293. Ibid.
294. *Skating Review*, "Book Taught," September/October 1942, 2.
295. *Billboard*, "Illinois Speedsters Meet in Arcadia."
296. *Skating Review*, "Racing by Dorothy Law," November 1943, 12.

297. *Billboard*, "Results of the Illinois State Roller Skate Championship," March 20, 1943, 44.
298. Hank Werner, "Record? What Record? Speed Coach Speaks Hard Words to Speed Skaters," *Roller Skating News*, November 1958, 7.
299. *Skating Review*, "Chicago Roller Bowl," Arena Gardens Issue, 1943, 17.
300. *Billboard*, "Phil J. Hayes," June 17, 1944, 43.
301. *Skating Review*, "Mastery of the 3 Turn," May 1944, 12.
302. Cairo-Purling Rink, "And Then What Happened?"
303. *Billboard*, "Madison Gardens, Chi, in Gala Bow for 37th Season," September 25, 1943, 37.
304. *Skating Review*, "The New Crop Looks Good," April 1944, 3.
305. *Billboard*, "Dance Skating Gains at Memphis Drome," March 31, 1945, 73.
306. Ibid., "25 Factors Govern Biz Volume in Today's Tussle for Dollar: Right Ads Keep Wheels Rolling!," May 22, 1948, 88.
307. Ibid., "The Twain Must Meet," August 12, 1944, 41.
308. Ibid., "Perry B. Rawson Explains New and Safety Instruction Devices," January 27, 1945, 39.
309. Ibid., "Rinks and Skaters," "Rink Owner Cries 'Out' at Capers of the Skaterbug," September 14, 1946, 85.
310. The Savoy Ballroom, located in Harlem, was managed by African American real estate businessman Charles Buchanon, who sought to run an upscale, luxury ballroom for those who wished to dance swing in an atmosphere of tasteful refinement. The Savoy attracted a clientele that was 85 percent black and 15 percent white.
311. *Skating Review*, "Garden Show Proposed as Annual Affair," March 1944, 3.
312. *Billboard*, "State Champs Set for ARSA Meet," April 22, 1944, 46.
313. Ibid., "Rinks and Skaters," October 24, 1942, 46.
314. Mason, "Impact of World War II on Women's Fashion," 18.
315. Ibid.
316. Ibid., 18, 32.
317. *Skating News*, "This Month's Cover Subject," January 1945.
318. *Billboard*, "New Speed Records during RSROA Championship Meet," May 27, 1944, 48. See also *Skating Review*, June 1944, 13.
319. *Chicago Daily Tribune*, "Roller Speed Titles Won by 3 Chicagoans," May 5, 1944, 25.
320. Ibid., "Brown Wins 2 Skate Titles; Nears Sweep," May 4, 1944, 24.
321. *Skating News*, "WPB Orders Brownout; Bright Lights Will Fade," February 1945, 2.

322. Mark Thornton, "The Real Reason for FDR's Popularity," Mises Institute, October 20, 2010, https://mises.org/library/real-reason-fdrs-popularity.
323. Wayback Machine, "V-E Day," https://web.archive.org/web/20080515065523/http://history.sandiego.edu/gen/WW2Timeline/qt/v-eday.html.
324. Fred A. Martin, "A Definite Plan!," *Skating News*, May 1945, 3.
325. *Skating News*, "Reconversion—This Is How It Looks!," September 1945, 5.
326. *Billboard*, "Sam Babb," July 28, 1945, 50. The story was told by Sam Babb about skate racer Tony Belvea.
327. Richard G. Budd, "Hints on Speed Skating," *Skating News*, March 1952, 9.
328. *Billboard*, "Madison Gardens, Chi, in Gala Bow," 37.
329. *Skating News*, May 1946, 16.
330. Ibid., 4.
331. *Billboard*, "Arcadia, Roller Bowl Open Door for Chi Braille Center Skaters," February 25, 1950, 79.
332. *Skating News*, "Illinois State Meet," June 1949, 21.
333. Justin Parkinson, "The Victorian Craze that Sparked a Mini-Sexual Revolution," *BBC News Magazine*, April 2015, http://www.bbc.com/news/magazine-31831110.
334. *Skating News*, "This Month's Cover…Dad Wins and Retires," May 1952, 3.
335. Ibid., "1952 American Amateur Roller Skating Championships," June 1952, 6.
336. Ibid., "Illinois State Meet," June 1952, 6.
337. Ibid., "Let's Go to Denver," June 1952, 9.
338. Jesse E. Bell, "A *Skating Review* Feature: Racing—Passing," November 1943, 12.
339. *Skating News*, "1952–53 All-American Champions," June 1953, 6.

Part IV

340. Philippa Gates. "Home Sweet Home Front Women: Adapting Women for Hollywood's WWII Home-Front Films," *Journal of American Popular Culture* 15 (Fall 2016): 2, http://www.americanpopularculture.com/journal/articles/fall_2016/gates.htm.

341. Smithsonian National Museum of American History, "Be with Him at Every Mail Call," poster, general history, http://amhistory.si.edu/militaryhistory/collection/object.asp?ID=553&back=1.
342. National Park Service, *World War II and the American Home Front*, 72.
343. Ibid., 17.
344. *Billboard*, "FSA Points to Home-Front Entertainment as Amusement's No. 1 Fall Job," July 31, 1943, 4.
345. Schwartz, *The Speculator*, 433.
346. *Billboard*, "The Lack of Entertainment Blamed for Lowered War Production," February 20, 1943, 3.
347. Ibid., "The New National Wartime Morale and the NEIC," July 31, 1943, 4.
348. A study of civilian agencies directed to support the war industry reveals overlap, redundancy and conflicting descriptions. While the U.S. Federal Security Agency report *Spare Time: A War Asset for War Workers* describes its role, elsewhere sources identify other agencies involved in civilian health, safety and recreation requirements—for example, the announcement in RSROA's May 1944 *Skating Review*, "An Important WPB Announcement," 17.
349. Peterson, *Planning the Home Front*, 4.
350. *Billboard*, "Skating Program Set by OCD Seen as Business Hypo," 44.
351. Ibid., "Ops (Operators) Overcome War Problems; Rosy Future to Follow Conflict," July 31, 1943, 60.
352. David J. Coles, "Keep the Home Fires Burning: Florida's World War II Experience," Florida Remembers World War II, Florida's World War II Memorial, http://www.museumoffloridahistory.com/exhibits/permanent/wwii/history.cfm.
353. Phillips J. Peck, "United States—A Nation of 4-F's! Federal Security Agency Committee Seeking to Bring Physical Fitness to Fifty Million," *Olean Times Herald*, March 9, 1944, 13, https://www.newspapers.com/image/38681840/?terms=John%2BB%2BKelly.
354. National Park Service, *World War II and the American Home Front*, 30.
355. Library of Congress, LC-DIG-highsm-23456, http://www.loc.gov/pictures/item/2013633913. The "Rosie the Riveter" poster symbolized the role of women in the war effort. The poster was stylized after a mural on an abandoned building in Sacramento, California.
356. U.S. Centennial of Flight Commission, "The American Aerospace Industry During World War II," http://www.centennialofflight.net/essay/Aerospace/WWII_Industry/Aero7.htm. Two girls on roller skates at Douglas Aircraft in El Segundo, California.

357. *Billboard*, "Skating Program Set by OCD Seen as Business Hypo," 44.
358. James Vannurden, director and curator, "Curator's Corner," *Rolling through Time*, National Museum of Roller Skating, May 1, 2014. http://www.rollerskatingmuseum.com/downloads/May%202014.pdf.
359. *Skating News*, "Letters to the Editor," September 1945, 7.
360. Ibid., "Our Boys Like to Skate," March 1945, 14.
361. National Park Service, *World War II and the American Home Front*, 78.
362. *Billboard*, "Twelve Super Spots in Works," July 8, 1944, 44.
363. Ibid., "Big PA Spots Are in Works for Post-War," October 7, 1944, 40.
364. Ibid., "Allies Release War Films to Spur Production, Fight 'War Is Over' Sentiment," September 9, 1944, 45.
365. Ibid., "Industry Asked to Aid Amputees in Govt.'s New Therapy Program," November 3, 1945, 55.
366. Ibid., "Artificial Legs No Handicap When 25 G.I.'s Don Wheels at Newark's New Dreamland," December 1, 1945, 89.
367. Ibid., "Operators Should Treat Disabled Veterans Same as Regulars," December 1, 1945, 89.
368. Government Research Library, "U.S. Fleet Activities, Yokosuka, Japan," http://www.globalsecurity.org/military/facility/yokosuka.htm.
369. *Rolling through Time*, "Featured Story: Chicago Roller Skating Company," National Museum of Roller Skating, December 1, 2015.
370. *Roller Derby Jesus: The Blog and Memoirs of Jerry Seltzer*, "Roller Derby and the Military: Was There Really a Game on an Aircraft Carrier," September 30, 2012, http://rollerderbyjesus.com/2012/09/30/roller-derby-and-the-military-was-there-really-a-game-on-an-aircraft-carrier.
371. Allison Batdorff, "Yokosuka Roller-Rink's Doors Shutting for Good," *Stars and Stripes*, May 3, 2006, http://www.stripes.com/news/yokosuka-roller-rink-s-doors-shutting-for-good-1.48499.

Part V

372. George Pickard, editor's column, *Skate*, Fall 1971, http://www.rollerskatingmuseum.com/members/magazine/USARS_Fall1971_Web.pdf.
373. U.S. Amateur Roller Skating Association, "About Us," http://www.usarsarollerskaters.org/about.html.
374. *Skating News*, "The Story of the RSROA: 20th Anniversary 1937–1957," April 1957, 3, 13.

375. Fred A. Martin, "What the RSROA Stands for: RSROA 1950 American Amateur Roller Skating Championships," National Museum of Roller Skating, July 1950.
376. *Billboard*, "URO Set for Action," December 12, 1942, 58.
377. National Museum of Roller Skating, *Why the RSROA Was Organized*, 1940 U.S. Amateur Roller Skate Championship program, 1940.
378. Ibid., "Amateur Skating Union, Letter to Attendees," U.S. Amateur Roller Skating Championship, 1940 RSROA.
379. *Skating News*, "Host to California and Southwest Pacific Regional Championships Offers Brand New Rink," April 1955, 15. This article describes the opening of a newly constructed rink in Fresno and rink amenities to attract skaters.
380. *Billboard*, "AAU Restricts Scope of RSROA," December 13, 1941, 47.
381. Ibid., "RSROA-AOW Fight Is Taken to Court," December 13, 1941, 47.
382. Turner and Zaidman, *History of Rolling Skating*, 36–37.
383. U.S. Amateur Roller Skating Association, "About Us."
384. *Billboard*, "See Benefits of New Org," December 19, 1942, 46.
385. Ibid., "New Association, United Rink Operators—Formed in the East," November 28, 1942, 56.
386. Arlis Snyder, "An Analysis of Competitive Judging," *Skating News*, October 1956, 7.
387. "AOW Preps Its 12th Annual Competition," April 19, 1952, 51.
388. Russo, "Salute to the Bygone AOW Chain."
389. *Skating Review*, "An Agreement Can Be Reached, Under a White Flag," November 1944, 1; Pickard, *Titans and Heroes*, 88–90. Pickard summarizes the initial meeting, the fallout of the *Skating Review* editor's appraisal of the meeting, Smith's editorial response and the subsequent RSROA withdrawal of financial support.
390. Edward Smith, "Take the Fun Out and You Kill Roller Skating," *Skating Review*, November 1944, 1. Somewhat simultaneously after Smith's editorial, RSROA withdrew its financial support of *Skating Review*. Shortly afterward, *Skating Review* folded, and RSROA introduced *Skating News*.
391. *Billboard*, "Why Be Foolish? Asks Giles in Plea for Unity in Skating," July 5, 1947, 89.
392. Ibid., "Schmitz—Martin Battle Resumes," December 4, 1948, 67.
393. Ibid., "Is RSROA-USARSA Merger Under Way?," May 17, 1952, 58.
394. Turner and Zaidman, *History of Rolling Skating*, 37.
395. *Billboard*, "RSIA Sets Up Shop in Chicago," October 16, 1948, 79.

396. Ibid., "Get on Bandwagon to Boom Skating, Urges Fuller of RSIA," August 14, 1948, 86.
397. Ibid., "RSROA Reply by Fred A. Martin," September 22, 1945, 59.
398. Ibid., "RSROA Rise Parallels Progress in Skating," January 31, 1953, 45.
399. *Skate*, "Stan Musial Says: Skating on My Fitness Team," December 1964, 1, http://www.rollerskatingmuseum.com/members/magazine/1964%20December.pdf.
400. *Skating Review*, "John B. Kelly," March 1942. As director of fitness within the Office of Civilian Defense, Kelly acknowledges the government's support of roller skating as recreation to keep war industry workers fit.
401. *Skating News*, "A Year 'Round March of Dimes," March 1955, 5.
402. *Billboard*, "Arcadia Rink," January 22, 1944, 45.
403. Ibid., "RSROA Garden Show Goes Over 13G for Polio Foundation," May 6, 1944, 45.
404. Ibid., "Walter Anderson," June 10, 1944, 44.

Part VI

405. *Decatur Daily Review*, "Old Craze Comes Back," October 11, 1904, 2.
406. *Inter Ocean*, "Shall We All Roll Again?," October 22, 1906, 1.
407. Tyler, "Rollin' Round Roller Rinks," September 25, 1941.
408. Library of Congress, Topics in Chronicling America—Roller Skating Craze, Newspapers and Current Periodical Reading Room, https://www.loc.gov/rr/news/topics/rollerskating.html.
409. Rob's Roller World website.
410. Colin Bane, "Roller Derby Pioneer Jerry Seltzer on the 75th Anniversary of Transcontinental Roller Derby," Westword, May 5, 2010, http://www.westword.com/arts/roller-derby-pioneer-jerry-seltzer-on-the-75th-anniversary-of-transcontinental-roller-derby-5804165.
411. Women's Flat Track Derby Association, "WFTDA History," http://wftda.com/history.
412. David Bachman, "Doctor Jock," *Chicago Tribune*, May 23, 1979, section 7, 4.
413. Roller Skating Association International, "Exercise Benefits of Roller Skating," http://www.rollerskating.com/pages/all+about+roller+skating/51.
414. A.L. Kennedy, "Roller Skating & Exercise," Live Strong, February 2, 2014, http://www.livestrong.com/article/107358-roller-skating-exercise.

415. National Roller Skating Museum, "Earliest Roller Skating Movie: The Rink," March 2015, http://www.rollerskatingmuseum.com/downloads/Mar%202015.pdf.
416. Fiona Ortiz, "Urban Roller Skating Survives as a Subculture while Rinks Close Nationwide," Reuters, February 4, 2015, http://www.huffingtonpost.com/2015/02/04/urban-roller-skating_n_6611610.html.
417. Poletti, "Residual Culture of Roller Rinks," 45.
418. Intza, "Images of Women on the Home Front," 52.
419. United Skates Documentary, "Sneak Peek," http://www.unitedskatesdocumentary.com/#!watch/cee5. A jam skater describes the process for mentally preparing for skate night at the big rink.
420. Erika Wolf, "11 Things You Might Not Know About Roller Skates," Mental Floss, August 12, 2013, http://mentalfloss.com/article/52168/11-things-you-might-not-know-about-roller-skates.
421. Carlesa Williams, "Rhythm Skating on Quad Skates," ThoughtCo, February 2, 2016, https://www.thoughtco.com/rhythm-skating-on-quad-skates-1963999. The author describes Paradise Valley, the black neighborhood and roller skating.
422. Shelley Griffith, "Paradise Valley," Encyclopedia of Detroit, http://detroithistorical.org/learn/encyclopedia-of-detroit/paradise-valley. Paradise Valley was a neighborhood of more than three hundred black-owned businesses that catered to the growing black migrants from the South who settled in the near East Side neighborhood of Black Bottom and filled the employment rolls of the Detroit automobile industry. The business district and neighborhood succumbed to urban renewal, and the construction of freeways as auto manufacturing moved from the inner city to the suburbs.
423. Williams, "Rhythm Skating on Quad Skates."
424. Poletti, "Residual Culture of Roller Rinks," 78.
425. Fred Bergin, "The Natural Style," *Billboard*, June 8, 1946, 81, 83.
426. Perry B. Rawson, "1947 Lab-Built Challengers Set Stage for Drive," *Billboard*, January 31, 1948, 72.
427. George Pickard, "A Look at Speed Skating: Part One," *Skate*, March 1964, 8; George Pickard, "A Look at Speed Skating: Part Two," *Skate*, April 1964, 8.
428. *Skate*, "In Speed—You Win on Your Own Skills," January 1966, 10.
429. Ibid., "Give Us Right Track: Modern Speedmen Speak Up!," February 1965, 2.
430. Ibid., "Old-Time Speedman Says Jack Is Really the Greatest," March 1965, 7.

Conclusion

431. Turner, *History of Roller Skating*, 92.
432. Emily MacKay, Oaks Park Rink, telephone conversation, April 19, 2017. The Oaks Park Rink has experienced an upswing in fitness, with senior classes being the most popular and largest.
433. Fiona Ortiz, "Urban Roller Skating Fights for Survival as U.S. Rinks Close," Reuters, February 4, 2015, http://www.reuters.com/article/us-usa-chicago-rollerskating-idUSKBN0L818N20150204.
434. Turner, *History of Roller Skating*, 92. Turner describes the separation over the decades of adults and their use of rinks as their primary source of recreation, addressing dedicated sessions, music and formal programs that target the adult social recreational enthusiast.

Appendix C

435. Laverne Larson, "The Roller Rink," *Suburbanite Economist*, October 7, 1953. Larson skated at the Roseland Roller Rink.

SELECTED BIBLIOGRAPHY

Baruch, Bernard M. *The Public Years*. New York: Holt, Rinehart and Winston, 1960.

Borzo, Greg. *Chicago Cable Cars*. Charleston, SC: The History Press, 2012.

Brooks, Lou. *Skate Crazy: Amazing Graphics from the Golden Age of Roller Skating*. Philadelphia: Running Press Book Publishers, 2003.

DeFiore, Evelyn. *My Journey through Time*. Bloomington, IL: AuthorHouse, 2011.

Grisham, William F. "Silent Movie Capital: Essanay Film Company." Chicagology, December 7, 1969. https://chicagology.com/silentmovies.

Hannah, Eleanor L. *Manhood, Citizenship, and the Formation of the National Guards, Illinois, 1870–1917*. Columbus: Ohio State University Press, 2006.

Haugh, Dolores. *Riverview Amusement Park*. Charleston, SC: Arcadia Publishing, 2004.

Intza, Carla E. "Images of Women on the Home Front, a Study of the Films Since You Went Away, Tender Comrade and Pin-Up Girl: What OWI and Hollywood Wanted Us to See." Master's thesis, Regent University, April 1, 2004.

Jimenez, Michael. "To the Core: The Congress of Racial Equality, the Seattle Civil Rights Movement, and the Shift to Black Militancy." Master's thesis, University of Central Florida–Orlando, 2012. http://stars.library.ucf.edu/cgi/viewcontent.cgi?article=3140&context=etd.

Life. "Vintage Roller Derby Bad Girls: SASS on Wheels." December 13, 1948. http://selvedgeyard.com/2009/08/04/vintage-roller-derby-bad-girls-sass-on-wheels. This article describes the roller derby finale in Chicago on June 22, 1947.

Mabe, Catherine. *Roller Derby: The History and All-Girl Revival of the Greatest Sport on Wheels*. Denver, CO: Speck Press, 2007.

Mason, Meghann. "The Impact of World War II on Women's Fashion in the United States and Britain." Master's thesis, University of Nevada–Las Vegas, 2011. http://digitalscholarship.unlv.edu/thesesdissertations/1390.

National Museum of the U.S. Air Force. "The Douglas A-24." April 10, 2015. http://www.nationalmuseum.af.mil/Visit/MuseumExhibits/FactSheets/Display/tabid/509/Article/196307/douglas-a-24.aspx.

National Park Service, U.S. Department of the Interior. *World War II and the American Home Front.* October 2007. https://www.nps.gov/nhl/learn/themes/WWIIHomeFront.pdf.

National Roller Derby League. "First Annual Roller Derby Year Book—1951." http://www.bankedtrack.info/Annuals/RollerDerby1951.pdf.

Peterson, Sarah Jo. *Planning the Home Front: Building Bombers and Communities at Willow Run*. Chicago: University of Chicago Press, 2013. https://books.google.com/books?id=Wu55uzCZdpkC&source=gbs_navlinks_s.

Pickard, George. "Series of Singles Skating: Backward Skating." *Skate*, January 1959.

———. *Titans and Heroes of American Roller Skating*. Lincoln, NE: National Museum of Roller Skating, 2010.

Poletti, Romy. "Residual Culture of Roller Rinks: The Media, Music & Nostalgia of Roller Skating." Master's thesis, McGill University, Montreal, 2009. http://www.collectionscanada.gc.ca/obj/thesescanada/vol2/QMM/TC-QMM-66673.pdf.

Powers, John R. *The Last Catholic in America*. Chapter 16, "Swank." Chicago: Loyola Press, 2004.

Rawson, Perry B. "The Art of Plain Skating." *Skating Review*, April 1942.

———. "The Art of Plain Skating." *Skating Review*, March 1942.

Schwartz, Jordan L. *The Speculator: Bernard M. Baruch in Washington, 1917–1954*. Chapel Hill: University North Carolina Press, 1981.

Sengstock, Charles A. *That Toddlin' Town: Chicago's White Dance Bands and Orchestras, 1900–1950*. Urbana: University of Illinois Press, 2004.

Smith, Preston H. "Congress of Racial Equality (CORE)." *Encyclopedia of Chicago*. N.p., 2005.

Travis, Dempsey. *An Autobiography of Black Chicago*. Chicago: Agate Bolden, 2013.

Treadwell, Mattie E. "United States Army in World War II: The Women's Army Corps." Center of Military History, United States Army, Washington, D.C., 1954. Retrieved from http://www.history.army.mil/books/wwii/Wac/index.htm.

Turner, James, and Michael Zaidman. *The History of Roller Skating*. Lincoln, NE: National Museum of Roller Skating, 1997.

Tyler, Charlie. "Rollin' Round Roller Rinks." *Chicago Herald-American*, 1941–44.

U.S. Office of Civil Defense and Office of Defense Health and Welfare Services. *Volunteers in Recreation, 1939–1945*. World War II Government Publications Collection, Ball University, February 1942. http://libx.bsu.edu/cdm/compoundobject/collection/WWIIGovPubs/id/584/rec/1.

U.S. Office of Community War Services, U.S. Federal Security Agency. *Spare Time: A War Asset for War Workers*. Retrieved from Google Books, University of Illinois–Urbana/Champaign, 1943.

Wolcott, Victoria W. *Race, Riots and Roller Coasters: The Struggle Over Segregated Recreation in America*. Philadelphia: University of Pennsylvania Press, 2012.

Filmography

This filmography is a selected bibliography of vintage videos, movie clips, Wurlitzer pipe organ clips and World War II propaganda clips that provide the sights and sounds from that era's conflict, 1950s roller skating and disco era skating—everything from Bob Hope and V-mail to Gloria Nord in 2014.

Blakey, Roy. "Star of the Show Gloria Nord on Harold Steinman and the Skating Vanities." 2014. Vimeo, https://vimeo.com/102836264. Roy Blakey interviews Gloria Nord.

Butler, Bill. "Quad Skating at Empire Roller Rink in Brooklyn." 1978. YouTube, https://www.youtube.com/watch?v=fi8DiG3NL8Q. The legendary Empire Roller Rink, where roller disco is purported to have started.

It's Always Fair Weather, clip. MGM, 1955. "Gene Kelly—Roller Skates." YouTube, https://www.youtube.com/watch?v=aZYS2rKh01U. Kelly sings and tap-dances on skates with steel wheels.

Russo, Rob. "Salute to the Bygone AOW Chain of Roller Rinks." Rob's Roller World. http://www.robsrollerworld.com.

———. "This Is Roller Skating—1950s." Roller Skating Foundation of America, circa 1950. Rob's Roller World. http://robsrollerworld.homestead.com/Nostalgia.html. A film clip from the early 1950s, capturing the roller skating styles of the 1940s and 1950s, showing figure, skate dancing and the variety of groups involved in skating.

Shall We Dance, clip. RKO Radio Pictures, 1937. YouTube, https://www.youtube.com/watch?v=LOILZ_D3aRg. Fred Astaire and Ginger Rogers spin around Central Park on roller skates and sing "Let's Call the Whole Thing Off."

Tony Tahlman at the Elm Rink, August 23, 2012. YouTube, https://www.youtube.com/watch?v=yF6z2EyVMWc. Tony Tahlman plays "Honky Tonk," composed by Billy Butler, on the 4/24 organ at the Elm Rink.

Tony Tahlman at the Elm Rink, May 19, 1975. YouTube, https://www.youtube.com/watch?v=yF6z2EyVMWc. Slideshow with Wurlitzer pipe organ accompaniment by Tony Tahlman, organist of the Elm Rink.

United Newsreel Corporation. "You Have V-Mail," 1944. Courtesy *Smithsonian* magazine, February 23, 2010. YouTube, https://www.youtube.com/watch?v=WR8cBKhgELc.

INDEX

A

America on Wheels
and Levittown Arena 85
chain of East Coast rinks 173
Arcadia Gardens Rink, Chicago
a brief history of 50
hosting RSROA state competions 102
Paddy Harmon link to Chicago Stadium 55
the visits of Gloria Nord 41
Arcadia Roller Rink of Detroit ("the Arc") 78
Arena Gardens Roller Rink
a brief history of 79
home of Detroit's premier sports palace 79
Armory Roller Skating Rink
a brief history of 52
reclaimed as an armory in 1942 51
Awful Skate, An 31, 181

B

Benny Goodman and His Orchestra, and the "Jersey Bounce" 110
Berry, Leon 37, 111
ace organist of Arcadia Gardens 50
as the dean of roller rink rock 50
at the Hub 61
Brown, Russell
and National Championship, 1941 121
at ARSA nationals, 1944 129
goes professional 122
joins the army 115
rivalry with Bill Hay 98, 118
speed record, 1941 37

C

Chicago as roller capital
champions of the postwar years 144

contribution of Paddy Harmon 55
its claim for 31
rocking in the New Year, 1944 123
Chicago Braille Center 53, 69
Chicago Coliseum
a brief history of 53
and Gloria Nordskog, 1938 99
as center of spectator roller events 37
as part-time roller rink 23
hosting early speed skate races 34
opening of Skating Vanities, 1942 19
Chicago riots 31
Chicago Roller Skate Company
and Chubby, the roller-skating horse 39
and WPB Order M-126 29
built skates as military supplies 159
celebrates fifty years 38
Four Hollywood Blondes 60
headquarters in Chicago 38
reconversion to skate manufacturing 133
Chicago Service Men's Center 162
Chicago Stadium
a brief history of 55
a part-time rink 23
Harmon and promotional tactic for 67
Harmon brings roller skating to 38
limitations as neighborhood rink 55
Chubby, first roller-skating horse 39
Cioni, Roland 38
Cleveland Rollercade Skating Rink, a brief history of 80
Community Facilities Act of 1940 (Lanham Act) 152
competition skating
Arena Gardens, first RSROA speed skating national 79
Chicago Coliseum, first roller derby, 1935 55
Cleveland Auditorium, first amateur roller skate championship, 1940 171
Mineola Skating Rink, first skate dance championship, 1939 114
Congress of Racial Equality (CORE)
protest of White City, 1942 31
protest of White City, 1946 76

D

dance ballrooms 46
at White City Ballroom 47
the Aragon 50
the Arcadia Ballroom 46
the Trianon 47
dancing on wheels
at Mineola Skate Rink 88
Davis, Jimmy 185
lobbies owners for one night skates at Savoy 72
organizes all-black Midwest speed skate league 36
D-Day 164
desegregation of recreational facilities
disciplined crusades of civil disobedience and CORE 31

lawsuit against White City Roller Rink 76
of Sefferino Rollerdrome 91
self-policing by white patrons, Skateland 91
Douglas Aircraft in El Segundo, California 156

E

Eastland steamer disaster 69
Elm Skating Rink, a brief history of 57
Empire Rollerdrome
a brief history of 83
as heart of roller disco craze 83
host of Skate Queen Contest 83
Essanay Film Company 31

F

Federal Security Agency 153
and fitness program 153
"Jenny on the Job" 128
recreational facilities for communities with wartime industry 152
Spare Time: A War Asset for War Workers 151
Fred A. Niles Studios, site of former Roller Bowl 70
Fritchle Automobile & Battery Company 87

G

Gay Blades Rollerdrome 84
a brief history of 84
Gladys and George Werner Senior Dance Challenge Trophy
won by Robert Shaffer and Jaci Zimmerman 144
Golden Age of Roller Skating
a brief profile of 17
its end in Chicago 31
legacy of
black subculture, the 185
competitive roller skating, set rules for 170
family-centered, rink ownership as generational 175
neighborhood recreation centers, as 137
wholesome, physical fitness, as 176
why it ended in 1959 30
Grable, Betty 20, 182, 183
"Gray Lady" 68

H

Hammond electric organ 30
Harmon, Paddy
and revival of roller skating, 1904 39
and Ware brothers 38
Chicago Stadium owner 55
Harpo Studios 69, 70
Hay, Bill 105, 119, 136
national trophy on display at Madison Gardens 102
rivalry with Russell Brown 118
won the 1940 national speed title 98
Henie, Sonja
as the Golden Girl 20
ballerina on ice skates 19

Herald-American
ease of learning skate dance lessons 102
Tyler reports on skate craze, 1941 179
Hollywood and roller skating
Four Blonds of 60
movies, pop culture and 181
OWI enlists favorable messages from 147
Hollywood Roller Rink, a brief history of 58
Hub Roller Rink, a brief history of 60

J

"Jenny on the Job" 128, 153, 182
Jersey Bounce
as noseart, B-24D Liberator 111
at Madison Gardens Rink shuffle skate 110
Backward Strut version of 110
in letters to the boys overseas 159
popularized by Benny Goodman orchestra 110
USS *New Jersey* does the 111
Joseph P. Seifert Challenge Trophy won by Teddy Rosdahl 126

K

Keep 'em Rolling
propaganda campaign of OWI 21
slogan for rink "getaway party" 112
Knight, Earl, 1952 national speed champion 142

L

Levittown Roller Rink
a brief history of 85
as member of AOW 174
Lombardo, Guy, records RSIA "Roller Skating Song" 175

M

Madison Gardens Rink
a brief history of 61
afternoon of December 7, 1941 102
and Anita Newquist 109
and floor size 47
and speed club 107
and the Jersey Bounce 110
as former cable car barn 63
doorman Big Bill 95
early history 37
early speed skate races 34
graceful skating contests 104
hosted 1915 skate race 61
national champions representing 121
"Oldest and Best-Known" 41
rink logo on display at Johnny's Icehouse 63
rink rats and skate dancing 95
Rockwell cable car powerhouse 99
Russell Brown, member of 105
site of Johnny's Icehouse 55
skate club sweater 126
thirty-fifth season and roller skate craze 179
Mammoth Garden Roller Skating Rink
1952 RSROA Nationals 141
a brief history of 86

Martin, Fred A. 23, 38, 79, 80, 186
Mineola Roller Rink
a brief history of 87
passing of Earl Van Horn 30
where skate dancing began, 1934 87

N

National Entertainment Industry Council 151
National Foundation for Infantile Paralysis 125, 167, 177
National Guard armories
1st Regiment 53
2nd Regiment 69
202nd Coast Artillery 51
Rollerdrome in Gary taken over by 104
New Planet Roller Rink, a brief history of 63
Nordskog, Gloria
and Betty Grable 182
appeal to *Seventeen* magazine audience 126
as a Chicago girl, 1938 17
discovered by Harold Steinman 19
media plays off Nord versus Sonja Henie 20
mother fashions outfits 128
not to confuse roller derby with Skating Vanities 186
performs at reopening of Arcadia after fire 50
servicemen's favorite pin-up girl, 1944 46
shortens name to "Nord" 17
Skating Vanities, 1943 20
the duties of professional skaters 45
works out new routines at Arcadia 37
North Avenue Rollerway Skating Rink
a brief history of 65
an ARSA-style rink 137
home of national dance champions 144
hosts national events 48
joined United Rink Operators, becoming an ARSA member 65
last large rink with pipe organ in Chicago, 1998, as 66

O

Oaks Amusement Park 89
Oaks Skating Rink
a brief history of 89
and Lanham Act funds 152
longest operating roller rink as of 2017 89
Office of Civilian Defense 21, 29, 152, 153
Office of Defense Transportation 152
Office of War Information
campaign to keep the home fires burning 145
established in 1942 147
Keep 'em Rolling campaign 21
skate industry adopts messages 152
women's role to write letters 158
Old Timers Roller Skating Club of Chicago 102, 107

Oprah Winfrey Show, The 70
organists, Chicago rinks
Al Melgard, the Stadium 56
Eddie Hollenbeck, the Roller Dome 70
Fred Arnish, North Avenue 66
Happy Johnson, Madison Gardens 61
Leon Berry, Arcadia 50
Norvel Hall, the Armory 52
Paul Grosnick, North Avenue 66
Tony Tahlman, the Elm 57
organ music and roller skating
adapted for the Jersey Bounce 111
as music of the war generation 30
dropped in favor of disco music 61
jazz bands at the Savoy 72
last rink in Chicago 66
used in silent movie era 30

P

Palace Roller Rink 165
Park City 31, 76, 144
Park City Roller Rink 31
Pasco Naval Air Station 165
Pickard, George
among first skaters at Detroit's Arcadia 79
roller skate organizations merge, 1971 169
Pin Up Girl 20, 183
Poletti, Romy 30
Port City Rollerz 185

R

Richardson Ballbearing Skate Company
as major skate manufacturer 38
conversion of ball bearings to military requirements 159
reconversion to skate manufacturing 133
Riverview Roller Rink 107
a brief history of 67
as host for Illinois championship, 1922 67
hosted Chicago Service Men's Center 68
Rodney R. Peters Senior Men's Speed Skating Trophy
won by Bill Hay 99
won by Earl Knight 142
Roller Bowl
a brief history of 68
and ARSA 1944 Nationals 70
as newest rink 41
as skate dance center 112
competitions and the war years 102
features when opened, 1942 109
Figure and Dance Club of 69
host state and national competitions 48
Ozzie Nelson at 125
sessions for blind skaters 138
soundproof floor 43
state speed contest results, 1952 139
to host 1944 RSROA nationals 121
roller derby
1940s fever for 25

and pop culture 181
Arcadia, home of Chicago Westerners 51
featured in *Life* magazine 25
revival of Women's Flat Track 180
rules and Damon Runyon 33
Roller Dome Rink, a brief history of 70
"Roller Romance" 23, 138
roller skate craze
1904 Decatur newspaper reported in 179
1979 runner's reference to Dr. Bachman 181
at the Savoy 72
Chicago's *Herald-American* in 1941 179
dancing on wheels at Mineola 88
derby craze 53
is it back in the twenty-first century? 187
Lou Brooks and Skate Crazy 30
roller disco craze at the Empire 83
Victorian "rink-o-mania" 138
roller skates, used at work
"Jenny on the Job," propaganda campaign 128
moving paperwork at Douglas plants 156
retrieve parts at White Motor Company 156
waitresses on skates at drive-ins, 1940s 25
Roller Skating Club of Chicago 35, 53, 69
Roller Skating Institute of America
best thing for skating since 1942 23
sweeps the nation with "Roller Skating Song" 175
Roller Skating Rink Owners Association 17
first national speed skate championship, 1938 35
formed in 1937 170
"Roller Skate to Health" 170
RSIA member of 175
start of in 1937, anchoring golden age 17
"Rollin' Round Roller Rinks" 102
Rosdahl, Teddy
1952 Figures National Champion 142
junior boys ARSA national champion, 1944 126
pro at North Avenue 123
Roseland Roller Rink
a brief history of 71
rebuilt from a former post office 71
Rosie the Riveter 154
rosin 38, 102, 182
the rise and fall at the Swank 74
Runyon, Damon 33

S

Savoy Roller Rink 72
a brief history of 72
only Chicago rink with jazz bank 72
site of Harold Washington Cultural Center 74
Sefferino Rollerdrome 45, 136
a brief history of 90
as target of desegregation actions 91

hosted first speed skate national, 1937 90
operation as a private skate club 91
Seipp, Carol
ARSA National Championship, 1953 144
Seipp, Tom
ARSA National Championship, 1953 144
Seltzer, Leo 33, 55
Shaffer, Robert
ARSA National Championship, 1962 144
at North Avenue Rollerway 65
Skate Crazy (Brooks) 30
skate fitness 181
Skating Vanities
and pop culture 181
and production of Harold Steinman 19
and television audiences 136
Billboard and fastest hours of spectacle 99
first season as Roller Follies 34
Gloria Nord stumbles 20
live performance versus TV derby 25
opens at Chicago Coliseum 17
versus Sonja Henie 20
Steinman, Harold 19, 99
Swank Roller Rink 138
a brief history of 74
cross-town rival of Roseland 71
hosted ARSA state meet, 1956 75

T

Transcontinental Roller Derby 33
at Chicago Coliseum 53
202nd Armory Rink
a brief history of 51
opens as world's largest in late 1930s 34
replaced by the Michigan Avenue Armory Rink 120
Tyler, Charlie
reports new armory to open, Arcadia, 1943 119
reports of skate dancing, 1941 102
tags Caroline Buchanan as "Red" 119
writes of new roller craze, 1941 179

U

United Rink Operators
as rival to RSROA 172
RSIA member of 175
United Service Organizations 162

V

V-mail
British adopted, 1939 159
developed by Eastman Kodak Company 159

W

Ware brothers 38

War Production Board
issues black-out orders 26
issues supply requirements for skate manufacturers 104
mobilized as emergency agency 25
supports rebuilding of Rollerdrome 29
war orders remained in effect until withdrawn 29
women's fashions affected by 126
war tax 29
White City Roller Rink
a brief history of 75
and CORE protest of, 1946 76
floor size 41
picketed by interracial groups, 1942 30
roller rink survives park fire, 1933 76
White Motor Company, employees use skates in parts department 156
Women's Army Corps
Madison Garden's Wanda Hoffman joins, 1943 117
Mineola's Pro Claire Miller joins up 118
"my best soldiers" 118
named full branch of the army, 1943 118
Wurlitzer theater organ 60, 61, 80, 98, 102, 103, 123, 183
and "Roller Romance" 23
at the Cleveland Rollercade 80
Axle sticks with during disco era 61
December 7, 1941 103
Geneva Cannock Chase, at the Elm 57
last live at a U.S. rink 90
scene at Madison Gardens 96
silent movie era 30

Y

Yokosuka Iron Works 165
Yokosuka Naval Base, roller rink at 165

Z

Zimmerman, Jacqueline
ARSA National Championship, 1962 144
at North Avenue Rollerway 65

ABOUT THE AUTHOR

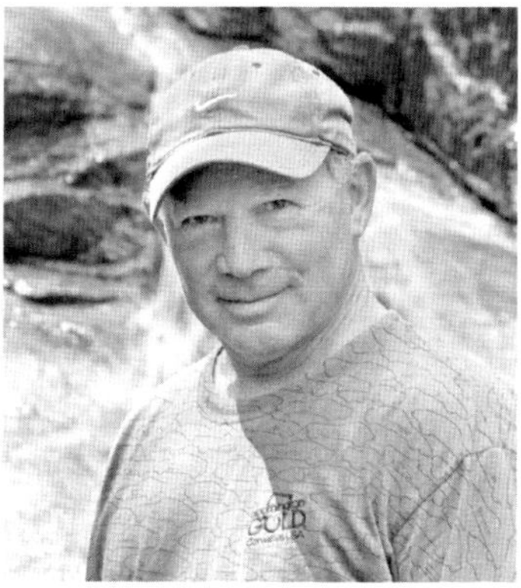

Born on the West Side of Chicago, Tom Russo grew up in the western suburbs of Northlake, Elmhurst and Melrose Park, where he skated, dismembered things that rolled and competed whether it was scrimmage ball games on asphalt, dirt or manicured ball fields or pulling a race car to Oswego Raceway.

He learned to skate in Northlake with his two sisters, waiting each winter for the creek to freeze over. Skating the length of the creek led to playing hockey as he met neighborhood boys. Over the years, he ice-skated and roller-skated on both quads and in-line skates. Today, as he travels, Russo seeks out local rinks to skate and feel the skate culture of those rinks and the communities they host. His skates of choice are quads!

Russo currently is an instructor, trainer and freelance writer. He has a degree in nutrition from Southern Illinois University, along with a master's in community health. He also has a Master of Arts degree in homeland security studies from the Naval Postgraduate School. As an adjunct instructor for Columbia College, he instructs courses on homeland security, emergency management and epidemics and bioterrorism.

His freelance writing topics range from hobby to professional, as well as from recreation to the technical. Whether the topic is Corvette restoration and preservation or the health and medical response for public health emergencies, Russo has an ability to navigate the application of core principles of preparedness and share those with students of the profession. He has written at length on pandemic policy and preparedness. He authored and self-published the *Corvette Buildsheet Book: A Study Guide for 1973–82 Build Records*.

Tom is a lifelong recreational enthusiast and a student of the coastal environment and currently lives in Myrtle Beach, South Carolina. He enjoys yearlong cycling, roller skating and the southern Lowcountry lifestyle that includes wandering the one hundred miles of the unpaved, untouched, undeveloped sixteen-thousand-acre refuge of Hobcaw Barony. He volunteers at Hobcaw as a docent and is a member of the Guestbook Research Committee. He has made a career of volunteer work and serves on the City of Myrtle Beach Bicycle & Pedestrian Committee.